PARALLEL
PROCESSING AND
MEDIUM-SCALE
MULTIPROCESSORS

SIAM PROCEEDINGS SERIES LIST

Neustadt, L.W., Proceedings of the First International Congress on Programming and Control (1966)

Hull, T.E., Studies in Optimization (1970)

Day, R.H. & Robinson, S.M., Mathematical Topics in Economic Theory and Computation (1972)

Proschan, F. & Serfling, R.J., Reliability and Biometry: Statistical Analysis of Lifelength (1974)

Barlow, R.E., Reliability & Fault Tree Analysis: Theoretical & Applied Aspects of System Reliability & Safety Assessment (1975)

Fussell, J.B. & Burdick, G.R., Nuclear Systems Reliability Engineering and Risk Assessment (1977)

Duff, I.S. & Stewart, G.W., Sparse Matrix Proceedings 1978 (1979)

Holmes, P.J., New Approaches to Nonlinear Problems in Dynamics (1980)

Erisman, A.M., Neves, K.W. & Dwarakanath, M.H., Electric Power Problems: The Mathematical Challenge (1981)

Bednar, J.B., Redner, R., Robinson, E. & Weglein, A., Conference on Inverse Scattering: Theory and Application (1983)

Voigt, R.G., Gottlieb, D. & Hussaini, M. Yousuff, Spectral Methods for Partial Differential Equations (1984)

Chandra, Jagdish, Chaos in Nonlinear Dynamical Systems (1984)

Santosa, Fadil, Symes, William W., Pao, Yih-Hsing & Holland, Charles, Inverse Problems of Acoustic and Elastic Waves (1984)

Gross, Kenneth I., Mathematical Methods in Energy Research (1984)

Babuska, I., Chandra, J. & Flaherty, J., Adaptive Computational Methods for Partial Differential Equations (1984)

Boggs, Paul T., Byrd, Richard H. & Schnabel, Robert B., Numerical Optimization 1984 (1985)

Angrand, F., Dervieux, A., Desideri, J.A. & Glowinski, R., Numerical Methods for Euler Equations of Fluid Dynamics (1985)

Wouk, Arthur, New Computing Environments: Parallel, Vector and Systolic (1986)

Fitzgibbon, William E., Mathematical and Computational Methods in Seismic Exploration and Reservoir Modeling (1986)

Drew, Donald A. & Flaherty, Joseph E., Mathematics Applied to Fluid Mechanics and Stability: Proceedings of a Conference Dedicated to R.C. DiPrima (1986)

Heath, Michael T., Hypercube Multiprocessors 1986 (1986)

Papanicolaou, George, Advances in Multiphase Flow and Related Problems (1987)

Wouk, Arthur, New Computing Environments: Microcomputers in Large-Scale Computing (1987)

Chandra, Jagdish & Srivastav, Ram, Constitutive Models of Deformation (1987)

Heath, Michael T., Hypercube Multiprocessors 1987 (1987)

Glowinski, R., Golub, G.H., Meurant, G.A. & Periaux, J., First International Symposium on Domain Decomposition Methods for Partial Differential Equations (1988)

Salam, Fathi M.A. & Levi, Mark L., Dynamical Systems Approaches to Nonlinear Problems in Systems and Circuits (1988)

Datta, B., Johnson, C., Kaashoek, M., Plemmons, R. & Sontag, E., Linear Algebra in Signals, Systems and Control (1988)

Ringeisen, Richard D. & Roberts, Fred S., Applications of Discrete Mathematics (1988)

McKenna, James & Temam, Roger, ICIAM '87—Proceedings of the First International Conference on Industrial and Applied Mathematics (1988)

Rodrigue, Garry, Parallel Processing for Scientific Computing (1989)

Chan, Tony F., Meurant, Gerard, Periaux, Jacques & Widlund, Olof B., Domain Decomposition Methods (1989)

Caflisch, Russel E., Mathematical Aspects of Vortex Dynamics (1989)

Wouk, Arthur, Parallel Processing and Medium-Scale Multiprocessors (1989)

PARALLEL
PROCESSING AND
MEDIUM-SCALE
MULTIPROCESSORS

Edited by Arthur Wouk

 Philadelphia

Society for Industrial and Applied Mathematics

PARALLEL PROCESSING
AND MEDIUM-SCALE MULTIPROCESSORS

Proceedings of the Workshop on Parallel Processing and Medium-Scale Multiprocessors, Stanford, California, January, 1986.

This workshop was sponsored by the Mathematical Sciences Division of the United States Army Research Office and the Department of Computer Science.

The views presented here are not necessarily those of the United States Army Research Office.

Library of Congress Cataloging-in-Publication Data

Parallel processing and medium-scale multiprocessors/ ed., Arthur Wouk.
   p. cm.
   "Papers ... presented at a research workshop on 'Parallel processing and medium-scale multiprocessors' which was held at Stanford University in January 1986 under the sponsorship of the Army Research Office with the cooperation and assistance of the Department of Computer Science"—Introd.
   Bibliography: p.
   ISBN 0-89871-238-6: $31.50
   1. Parallel processing (Electronic computers)
2. Multiprocessors. I. Wouk, Arthur, 1924- . II. United States. Army Research Office. III. Stanford University. Computer Science Dept. QA76.5.P31484 1989
004'.35—dc20

89-6435
CIP

PREFACE

For some time, the community interested in large-scale scientific computing has been attempting to come to terms with parallel computation using a number of processors sufficient to make their concurrent utilization interesting, challenging, and, in the long run, beneficial. Unexpected consequences of parallelization have been discovered. It is possible to obtain reduced performance, both relative and absolute, from an increased number of processors, as a result of inappropriate use of resources in a multiprocessor environment. This exemplifies one of the paradoxes which result from our cultural bias towards sequential thought processes. As a consequence there is a bias for sequential styles of program development in a multiprocessor environment.

We have learned that the problem of automatic optimization in compilation of parallel programs is computationally "hard". Early hopes that automatic, optimal parallelization of sequentially conceived programs would be as achievable as earlier automatic vectorization had been, have been dashed. We lack the insights and folklore which are needed to develop useful methodologies and heuristics in the area of parallel computation. We are embarked on a voyage of exploration of this new territory, and the work described in this volume can provide helpful guidance. We have to explore fully the differences between distributed memory systems, shared memory systems, and combinations, as well as the relative applicability of SIMD and MIMD architectures. Based on the information obtained in such exploration, useful steps towards efficient utilization of many processors should become possible.

The papers in this book were presented at a research workshop on "Parallel Processing and Medium-Scale Multiprocessors" which was held at Stanford University in January 1986 under the sponsorship of the Army Research Office with the cooperation and assistance of the Department of Computer Science. This workshop was a follow-up to an earlier workshop "New Computing Environments: Parallel, Vector and Systolic" held at the same location in 1984, under the same auspices. The efforts of the staff of the Department of Computer Science and of Professor Gene Golub contributed significantly to the success of these workshops, and is hereby acknowledged.

This workshop was intended to bring together research workers with strong connections to scientific computation, yet with an interest in the systems programming problems which are restricting the application of the new hardware being developed. It did initiate considerable interaction among those present, and the record of its contents should continue to be useful in current developments.

The papers contained in this volume cover several areas: systems programming, parallel/language/programming systems, and applications programming. The work reported includes investigations into debugging of parallel programs, portability of applications programs and parallel operating systems, efficient resource allocation in multiprocessors, parallel constructs for applications programming languages, and applications programming efforts on diverse architectures.

It is widely recognized that large-scale parallelism will be required for the next step in computational mathematics: the solution of realistic three dimensional problems of mathematical physics. However, before we can run, we must walk, and it is hoped that these proceedings will help us in learning to walk.

Arthur Wouk
Mathematical Sciences Division
Army Research Office
Research Triangle Park, North Carolina

Richard H. Byrd, Department of Computer Science, University of Colorado, Boulder, Colorado 80309

A. Couch, Department of Computer Science, Tufts University, Medford, Massachusetts 02155

George Cybenko, Department of Computer Science, Tufts University, Medford, Massachusetts 02155

Cornelius L. Dert, Econometric Institute, Erasmus University, Rotterdam, The Netherlands

J. J. Dongarra, Mathematics and Computer Science Division, Argonne National Laboratory, Argonne, Illinois 60439

W. Morven Gentleman, Division of Electrical Engineering, National Research Council of Canada, Ottawa, Ontario, Canada K1A 0R8

Alan George, Department of Computer Science, University of Waterloo, Waterloo, Ontario, Canada N2L 3G1

William D. Gropp, Department of Computer Science, Yale University, New Haven, Connecticut 06520

Michael T. Heath, Mathematical Sciences Section, Oak Ridge National Laboratory, Oak Ridge, Tennessee 37831

Ching-Tien Ho, Department of Computer Science, Yale University, New Haven, Connecticut 06520

Jung Pyo Hong, Advance Computing Systems, Los Alamos, New Mexico 87545

S. Lennart Johnsson, Department of Computer Science, Yale University, New Haven, Connecticut 06520

Harry F. Jordan, Department of Electrical Engineering, University of Colorado, Boulder, Colorado 80309

David W. Krumme, Department of Computer Science, Tufts University, Medford, Massachusetts 02155

Joseph Liu, Department of Computer Science, York University, North York, Ontario, Canada M3J 1P3

Cleve Moler, ARDENT Computer Corporation, Sunnyvale, California 94086

Esmond Ng, Mathematical Sciences Section, Oak Ridge National Laboratory, Oak Ridge, Tennessee 37831

David M. Nicol, Department of Computer Science, College of William and Mary, Williamsburg, Virginia 23185

D. P. O'Leary, Computer Science Department, University of Maryland, College Park, Maryland 20742

Nisheeth Patel, United States Army Ballistic Research Laboratory, Aberdeen Proving Ground, Maryland 21005

Alexander H. G. Rinnooy Kan, Econometric Institute, Erasmus University, Rotterdam, The Netherlands

Joel H. Saltz, Department of Computer Science, Yale University, New Haven, Connecticut 06520

Robert B. Schnabel, Department of Computer Science, University of Colorado, Boulder, Colorado 80309

David S. Scott, Intel Scientific Computers, Beaverton, Oregon 97006

D. C. Sorensen, Mathematics and Computer Science Division, Argonne National Laboratory, Argonne, Illinois 60439

Darlene A. Stewart, Division of Electrical Engineering, National Research Council of Canada, Ottawa, Ontario, Canada K1A 0R8

G. W. Stewart, Computer Science Department, University of Maryland, College Park, Maryland 20742

Bob Tomlinson, Los Alamos National Laboratory, Los Alamos, New Mexico 87545

Robert van de Geijn, Department of Computer Science, University of Texas at Austin, Austin, Texas 78712

K. N. Venkataraman, Compass Incorporated, Wakefield, Massachusetts 01880

CONTENTS

1   Debugging Multi-Task Programs
W. Morven Gentleman and Darlene A. Stewart

16   Matrix Computations and Game Playing on the iPSC
Cleve Moler and David S. Scott

25   DOMINO: A Transportable System for Parallel Processing
D. P. O'Leary, G. W. Stewart, and Robert van de Geijn

35   Statistical Methodologies for the Control of Dynamic Remapping
Joel H. Saltz and David M. Nicol

58   Sparse Cholesky Factorization on a Local-Memory Multiprocessor
Alan George, Michael T. Heath, Joseph Liu, and Esmond Ng

76   Concurrent Global Optimization on a Network of Computers
Richard H. Byrd, Cornelius L. Dert, Alexander H. G. Rinnooy Kan, and Robert B. Schnabel

97   Heterogeneous Processes on Homogeneous Processors
George Cybenko, David W. Krumme, K. N. Venkataraman, and A. Couch

108   Matrix Multiplication on Boolean Cubes Using Generic Communication Primitives
S. Lennart Johnsson and Ching-Tien Ho

157   The Force on the Flex: Global Parallelism and Portability
Harry F. Jordan

177   SCHEDULE: An Aid to Programming Explicitly Parallel Algorithms in Fortran
J. J. Dongarra and D. C. Sorensen

192   Dynamic Grid Manipulation for Partial Differential Equations on Hypercube Parallel Processors
William D. Gropp

204   Solving Compressible Euler Equations on a Hypercube Simulator
Jung Pyo Hong, Bob Tomlinson, and Nisheeth Patel

Debugging Multi-Task Programs*

W. Morven Gentleman[†]
Darlene A. Stewart[†]

Abstract. Techniques used to debug sequential programs can, of course, also be used for debugging concurrent or even parallel programs. Especially when concurrentness or parallelism is explicit in the program, or when the program must respond to asynchronous external events, however, these techniques may be insufficient. Debugging such programs is difficult because timing of events can be critical. This is particularly true for performance bugs, even more than for correctness bugs. Whereas the traditional debugger for sequential bugs is based on the "stop the world, I want to get off" breakpoint, in a multi-task program normally you only want to stop a specific task, and indeed halting all the processors may not be possible even if you want to. In addition to breakpoints, other techniques have been found useful.

This paper describes the techniques supported by the new debugger currently being built for use with the Harmony[1] operating system. Three categories of features are discussed: non-realtime (traditional) tools, realtime (multi-tasking multi-processor) tools, and the user interface.

1. Debugging techniques. Most programs require debugging. This is particularly true for complex programs, which realtime programs or parallel programs tend to be. Although this statement is trite, few programmers have a disciplined methodology of debugging and few schools teach how to debug programs. Before focussing on the topic of this paper, let us look more generally at how debugging is done today.

All too often the debugging technique practiced can best be described as wild optimism. A large program is written in its entirety, and then debugging is attempted by running it over and over with trial data, looking for aberrant behaviour. Initially the program often fails spectacularly, but as bugs are found and fixed, hopefully a stage is eventually reached where the program usually behaves as expected. Sande [12] once called this "debugging by friction" — if the program is run through the machine often enough, maybe the bugs will wear off!

Criticism of this approach usually focusses on the fact that one can never be sure of finding the last bug, that one can never be sure the program is correct. Instead, we prefer to make the observation that this approach is highly inefficient of the programmer's effort. The essential steps of debugging are, first,

---

* NRCC No. 27640. Also available as NRC/ERB-1008, National Research Council of Canada, Ottawa, Canada.

[†] National Research Council of Canada, Ottawa, Canada, K1A 0R8.

[1] Mark reserved for the exclusive use of Her Majesty the Queen in right of Canada by Canadian Patents and Development Ltd./Société canadienne des brevets et d'exploitation Ltée.

detecting that something has failed and, second, tracing back through the derivation of that something in order to locate the cause of the failure. Given all the output of a complete program, it is often exceedingly difficult to detect that it has failed, unless the failure is something spectacular such as an address exception. Faced with a complex mass that has failed, the programmer often has an immense job tracking back from the symptom to the cause. Trying to debug everything at once often means that several bugs interact, some disguising the effects of others and making cause and effect relationships difficult to establish. Moreover, even after identifying bugs found at this stage, properly correcting them often results in major redesigns that throw away much of the code that was written, clearly showing that effort was wasted. We believe that this approach stems from a misguided belief that the program must be written in its entirety for the programmer to grasp fully its interlocking intricacies and to settle design issues, combined with the pious hope that maybe this time the coding will all be correct. Simplistic "program proof" can actually exacerbate this effect. We believe instead in planning for debugging.

The key idea in planning for debugging is that of using systematic testing. Typically, for a given program, we want to develop a strategy whereby a sequence of tests can establish, at each step, that part of the program is probably working correctly, which can be used at the next step to show that another part of the program is probably working correctly. Unit test, i.e., separately testing individual components, is one such way. Another simple and popular way to do this is by recognizing that most programs have milestones, which are points in the execution where some phase of the computation is complete and testable properties should hold for the data structures that have been built and for the values in these data structures. Even just reaching a milestone can be significant, but the testable properties are more important. Verification and display of these properties are probably not part of the normal output of the program running in production mode, but debugging code can be used to do this when the program is run on test data for which the expected properties can be derived. Note that working with such test data alleviates the first step of debugging, that of recognizing when something is wrong. Note also that proceeding from milestone to milestone limits how far back the programmer must search to locate the source of the problem. Note that often milestones can be chosen at stable points in the program so any parallelism or concurrentness, even indeterminacy, used in advancing from the previous milestone can be ignored in subsequent analysis. Note finally that often the probable correctness of milestones can be established during development while later code still only exists as stubs.

We have stressed "probable correctness" in the previous paragraph because it is well known that the dominant proportion of the persistent bugs in large programs are due to the programmer incompletely recognizing the complexity of the situations his code must handle, indeed that often this failing is also present in the problem specification [9]. Thus systematic testing, like proof of correctness, will almost certainly have the deficiency of falling only within the domain of the problem as the programmer understood it [1]. However, once the machinery for testing is in place, and confidence established in the normal case properties of the program, we are in a much better position to examine those properties in realistic situations or in situations where anomalous behaviour has been observed. Simply examining the program state at milestones often reveals situations that the program will not be able to handle in its subsequent computation.

Typically, the examination of properties described above is done manually. This can be valuable for exposing unanticipated aspects of the data, but is tedious and error prone. Consequently, a better approach is to automate the examination, by the programmer making assertions in the code as to what properties should hold at indicated milestones, and providing code in the form of audit routines that can be executed on intermediate data structures to verify the assertions.

To make this discussion more concrete, let us consider some specific examples. A program that constructs a doubly linked list of records, and then uses the list, has a possible milestone at the point where the construction of the list is complete. Properties that might be tested include those of individual records, such as that values in various fields are plausible and that predecessor pointers in successor records point back to the record itself. Other properties that might be tested include those of the list as a whole, such as that the list terminates properly, that all necessary records are in fact on the list, and that if the list is supposed to be ordered with respect to some field then that it is so ordered. Notice that properties such as the preconditions, postconditions, and loop invariants that are used in proof of program correctness are also candidates to examine, but they are not the only properties one would look at.

Another example might be an engineering program, based on the finite element method, where a stress matrix is set up, then solved for various right-hand sides, perhaps with perturbations to the elements of the matrix. A possible milestone could be where the matrix has been formed, and a property that might be examined is that the eigenvalues of the matrix are sufficiently far from zero. By construction the matrix will be symmetric and positive semidefinite, so what this property is really testing is whether the chosen basis actually spans the space of solutions satisfactorily. What is interesting about this example is that the property is not immediately evident in terms of data normally available at the milestone (indeed the audit routine must do more work than the next stage of the normal computation). Even after the audit calculation, judgement is required to decide if all is well.

Returning to general techniques of debugging, one that is often suggested is simulation. In many cases what is meant is that a separate program should be written that is a simplification of the real program. This is sometimes suggested because the real program is too difficult to understand, or too expensive to conduct experiments on, but more commonly it is suggested because it is hoped that the simulation can be programmed more quickly and more cheaply than the real program, so that design decisions for the real program can be anticipated and evaluated in the simulation. Though such an approach is frequently suggested, it is hard to find cases where it has been followed, and even more difficult to find cases where it has been effective. There are a number of reasons for this. Clearly such a simulation will not find detail coding errors but at best might identify design shortcomings. However, it is exceedingly difficult to ensure that the simulation faithfully reflects how those design decisions will affect the real program, especially before the real program exists. A faithful simulation is likely not to be cheap, in particular requiring a scarce resource — the people capable of building the real program. Few organizations can tolerate the delay of building a comprehensive simulation before building the real program. Finally, because the simulation is not the real program, it usually cannot do the full job of the real program, but can only be used in a subset of the situations the real program might face, which means it is likely to share design oversights with the real program and not to be exercized so as to reveal them. The two situations where simulations have proved effective are when the simulation is intended to measure performance of a real program by adding instrumentation that the real program does not contain, for instance, because the hardware does not provide the information sought, and when hardware must be simulated because it is not available.

(The current round of promotion of prototyping tools for microcomputer applications may obsolete the comments in the above paragraph, at least for user interface design, because the tools make the cost of simulating the interface orders of magnitude cheaper than the cost of writing the actual program. Whether these tools are as effective in practice as claimed remains to be proved.)

In the context of parallel computing, however, what is usually meant by simulating the parallel program is something quite different. Programmers new to the world of concurrentness are often uncomfortable with the loss of control over the order in which things get done and want to debug the data structures and algorithms of their programs in a sequential mode, before addressing problems, such as deadlocks or critical races, which might arise from their use of multiple processors. In many parallel execution environments, whether with the anonymous tasks often used with the shared memory model or with the explicit tasks used with message passing systems, this is actually quite easy to do as the tasks are distributed over the available processors, and if only one processor is made available (and it has enough resources to run the program at all), then the same code, unchanged, is a sequential program. In our experience, this is not a useful thing to do.

Part of the reason for such a heretical statement is the observation that even on a single processor, the context switching among concurrent tasks induces much the same unpredictability of order of execution that caused the discomfort in the first place, and escaping from this can require such major code changes that one is not really debugging the same program. A deeper issue is that we observe that with good debugging techniques, working in appropriate programming abstractions (such as the explicit multi-tasking system based on remote procedure call that we use), the classic hazards of concurrent programming are rare. Indeed, the artificial sequentialization of things that were intended to run in parallel induces effects much harder to anticipate and understand. It really is much nicer, for instance, to have a debugger running in a separate processor, unaffected by the whims of the program being debugged.

What does happen when a parallel program is forced to run on one processor is that an amazing number of things that are seriously wrong work accidentally because the forced sequentialization resolves critical races, hides mistakes in preemptive priorities, etc. Consequently, the program gets far beyond where the real problem lay before exhibiting suspicious behaviour. Even just two processors is often enough to alert the programmer to the problems, whereupon such problems are not hard to find or to cure.

Of all debugging tools, the most important, in our experience, is a good interactive debugger used well. Because debuggers are unfashionable in certain parts of the computer science community, this statement needs amplification. The argument against debuggers is usually that they are unnecessary and promote sloppy work because programs should be designed and coded to be correct. This argument is based on the naive view that a sufficient alternative is to prove programs correct. Program proof is, of course, a useful tool for a programmer to have. However, program proof usually means just that the program implements its specifications. In real programs, the question of what to prove is not trivial. There are few interesting programs with a rigid specification — more commonly the program has an intended objective that could be met in many quite different ways. The engineering technique of breadboarding is essentially aimed at defining the specification from experience with prototypes. Also it is well known that oversights are the most common error both in designs and in mathematical proofs, so a manually created proof cannot be trusted.

A different criticism is that misuse of debuggers wastes time. One advantage of debuggers is that through techniques such as setting switches, correcting values, or patching code, they can shorten the edit-compile-link-download-execute cycle, which can be painful on realtime systems [8]. However, it is true that if the debugger is not used in a disciplined way, the programmer can lose track of what has been done and may not update the source code appropriately. Also, unless the programmer uses a systematic strategy to locate and eliminate bugs, there can be a tendency to poke aimlessly at the program, learning little.

A significant aspect of the use of debuggers is to analyze "correct" programs, i.e., those that compute what they were supposed to, but where we are worried about run time or resource usage. This is associated with the idea of a performance bug. Often the resource usage of a program is too difficult to analyze, so using an interactive debugger for "dynamic behaviour monitoring" gives a probe whereby data structures and algorithms can be examined as they work with real data to see whether any bottlenecks can be identified and whether any improvements are suggested.

A legitimate criticism is that too many debuggers are hard to use, indeed hard to remember, thus leading to programmer inefficiency. We will return to this later when we address user interface issues.

2. Why multi-task programs are different. Debugging multi-task programs, whether these are programs exhibiting true multi-processor parallelism or merely concurrentness, has the reputation of being more difficult than debugging conventional sequential programs. While this has not been our experience, it is true that a number of ways in which multi-task programs differ from sequential programs do affect debugging.

A major issue in the design of multi-task systems is whether they should be constrained to be deterministic; that is, given the same data, should the program always produce the identical results. A sequential program is always deterministic, but in a multi-task program the independent tasks can proceed at different rates at different times due, for instance, to resource availability. We note that in many cases determinacy is not a consequence of the original problem: for example, eigenvectors are only determined up to a scaling factor even when they correspond to an isolated eigenvalue and merely lie in the appropriate subspace for a multiple eigenvalue; a graph may have many minimal spanning trees rooted at the same node; an iterative floating point computation may guarantee to reduce the error below some bound but many different approximations would meet that criterion. In such cases there are many equally good results of the computation: the motivation for requiring determinacy is solely to make debugging easier. (Abandoning determinacy in such cases means a check that the answer is correct must be more sophisticated than merely bitwise comparison with an independently computed result, but rounding error often has similar effects.) Behind the desire for determinacy is the intent to run the program again on the same data, but in programs that interact with the external world this is often infeasible because the external conditions are not exactly reproducible, so other debugging techniques must be used. We should also note that requiring determinacy may rule out more effective algorithms (e.g., chaotic relaxation has sometimes been shown to be faster than practical sequential equivalents) and may even make certain problems impossible to formulate (e.g., realtime interception problems where the choice of whether to extrapolate a trajectory from old data or new depends on when the new data become available).

One approach that does not go as far as determinacy is to insist that all failure handling is under the programmer's control. This often makes it possible to guarantee that, at least as seen at synchronization points, the computation is repeatable except where driven by external events. In particular, it means that unpredictable results cannot occur outside of the programmer's control, for instance by resource exhaustion beneath the programming abstraction. A corollary is that the programming abstraction support some form of flow control on tasks that produce data or produce other tasks.

The classic bugs ascribed to multi-task programs are timing errors: critical races, deadlocks, livelocks, etc. Do these problems really occur and are they serious bugs? The answer to this question depends on the programming abstraction that is being used. Sometimes with a particular abstraction the error cannot happen or sometimes with that abstraction the error is very infrequent. If the abstraction does not support shared variables, for instance (as with a pure message passing abstraction), then there can be no critical race on the update of a shared variable, there can be no unintentional sharing of a variable, and there can be no variables intended to be shared but for which by mistake each task got its own copy. Semaphores are prone to errors of forgetting to signal that the semaphore is free when this is not done textually close to the wait on the semaphore, as well as being prone to loss of resources when a task holding those resources is destroyed, neither of which are common errors when synchronization is instead achieved by remote procedure call blocking communication. (Of course, errors made by users of an abstraction can be very different from those made by implementers of that abstraction.) In any case, experience with many abstractions suggests that some timing errors, deadlock, for instance, are not serious errors, in that if they occur they are obvious and are readily fixed. On the other hand, critical races for shared variables, especially inadvertently shared variables, are serious because they are hard to detect. Protocol errors are serious because programmers appear to find it hard to anticipate all the implications of repeated passes through a state table or all the situations that can occur. The more subtle experience is that many performance bugs are associated with timing errors. For example, to avoid critical races the execution order of some set of tasks is overconstrained, with consequent loss of potential parallelism.

An important consequence of multi-task programs no longer having a single thread of control is that, in understanding the program, there is a shift in emphasis from following the flow of control to concentrating instead on the protocol of interaction among the tasks. In many cases this protocol is over several interactions, not just communication at a single instant in time. Traditional debugger breakpoints are not very helpful here, as the breakpoint event is associated with control flow only and provides only a snapshot of the program at that point. Even simple sequential triggering is not provided. In general, for explicit tasking abstractions based on message passing there is a shift from being code oriented to being object oriented, i.e., task oriented. This means that a breakpoint is usually not usefully tripped when just any task executes that instruction, but only when a specific task does. (There are, of course, exceptions.)

Whereas a sequential program running into a breakpoint stops everything, and the first thought of what might be desirable in parallel computation (regardless of how hard it might be to implement) is a similar "Stop the world, I want to get off!" approach, it turns out frequently to be quite sufficient to stop only the task that tripped the breakpoint (and, of course, those that become blocked because of that task's unavailability). This is most important in realtime situations where critical activities cannot be stopped, but it is also desirable in general, for it means the debugger can just be a group of ordinary tasks within the abstraction and audit routines can also be run as ordinary tasks.

3. A troubleshooting guide. For cars, household appliances, and other common products the problems arising in practice are so repetitious that manufacturers supply a troubleshooting guide of standard faults, their causes, and their cures to be tried before looking for something unique. It has been our experience that this is worthwhile for bugs in programs also; for any programming environment, independent of the programmer or the program, the most common faults tend to be similar and the same techniques work to locate and cure them. Here, then, are the troubleshooting techniques we use to find bugs in programs written for Harmony [6], our multi-tasking, multi-processor message passing portable realtime operating system.

3.1 Examination of the state of tasks. The first thing to do when a program is halted (at a breakpoint or post mortem) is to examine the state of the relevant tasks in the system, maybe even of all tasks. Although the tasks in our system are explicit, tasks are created dynamically and are not necessarily uniquely associated with textual names, a task being identified instead by a system-supplied numeric task_id. Consequently the debugger provides a command to list currently existing tasks and summarize their states. Because there might be a very large number of tasks, and because processors are multiprogrammed and tasks do not migrate among processors, this debugger command takes as an argument a processor number and lists all the tasks currently existing on the specified processor. Another debugger command, given a specific task_id, displays the complete state that the system has recorded for that task, including the template from which it was created (what in Ada would be called the task type). Of particular interest is whether the task is eligible to run or is blocked and, if it is blocked, what condition it is waiting for and what queue it is on. In the remote procedure call style of programming, at any time most tasks are blocked awaiting communication, so understanding the blocking conditions and identifying which tasks are attempting to communicate with which others goes a long way toward understanding what the program is doing at that moment. Because the client-server idiom [5] is used heavily in Harmony programs, it is sometimes of interest to examine the request messages of clients awaiting service or of workers awaiting new work assignments.

3.2 Examination of standard system data structures. The next thing to do once the states of relevant tasks have been examined is to examine standard system data structures. Depending on what we are looking for, these could include the ready queues on a specified processor, the table of tasks on a specified processor that are awaiting interrupts, the storage pool on a specified processor, the directory task's list of symbolically known server tasks, the storage blocks allocated to a specified task, the tasks to which a specified task has opened connections, etc. It is important that the debugger be aware of such system data structures, to be able to display them effectively and to perform simple consistency checks on them. It is also an important part of system documentation to alert the programmer to what system data structures exist that might aid in understanding what his program is doing.

3.3 Using a spy task. There is another general technique of examination that should be mentioned: the use of a spy task. Any attempt to monitor the activity of a program introduces the Heisenberg effect: an artifact of the monitoring is to change the behaviour being monitored. Clearly it is desirable to minimize such interference. The spy task is a powerful technique for doing this. All the monitoring is put into a task different from the tasks being monitored, and this task then relies on sharing address space with the tasks being monitored to enable it to inobtrusively sample their data while they are running. This works particularly well when processors share address space, so the spy task can run on a different processor from the tasks being monitored and only steals a few memory cycles. Running the spy on a different processor also avoids having sampling correlations with the scheduling of the activity being monitored. Even dynamic data structures can be monitored with only the slightest collusion on the part of the monitored tasks; if the monitored task maintains a generation sequence number for the data structure, and the spy checks it before and after reading the structure, then as long as it is the same the spy got a consistent snapshot. Care must obviously be taken in following pointers lest they change underfoot.

3.4 Check for stack overflow. When we come to actually identifying causes of trouble, there is no question that the most frequent culprit is stack overflow. It is also the most insidious, as the symptoms appear inexplicable: storage pool corruption, variables suddenly changing value without having been assigned to, wild transfers because return addresses have been damaged, in general the programmer's abstraction of the computing environment having been violated. The fundamental issue is that to get many of the benefits of lightweight tasks, such as simple semantics for the behaviour of a single task, requires that many tasks execute in the same address space, in particular that their stacks lie in the same address space. This is, however, not properly supported in hardware, nor by commercial compilers. It would be possible for individual stack frames to be separately obtained from the storage manager, but commercial compilers almost never support this, and indeed it implies undesirable and unpredictable overhead. Consequently, stacks are allocated as fixed-size contiguous storage obtained from the storage pool, and stack overflow detection needs to be by a hardware or software check against the limit of the allocated block. Conventional stack based systems, such as the Unix implementations of Pascal or C, have a single stack that relies on memory mapping hardware. The stack grows toward address space beyond the bounds of mapped memory, so the stack can be grown effectively without limit so long as memory mapping violations by stack manipulations result in the bounds being extended to map more real memory. Thus, compilers do not check for stack overflow and the only hardware check is the memory mapping violation. Conventional Pascal or C systems without memory mapping hardware grow the stack toward the storage pool, so the stack could grow until it collided with the high water mark of blocks allocated from the pool, and although the stack size is not fixed, similar stack overflow detection is needed to what is needed for the multiple stack case, and many systems similarly do not check.

Although automatic monitoring for stack overflow is not usually provided, and consequently a stack can grow so as to overwrite whatever was adjacent in memory and then shrink back to hide the evidence, it is easy to detect at a breakpoint whether a stack is currently overflowed, and indeed it is easy to provide a runtime function that determines whether the task calling it has currently overflowed its stack. More importantly, use of a program development tool called a stack bounder guarantees that stack overflow cannot happen. A stack bounder determines, from compiler provided information or from pseudo-execution, the maximum stack requirement for every function potentially called by the task, then from the call graph determines a bound on the maximum stack requirement of any possible nesting list by summing the individual requirements. Recursion and indirect function calls are resolved through programmer interaction.

Thus checking for stack overflow any time a program is examined and upon any suspicious behaviour using the stack bounder to confirm that stacks are sufficiently large is a cheap investment that completely eliminates this problem.

3.5 Check for storage pool corruption. Another potential problem worth checking for is corruption of the storage pool. This can be a consequence of stack overflow, using dangling pointers or uninitialized pointers, running off the ends of arrays, allocating record variants that are too small, etc. Each block in the storage pool is preceded by a header indicating block size, whether the block is allocated or free, and, if the block is allocated, a link to other blocks allocated to the same task. If the block is free, the part that would be available to the user if it were allocated contains an unlikely bit pattern. Damage to these fields is likely if there is any corruption of the storage pool, and the debugger can readily check them for consistency (with care, even while the system is running). Tasks owning nearby blocks are prime suspects if corruption is found.

3.6 Check for deadlock. The next potential trouble worth checking is deadlock, not because it is frequent (as discussed above, we find it rare) but because programmers are concerned about it. Deadlock, by definition, is when there is a cycle of tasks waiting on each other. For system level deadlocks in Harmony, this means that each task in the cycle is either send-blocked on another (i.e., it has sent a message that has not yet been received), reply-blocked on another (i.e., it has sent a message that has been received but not yet replied to), or receive-blocked on another (i.e., it is blocked awaiting a message from that other task and only that other task's message will be accepted). Examination of state (especially blocking conditions) and examination of the system queue data structures readily detects this condition, if it exists, and identifies the tasks involved. Since receive specific is rarely used, such a cycle would likely only involve send-blocked and reply-blocked tasks. The methodology of task structuring in hierarchies with the client-server paradigm, combined with the graphic representation of blocking diagrams for tasks [4], [5], means that cycles do not arise naturally, and are in any case eliminated at design time, except when the programmer is unaware that an apparently innocuous procedure invocation hides intertask communications with consequent possible blocking.

System level deadlocks are, however, not the only type of deadlock that can occur in Harmony. A server can induce a conventional type of deadlock by choosing not to reply immediately to a client's request. For example, a file system server that permits only a single writer on a file can produce a conventional deadlock when task A that has file X open for write attempts subsequently to open file Y for write but task B already has file Y open for write and is also attempting to open file X for write. The deadlock here occurs if the server does not recognize the situation and handle it in the conventional way. Because the deadlock is inside the server, both tasks A and B will be reply-blocked on the server, but the server itself is not blocked, and without examination of the internal state of the server, there is no way to recognize that tasks A and B form a deadlocked cycle. The situation can be more complicated in that the deadlock can arise from conflicting requests for services provided by different servers, so the deadlocked tasks may be reply-blocked on different servers. Moreover, the open architecture of Harmony, where there is no central management of resources, means that conventional deadlock prevention schemes, such as forcing resources to be acquired in fixed order, are inapplicable. Fortunately, conventional deadlocks like this also seem rare in practice.

A more subtle problem is livelock, where tasks are not actually permanently blocked, but make no progress toward their objective because some task cannot make progress until some other task has performed an action that it does not get around to doing. Because task interaction in Harmony is through message passing, livelock in Harmony usually takes the form of an administrator task, which receives messages from anyone and implements an automaton, getting stuck in an internal state that only a certain message can change despite what other messages the task receives and handles. Examination of system state and system data structures do not help here, except to rule out deadlock as the problem. However, examination of the internal state of the administrator task exposes the problem, and that internal state can usually be probed and changed by sending it messages from the debugger.

3.7 Check for unexpected implications of preemptive priority. One difference between parallelism used to increase computational capacity and concurrentness used for realtime computing is that the scheduling discipline for runnable tasks is rarely an issue for the former, whereas it is often the essence of the latter. Although other scheduling disciplines, such as deadline scheduling, may better meet problem specifications, preemptive priority scheduling is almost universally provided because it is the discipline we know how to implement efficiently and other disciplines can be approximately implemented with it. Preemptive priority scheduling is important for several reasons. From the point of view of high priority tasks, it permits lower priority tasks to be ignored in meeting scheduling requirements. From the point of view of low priority tasks, it permits actions of higher priority tasks to be regarded as atomic. When integrated with the interrupt hardware priority system, it arranges for an interrupt to be held off until the appropriate task is waiting for the interrupt. It can be used to ensure a set of tasks runs in a specific order.

Unfortunately, preemptive priority scheduling does what the programmer specified, not what the programmer expected. Not infrequently tasks at different priorities will be observed to become ready and to run in an unexpected order. When analyzed, what is happening is correct for what was specified, but it is not what the programmer intuitively expected. Unwise choice of priorities can also lead to tasks hogging the processor. Consequently, sequencing problems and performance problems, as well as problems of cpu starvation for tasks, call for careful examination of task priorities.

The integration of interrupt hardware priorities with preemptive priority scheduling for tasks has associated a very common configuration error. The interrupt hardware priority level of a particular device is usually set in hardware, e.g., by jumpers, DIP switches, PALs, or PC board traces. The task awaiting the interrupt from that device must run at the corresponding preemptive priority scheduling level, which is declared in software. This is one of many aspects of device drivers where hardware and software must correspond. In general there is no automatic way to confirm that hardware and software configurations correspond, and again and again we have seen it wrong, with baffling effects.

3.8 Consider the consequences of task destruction. Dynamic task destruction has many benefits, but it introduces complications. There are two ways to implement task destruction: poison pill destruction where a task is sent a message to destroy itself and system imposed destruction where the system immediately stops the task from further execution. Poison pill destruction has the disadvantages that the task may ignore the message for some time, that it may improperly clean up thus losing resources, and that the code for destruction is repeated (with minor differences) in every task. Harmony therefore uses system imposed destruction, but that has the difficulty of arranging to clean up properly without knowing exactly what the task being destroyed was doing. By recording resources allocated to a task, it is straightforward for the system to scavenge resources; by recording the connections the task has open, it is straightforward for the system to notify the servers to close those connections; and by recording descendants of a task, it is straightforward for the system to eliminate orphan tasks. What the system cannot do, and thus is the programmer's responsibility, is to arrange that message protocols will recover appropriately when one of the participants is destroyed. The atomicity of the message passing primitives helps, the connection mechanism is safe, and in particular the client-server paradigm is safe provided that the server checks the result of the reply primitive to ensure the client was not destroyed before being replied to. Programmer-designed custom protocols, however, often are ill-behaved when tasks are destroyed unexpectedly.

A different aspect of task destruction that can cause problems is the fact that task destruction takes finite time, during which other tasks are running, and that it involves message passing between tasks, which is then subject to scheduling priorities. Task destruction in Harmony is complete, in that the destroy primitive does not return until all resources associated with the victim and its descendants have been released, but it is not atomic, and is not even immediate for the victim until the local task manager on the victim's processor has had a chance to receive and act on the destruction request. Unfortunate combinations of priorities can have predictable but awkward consequences, and unexpected intermediate situations can be exposed if the task desiring the destruction uses another task as an agent to call the destroy primitive in order to avoid blocking.

3.9 Look for unnecessary sequentialization. Harmony and related systems have been used extensively by programmers from novice to professional. The realtime programming course at the University of Waterloo alone has been taken by thousands of students over the last decade. What stands out as the most common design error in programs is that the message passing primitives are used in such a way as to cause unnecessary sequentialization. In other words, what is computed is correct, but opportunities for concurrentness or parallelism are prevented, with consequent loss of throughput or responsiveness. This error is called "subroutining", because the remote procedure call communication between tasks is used to induce a single thread of control, exactly as with subroutines. Clues leading one to suspect this problem are indirect, such as unsatisfactory throughput or responsiveness, or casual observation that the ready queues have fewer tasks on them than might be expected. Correspondents and blocking conditions of tasks that are not ready might also suggest the problem, but we must admit that our prime technique for identifying it has been reading the source code.

3.10 (Look for critical races and unsuspected shared variables). This is included as a final topic because it is a concern in some systems and in some design methodologies. Tasks on the same processor do share address space in Harmony and in many realizations of Harmony a pointer passed from one task to another can be used to access shared data even if the tasks are on different processors, so these problems can potentially happen. The converse problem, where each task accidentally ends up with a private copy of data that was intended to be shared occurs even more easily. Nevertheless, the effect of the message passing design methodology is such that only the most hardened miscreants schooled in the shared memory style of programming ever actually directly share data among tasks unless those data are constant or unless the protocol among the tasks involves a clear transfer of ownership of the data, with only the current owner ever accessing them. Consequently we have titled this topic in parenthesis, because we do not actually recommend taking the trouble to try it.

4. Features for debugging sequential programs. In considering design issues for an interactive debugger to be used on multi-task programs, the first observation is that much of a multi-task program is sequential, and hence the first issues to consider are features desirable for debugging sequential programs.

The key feature in interactive debuggers has been the breakpoint. A breakpoint is a mechanism for stopping the execution of the program when a specified event has occurred. Ideally, there are many kinds of events one might want for breakpoints: the execution of the instruction at a specified address, the use of data at a specified address, the use of data in a specified range of addresses (any field of a record or any element of an array), the use of a specified data value, the use of a specified addressing mode under specified conditions (use of a specified local variable in a specified function, regardless of the value of the stack pointer when the function is called), occurrence of a specified sequence of subevents, occurrence of a specified sequence of subevents without other specified subevents intervening, etc. With appropriate hardware support (e.g., an in-circuit emulator [7]), all these and more can be breakpoint events while the program runs at full efficiency. Unfortunately, adequate hardware support is rarely available (e.g., on every processor of a parallel computer), and interpretive execution is rarely acceptable, so most debuggers have had to make do with only the first kind of event, control passing through a certain address.

The simplest breakpoint mechanism is to compile a call to the debugger, as a subroutine, at the point of interest. The debugger as a subroutine is often considered unsatisfactory because the only options after a breakpoint are to quit or to resume; however, this restriction would probably apply in any case because the ability to restart execution anywhere, familiar from assembler level debuggers, is difficult to make work for high level languages. More seriously, the debugger as a subroutine is regarded as unsatisfactory because it imposes the slow edit-compile-link-download-execute cycle in the debugging process, so breakpoints that can be planted and removed as debugger operations are demanded instead. It should be noted that the debugger as a subroutine implies that it uses stack space, and we have already observed that stack overflow is a serious problem. If breakpoints are compiled in, then the stack bounder will allow for them as for any other procedure, but if they can be planted at run time, the worst case assumption of increasing the size of every stack is necessary, which can be costly if there are many lightweight tasks. Alleviating this problem suggests that the debugger should instead be a separate task, so a breakpoint only needs message sending stack space. This solution is attractive in that it also facilitates enhanced functionality, and so we use it with the Harmony debugger, nevertheless it does have drawbacks. For example, it means that breakpoints cannot be set in the lowest level of interrupt handling, because that is below the task abstraction and message passing can only be used within the abstraction. Using standard system services for handling breakpoints complicates the basic requirement of saving the task state so it can be examined and later restored, as the state that might change is more than just a few registers — to avoid this, some operating systems essentially duplicate their normal intertask mechanisms just for the debugger.

The usual method of planting breakpoints involves replacing the instruction to be breakpointed with a trap to a toehold of debugger code. The toehold can send a message to the debugger task, which then can determine whether the breakpoint applies to this task, can execute planted code, can initiate an interactive dialog, and so forth, but eventually will probably want to return from the breakpoint. To do this requires that the breakpointed instruction either be emulated or be replaced and executed in a controlled manner so that the breakpoint can be replanted immediately. When implementing breakpoints on a multi-tasking multiprocessor, there are some critical races that must be allowed for. Higher priority tasks can preempt a task that has tripped the breakpoint even while it is executing the toehold or emulating the breakpointed instruction, and of course they too may hit the breakpoint. It turns out that the most delicate critical races concern deleting planted breakpoints, and we have not found a satisfactory way to do this from another processor that shares address space. Instead we have been forced to use an agent task on the affected processor or to integrate this operation into the operating system kernel.

While the machinery for breakpoints exists to support interactive examination of the program, it can be used in a more general way to provide for planted code, of which a call to the interactive debugger is only one possibility. The immediate benefit of this approach is that it provides conditional breakpoints, where the interactive debugger is not entered every time control passes the trigger address, but only when some computable condition is satisfied. Another benefit is making temporary changes, especially repairs, to a program, thus deferring the edit-compile-link-download cycle, although this must be used with discipline so the changes are properly reflected in the source code. Planted code is often implemented as interpretive text executed within the context of the debugger, thus avoiding aggravating the stack overflow problem (and incidentally often fitting in more easily with a program compiled from a high level language). There are some interesting scoping questions about planted code, as to whether variables are evaluated in the context of the debugger or the context of the point at which the code is planted.

Where can breakpoints be placed? Users familiar with assembly level debuggers often want the ability to do single stepping of their programs. It is not always clear what this means in many high level languages, but there are examples of debuggers for such languages that do provide effective source level debugging. Unfortunately, most commercial compilers, especially those with significant optimization, leave little correspondence between the source level program and the machine language image that executes [13] — and provide inadequate symbol tables and no debugging schema to assist symbolic debugging. Function calls and returns are usually identifiable, and can be used as possible breakpoints, as sometimes can basic blocks, especially those with explicit labels. Often this is enough, which is perhaps not surprising, given that tracebacks of the stack are recognized as useful information for a debugger to display. This is also fortuitous, because in general, without help from the compiler, doing any more requires understanding and working with the compiler generated machine code. Working with compiler generated machine code is only practical with the aid of a disassembler.

The previous discussion of breakpoints focussed on what happens at a single breakpoint but, particularly when trying to understand performance issues or locate performance bugs, it is often useful instead to look between successive breakpoints or across several. A simple timer started by the resume command of the debugger and stopped when the next breakpoint occurs is a very effective tool for assessing particular critical paths. Program profiling can be done other ways, but building a profiler on a debugger, with counts and times taken at breakpoints, is attractive, especially when not all the source code is available, for instance when working with proprietary libraries.

Let us turn to the interactive aspect of the debugger. We have already indicated the importance of displaying state, and most state is recorded in complex data structures. While almost any debugger can display satisfactorily the value of a simple scalar variable, few will display an isolated record or an array in an intuitive way, and the insightful display of complex data structures is a real challenge [11]. Often the values the user needs to see are not directly available but must be derived. The first step in this is for the debugger to provide expression evaluation. These expressions should not just involve literal values, but also variables from the program, and debugger variables that provide a way to use values from earlier breakpoints. This statement implies that it should be possible to save expression values in debugger variables. It is also valuable to be able to store them in program variables. Patching values this way is of tremendous significance in its primary use to steer control flow: it is often the only practical way to explore error handling code when the errors are rare. It has a secondary use when an incorrect computation has been identified — if the correct input for the next stage of the computation can be patched in, it may be possible to defer the edit-compile-link-download-execute cycle until after the next problem is uncovered.

Expression evaluation is only the first step, however, and we have already described the significance of audit functions. Traditionally these are supported by being able to call procedures from the debugger. Again there are interesting scope problems, as to whether these are evaluated in the context of the debugger or the context of the breakpointed task. Other than supporting audit functions, calling procedures from the debugger has another important application, in that often the best way for the programmer to provide a problem-specific way to display a complex data structure is to provide a procedure the debugger can call to display it.

Many assembler level debuggers provide the ability to search memory for occurrences of specific (possibly multi-word) data. This has a role in high level language debugging also. When data structures are dynamically allocated, it may be easier to search the heap directly for a record you know should exist than to chase every possible chain it might be on. A search of the heap may be essential if you know the record has just been unlinked from a chain but has probably not yet been linked somewhere else or reallocated.

5. Features for realtime or parallelism. Whereas features useful for debugging sequential programs are relatively well understood, features for debugging realtime or parallel programs are still very much a research area, and there has been little experience [10]. Here are the things we have found useful, either ad hoc or as part of the Harmony debugger.

In preceding sections we discussed how the decreased role of control flow, and the increased significance of understanding state, resulted in the importance for multi-task programs of examining standard system data structures, and we also discussed audit routines as preferable to manual examination. Exactly because these data structures are important and are standard, and because their noteworthy aspects are also standard, audit and display routines for them should be provided with the debugger.

The first significantly different tool of realtime or parallel debugging, invented seemingly independently by each group of programmers with extensive realtime or parallel debugging experience, is the history buffer. To avoid having to rerun the program to learn how some situation occurred, with consequent questions of determinism or feasibility, we simply record significant events as they happen, so that we can go back and look at them later, if necessary. Normally this log is kept in a circular buffer, overwriting events no longer of interest, thus avoiding unbounded storage requirements and possibly even the costs of external I/O. Sometimes multiple buffers are kept with different wrap rates. What is written to a history buffer is a sequence of records, giving event type and parameters. The question of what events to write to history buffers is clearly up to the programmer and should be available both compiled in and planted, just like breakpoints. A history buffer can be read from the debugger without stopping the logging tasks. Experience indicates that recording too much is even worse than recording too little, as the log may not be long enough and even if it is, filtering out the events of interest can be too hard. It is worth noting that some people have explored correlating events from disjoint history buffers to reduce interaction artifacts from too many tasks contending over the same shared history buffer, and also that interactive dynamic graphics has been found useful to replay events leading up to something.

A tool similar to the history buffer, but which trades resolution in time for reduced synchronization overhead, is the vector of use bits. The name comes from the use bits and dirty bits that often support demand paging systems, providing an inexpensive record of access. A use bit in our context is explicitly cleared and is set by a compiled in or planted command. Often it is useful information to know that some piece of code, containing the set command, was not executed since the bit was cleared — and equally it is often useful information to know that the piece of code was executed at least once. A bit in the use bit vector might, for instance, be set in the code for a function so we can find if that function was ever called, or another bit might be set in the code for a task so that we can monitor to find how frequently the task is dispatched. Sometimes clearing and reading a group of use bits must be atomic to be useful.

It would be nice to have something like use bits for data structures, and of course we could set a use bit everywhere the data structure is referenced, but for many data structures this would be impractical, even if we just tried to identify where the data structure was changed. A tool that can be valuable is the ability to checksum an arbitrary block of memory. Checksumming blocks of memory (possibly containing many records) is useful for confirming that nothing has changed since the last time the block was checksummed, or for checking that something has actually changed as a precursor to a detailed exploration of the changes. There are some difficulties, however, in deciding what it means to say a data structure was unchanged. Is a list structure unchanged if the heap from which the records come is compacted, with pointers updated appropriately? If a record is deleted from a singly linked list by copying its successor over it, is the successor unchanged? Demanding this kind of equivalence makes monitoring difficult, even with hardware assistance.

Under features for debugging sequential programs we discussed the advantages of being able to call procedures from the debugger. The major problem in a multi-task situation is stack overflow again: as with planted breakpoints, the possibility of procedures called from the debugger cannot be predicted by the stack bounder. The solution is again the same, i.e., in a multi-task program, instead of calling procedures from the debugger, we need to create and destroy tasks from the debugger and most importantly we need to be able to create request messages, send them to such tasks, and interpret the reply messages. This facility is also useful for probing actors, such as the administrator task mentioned in the section on troubleshooting. It can also be used for stimulating execution of exception handling since in a multi-task program exception handling is often done by separate tasks.

We have already indicated that performance problems are a major concern in realtime and parallel computing. Load balance can be part of this. One way to detect problems, especially when tasks do not migrate between processors, is to look for excessive idle cycles on a processor. In many multi-task systems an idle task runs when a processor has no other work — if the idle task increments a counter that can be monitored by, say, a spy task, then excessive idle cycles can be detected easily.

For many message passing systems, the suggestion has been made that a useful debugging technique would be to intercept the messages, or to tap the I/O streams. This would be technically difficult to do in Harmony for two reasons. First, the use of remote procedure call semantics instead of asynchronous message sending means that the sender or receiver may, and often does, depend on the blocking behaviour of the other, and another task inserted between them might have difficulty duplicating that behaviour. Second, the fact that messages in Harmony are sent directly to a specified task_id instead of indirectly through some named channel, say, means there is no central place where intercepting the selected messages would be easy. We have not regarded this as a problem because our history buffers provide similar facilities.

6. User interface issues. All too often debuggers are unused because they are hard to learn and remember or because their output is confusing. Just distinguishing the dialogue you are having with the debugger from the dialogue you are having with the program being debugged is often a trial. Ever thought about using a traditional glass teletype oriented debugger to debug a new version of the debugger itself while it is being applied to some program? The user interface can make or break a debugger.

Program development requires learning a mass of details about the language, the libraries, the text editor, the problem specification, and so forth, and these details are memorized by continually working with them. If a debugger is to be powerful, that is, if it can provide needed facilities succinctly instead of forcing the user laboriously to concoct them manually from primitive operations, then the debugger interface must be rich, which, if it is command driven, means the user has a lot of notation and syntax to learn. Debuggers are not used as frequently as some other program development tools, however, so few programmers learn them well. The design of some debuggers attempts to reduce the burden by using the syntax and semantics of the language being debugged where possible in commands to the debugger, and similar benefits can be gained by the debugger being cognizant of system semantics. There are still gaps, however, in that one wants to do things with debuggers that are outside the language (such as to examine variables not currently in scope), and stretching semantics sometimes produces nonintuitive idioms or even clashes. Striking benefits have been seen when the debugger interface is driven instead by the modern facility of context sensitive pop-up menus [2], [3], where the user chooses only among options possible at the current point. People have even productively used such a debugger without being aware that a manual exists!

Even more important is the effect of the modern facility of multiple windows. Multiple windows are always nice, but one might go so far as to assert that for satisfactory debugging of multi-task programs they are essential. A number of features matter. First is the management of screen real estate. There is a lot of information a debugger can extract from a program, much of it only intelligible with highly structured display. The screen is never large enough, and if it were, things of interest might be too widely separated by clutter. It is not just that a scrolling glass teletype dialogue, losing items off the top, is unsatisfactory, but also that fixed form screens are inadequate. The user at the screen must have the ability to rearrange displays to bring together items he wants to focus on. He must also have the power of elision, to hide displays not currently of interest, yet be able to show those displays again when his focus changes. A second feature of importance is that the user should never have to retype data already displayed somewhere on the screen. Over the course of a debugging session so much has to be specified, detail is so important, and typing errors are so easy, that in traditional debuggers repeated attempts to get particular information are common, which is especially frustrating when that information had been displayed before! This problem is largely finessed by a pointing-based copy-and-paste ability. A third feature, alluded to in the opening of this section, is that separate windows for debugger dialogue and application dialogue immediately solves a traditional headache. This can be carried further by using disjoint windows for other functions such as symbol tables, crossreferences, source code display, etc. It is the fourth feature, however, that clinches the issue, and that is that separate windows can be used for the dialogues associated with debugging separate tasks. Because we recommend that debugger directives be associated with specific tasks and because tasks proceed asynchronously, a single debugger dialogue quickly loses track of less frequent activities.

Of course, ideally, the debugger dialogue should involve communication with the user at the level at which he thinks about his program, which is often described as symbolic debugging. Identifying variables and procedures by their symbolic names, relying on declared type information to automatically generate data structure display, and setting breakpoints or planting code in terms of the original source text contribute to this. We must note, however, that this ideal is not always achievable. There can be problems with the application itself. Deficiencies in the programming language may mean that the programmer actually thinks about his program in abstractions above the level of the language (dynamic storage management or use of records in Fortran, for instance), so it is desirable if at least the debugger lets such constructs exist. On the other hand, detailed pursuit of something (a timing dependent bug or a compiler bug, for instance) may force the programmer to think about his program at a much lower level than the language in which he wrote it, and the debugger needs to support that too.

More seriously, the ideal of communication at the user's level may not be achievable because of the environment. We already observed that most compilers do not support this because the symbol tables they produce are inadequate and they produce no debugging schema. If we want to be portable across development systems, this problem cannot be dismissed by sticking to a compiler that is good enough. A completely separate tool to process the source text and with access at most to load maps can alleviate but not remedy the problem. Even if we had no compiler problems, however, we still might not achieve the ideal. Most realtime computing, especially for embedded systems, is done on a target machine that is different than the host on which development was done, so the source code and other debugging information may not be available at run time and the original development host may not be attached. Proprietary libraries that are available only in object form have much the same effect. Production code distributed to the field, whether in embedded systems or mass market commercial products, again often exhibits this effect. In short, we cannot always count on source code being available nor on the executable image including debugger support, so we are forced to think of the debugger itself having access to a file system and building up there the information we need. Relying on a microcomputer as a smart terminal for the debugger is one approach.

The preceding discussion has brought out a point that is often overlooked, that serious debugging requires persistent context and conversely that persistent context can facilitate debugging. The simple observation is that a single snapshot of a program is not enough and that breakpoints tripped on instantaneous events only are not enough. We have already observed that debugger variables, to record values found earlier, qualitatively enhance expression evaluation and value patching, and that sequential triggering of breakpoints qualitatively enhances the ability to locate protocol bugs. Now we observe that understanding a complex program, debugging it and tuning it, does not happen in a single debugging session and that retaining context from one debugging session to the next can save a tremendous amount of time. Whether or not the executing program is saved and restarted, there is enormous value in the debugger being able to save things it has learned and read them to restart the next time.

The final user interface topic we want to touch on is how the debugger gets associated with the program in the first place. Traditionally, debuggers were linked in with test versions of programs, or the debugger was called as a command that then invoked the program it was to control. What this means is that when the program running in production fails, perhaps because of a rare and unanticipated event, the debugger is not available as a tool to locate the problem and get around it. When the debugger is a separate task, the cost of having it present even when the program is running in production is often small compared to the potential benefit. A programmer might even occasionally dial up such a program by remote access to monitor the program's health. Of course, in general, there would be no programmer conversing with the debugger as the program runs, and even if a human operator was interacting with the program when it suddenly took an exception, there is no guarantee that he would know what to do, or that adequate support information to recover would be available. Nevertheless, automatic entry into the debugger is a better last response than the traditional abnormal termination message!

7. Conclusions. When working in the right programming abstraction, supported by the right tools and techniques, debugging multi-task programs is no worse than debugging any other programs.

REFERENCES

[1] P. ABRAHAMS, *The role of failure in software design*, Commun. ACM, 29, 12 (December 1986), pp. 1129-1130.

[2] T. A CARGILL, *The Blit debugger*, J. Syst. Software, 3, 4 (December 1983), pp. 277-284.

[3] ———, *Implementation of the Blit debugger*, Software Pract. Exper., 15, 2 (February 1985), pp. 153-168.

[4] D. R. CHERITON, *The Thoth System: Multi-process Structuring and Portability*, North Holland, New York, 1982.

[5] W. M. GENTLEMAN, *Message passing between sequential processes: the reply primitive and the administrator concept*, Software Pract. Exper., 11, 5 (May 1981), pp. 435-466.

[6] ———, *Using the Harmony operating system*, NRC/ERB-966, National Research Council of Canada, Ottawa, Ontario, December 1983, revised March 1987.

[7] W. M. GENTLEMAN AND H. HOEKSMA, *Hardware assisted high-level debugging*, J. Syst. Software, 3, 4 (December 1983), pp. 309-314.

[8] R. L. GLASS, *Patching is alive and, lamentably, thriving in the real-time world*, ACM SIGPLAN Not., 13, 3 (March 1978), pp. 25-28.

[9] ———, *Persistent software errors*, IEEE Trans. Software Eng., SE-7, 1 (March 1981), pp. 162-168.

[10] M. S. JOHNSON, ed., *Proceedings of the ACM SIGSOFT/SIGPLAN Software Engineering Symposium on High-Level Debugging*, Pacific Grove, CA, March 20-23 1983; ACM SIGPLAN Not. 18, 8 (August 1983).

[11] B. A. MYERS, *Displaying data structures for interactive debugging*, Report CSL-80-7, Xerox PARC, Palo Alto, CA, June 1980, reprinted June 1982.

[12] G. SANDE, personal communication, 1971.

[13] P. T. ZELLWEGER, *Interactive Source-Level Debugging of Optimized Programs*, Ph.D. Dissertation, Computer Science Division—EESC, University of California, Berkeley, 1984; also Report CSL-84-5, Xerox PARC, Palo Alto, CA, May 1984.

CHAPTER 2

Matrix Computations and Game Playing on the iPSC*

Cleve Moler[†]
David S. Scott[†]

This talk discussed implementation of matrix computations and a game playing program on the Intel hypercube. The matrix computations are documented elsewhere [2], so this paper discusses only the game playing program. The original Othello program is described as well as the improvements that were incorporated in the second version. Also, our future plans for a chess program are given.

1. Introduction

This talk discussed two very different applications on the Intel hypercube--dense matrix computations and a game playing program. A write-up of the matrix computations has appeared elsewhere [2]. This paper will describe the game playing program.

Game playing programs have a long history in computer science. Chess has received the greatest attention, but many other two player games have also been investigated. For any given position, a game program will try to determine the best move to make. The rules of the game must be encoded so that all of the legal moves can be generated from any legal position. From a starting position, it is possible to create a game tree of all possible legal continuations. The arcs of the tree are the legal moves and the nodes are the resulting positions. By the rules of the game, certain positions have no legal moves. These terminal positions are wins, losses, or draws. Assuming that the game is finite, then it is possible to generate the complete game tree to determine whether a particular move leads to a win, a loss, or a draw.

In practice, the number of nodes in the game tree grows exponentially with the depth of the tree and computing a complete game tree for anything much more complicated than tic-tac-toe is impossible. Instead, the tree must be truncated and some method of evaluating the resulting positions must be used. This evaluation function requires much more game specific knowledge than the move generator and it is

---

* iPSC is a trademark of Intel Corporation
† Intel Scientific Computers, Beaverton, Oregon, 97006.

the heart of any game program. Finally, a technique is needed to
propagate the values of the leaves up through the tree until the
moves at the root can be scored. (The usual technique is called
alpha-beta searching (see section 4).) The highest scoring move is
then played by the program. Game programs require much of the same
kind of symbolic manipulation that other types of artificial intell-
igence programs require. They have the further advantage that they
are easy to validate. They can be played by expert human players or
by other programs to test how effective they are.

2.   Rules of Othello

Othello[2] was chosen over chess for the first game program to be
implemented on the iPSC because Othello is simpler, both in rules and
in strategy, than chess. At the same time, Othello is sufficiently
complicated to be a fair testbed for the tree construction and
searching algorithms. Othello is a two person strategy game. It
is derived from an earlier game called Reversi which was played in
England in the late 1800's. Two players, called black and white,
place discs on an 8X8 grid to try and capture their
opponent's discs and end up owning the most discs at the end of the
game. The initial position is as follows:

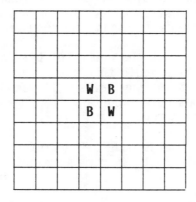

The rules are:

1.   Black moves first.

2.   Players alternate moving.

3.   If a player has no move available, he loses his turn.

4.   If neither player can move, the game is over.

5.   When the game is over, the player with the most discs wins.

6.   To make a move, you must make a capture.

7.   A capture occurs when the disc played makes a straight line
     (horizontally, vertically, or diagonally), with one or more
     enemy discs and a friendly disc at the other end (without any
     intervening spaces). All the intervening enemy discs are
     captured (turned over) and become friendly discs.

8.   All possible captures created by a play must be taken.

(2) Othello is a trademark of CBS toys.

3. Board Representation and Programming Language

There are 64 squares on the Othello board. Each square has three
possible states (black, white, and empty.). Thus, a total of 3^{64}
states must be represented which requires a minimum of 101 bits.
Actually, the four central squares are never empty and so 99 bits
are sufficient. However, such a compact storage scheme makes it
very difficult to manipulate the position (such as determining legal
moves and updating the position after a move is made). Alternatively,
the position could be represented using an 8X8 array of integers.
This is quite inefficient in space since it uses 16 bits per square
when only two are needed. It was decided to use bit boards in which
each bit position represents a square on the board. Two bit boards
are needed, one for the black pieces and one for the white pieces.

The move generator must be able to determine whether moving to a given
square is a legal move. This requires that the square is empty
(which is easy to check by examining the corresponding position in
the two boards) and that the move makes a capture. To verify a
capture, it is necessary to check the eight possible directions to
see if a nonempty sequence of enemy discs has a friendly disc at the
end. Care must be taken to avoid falling off the edge of the board.
This search is significantly simplified by surrounding the real board
by a set of permanently empty squares. This means that a search always
terminates normally without ever worrying about edges.

Unfortunately, this increases the number of bits per row from 8 to 10.
Perfect packing of the bits would then cause rows to start at arbitrary bits rather than on byte boundaries. It was decided that the
simplified addressing was more important than the extra space and so
16 bits were used for each row.

The decision to use bit boards made c the preferred programming
language over FORTRAN since it has much more powerful bit manipulation capabilities.

4. Alpha-beta Search

Given a full game tree of a specified depth and values for each of
the leaves, it is possible to propagate the values back up to the
rool using what is called the minimax algorithm. Assuming that the
values are computed with respect to the machine, then a node at which

the machine is to play is assigned the maximum value of all of its
children (the machine will make the best move) but a node at which the
opponent is to play is assigned the minimum value of all of its
children. However, it has been known for a long time that it is
not necessary to compute the value of all the leaves in order to
determine the value of the root. This truncation of the tree is
called alpha-beta searching (or pruning) [1]. The optimal number of
nodes that must be searched is much smaller than the total number of
nodes in the tree, but is is still exponential in the depth of the
tree. In the following game tree, the root has been assigned the
value 20. However, the value 20 could be computed without ever
computing the value 100 for the right most leaf. This branch (and
any other siblings) is "cut-off" by the value 10.

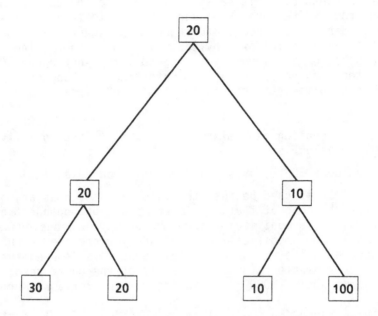

A standard alpha-beta searcher will do a depth first search of the
tree down to the specified depth. The alpha-beta pruning causes some
branches to be discarded without being searched. The amount of pruning
is strongly dependent on the order in which the children of a node
are searched. Two approaches can be used to try to obtain a good
ordering of the children. First, some game knowledge can be used to
try to order the moves as they are generated. This is the only
approach that can be used if only the current path from the root is
maintained in memory. Alternatively, if there is sufficient memory,
the entire tree can be stored. This saves time since previously
generated positions do not have to be regenerated and furthermore,
when a new level of the tree is generated, the old values of the
existing nodes can be used to order them. This procedure is called
iterative deepening. Finally, it is not even necessary to determine
the exact value of the root. It is only necessary to verify that
one move is better than the others.

5. Evaluation Function

Othello is an unusual game in that positions are very fluid. A disc
in the center of the board may be captured and recaptured many times.
On the other hand, discs on the edge are relatively stable and corner
discs are absolutely stable (can never be captured). Once a corner
has been captured, then it is possible for many more discs of the
same color to be absolutely stable by being adjacent to the corner.
Since the object is to own the most discs at the end, corners are of

utmost importance. Unfortunately, corners cannot be occupied unless
they create a capture. This makes plays next to the corner potentially dangerous. The squares diagonally next to the corner are
particularly dangerous since capturing central squares is usually
easy and this will be followed by capturing the corner. The early
part of an Othello game involves trying to force your opponent into
playing in these dangerous squares. Unfortunately, opponents tend
not to do this so the strategy is to eliminate all safe moves for the
opponent.

The evaluation function is a mixture of stability and mobility. The
basic mobility value is

$$value = 30*(mymoves - yourmoves)/(yourmoves + 1)$$

(the factor of 30 is used because the value is stored as an integer).
This captures the concept that the fewer moves your opponent has,
the better. This is modified by terms for occupying dangerous squares.
Further (and larger) modifications are made for occupied corners and
adjacent squares. The exception to this procedure is when the game
is over. Then evaluate returns the result of the game: zero if the
game is a draw and +/-(1000 + 10*winning margin) for a win or a loss.

Little time was spent on the evaluation function. The largest
improvement could be obtained by evaluating the four edge positions.
Some edge positions are very safe and others are very dangerous. The
current evaluator looks at each corner area separately and does not
look at whole edges. Another area of improvement would be in including potential mobility, in addition to current mobility, in the
function. On the other hand, this evaluation function combined with
a 3 or 4 move look ahead is sufficient to beat most human players.

6. Distributed Tree Alpha-Beta Search

The main reason for writing the Othello program was to produce and
test a distributed alpha-beta tree search algorithm. Distributed
algorithms can perform badly for two reasons. An algorithm has poor
load balancing if most of the processors are idle while a few
processors do most of the work. An algorithm has high **communication
overhead** if most of the time is taken in passing information between
nodes rather than in computation. Suppose that a task is divided
into np subproblems and each subproblem is solved by a separate
processor. Unless this subdivision is done very carefully, there is
a serious danger of load imbalance since, if one of the tasks takes
twice as long as the rest, then half of the processing power will
be wasted. The simplest way to obtain good load balancing is to
divide the total computation into many small tasks. Each processor
takes a task from a queue of available tasks. The completion of the
task may put new tasks on the queue. The problem is finished when
all the processors are done and the queue is empty. This procedure
is often called the problem heap paradigm (see [3]). The only load
imbalance is at the end, when only a few tasks are finishing but there

are no new tasks to hand out.   Provided the total number of tasks is
large enough, this imbalance can be made arbitrarily small.   Unfortunately, the communication overhead of starting a task is almost
independent of the size of the task.   To produce more tasks for the
same problem requires that each individual task is smaller.   This
means that communication overhead will eventually dominate and no
further speedup can be obtained (in fact, the time taken to solve the
problem actually increases).

For game problems, it is easy to visualize two kinds of tasks:
expanding a leaf by invoking the move generator, and evaluating a
leaf and propagating the value upwards.   Unfortuantely, the second
task may require access to the entire path back to the root.   It may
also have the effect of pruning other branches in the tree.   In order
to minimize the internode communication, it was decided to keep large
branches of the tree on the same processor.   The final decomposition
was as follows.

Node0 keeps the highest part of the tree and handles all communication with the host (which runs the user interface).   Each leaf in the
high tree is sent to another processor for evaluation.   The evaluation
(or **solve**) task runs standard sequential alpha-beta starting with the
received leaf as the root and expanding to a given depth (which is
set by the user at the beginning of the game).   The value of the
leaf is then sent back to Node0 which propagates it up the tree.   The
Node0 alpha-beta algorithm is somewhat different from the sequential
one since the values of the leaves may not return in a left to right
order.   This requires an extra field in the node to keep track of how
many children have returned values so that the algorithm knows when
to propagate further upward.

It is also necessary to build the tree in Node0 (both initially and
after each move is made).   A second kind of task (called **build**) is
used in which individual positions are sent to a processor for
expansion.   Movegen is called for the position and a list of new
positions is generated and sent back to Node0.   A slight savings was
obtained by delaying the update of a position with a given move as
long as possible.   In particular, the nodes of the Node0 tree contain
the old position and the new move.   When sent to another processor,
the first step is to update the position.   For a build task the
updated position is returned along with the list of new moves.   For
a solve taks, only the value is returned.   In both cases, a pointer
to the location of the leaf in the Node0 tree is sent from and
returned to Node0 so that the information can be attached to the
appropriate part of the tree.

Rather than have the other processor ask for tasks, it is simpler
for Node0 to maintain a queue of available processors in addition to
a queue of tasks.   The task queue is simply a list of pointers to the
current leaves of the Node0 tree.   Build tasks send leaves out to be
expanded while solve tasks send leaves out to be evaluated.

A completed build task adds more leaves to the tree (and the task queue) while a completed solve invokes parallel alpha-beta to propagate the returned value up the tree. All that is needed is a criterion for switching from building to solving. To obtain good load balancing, it is needed that the number of leaves to be solved be rather more than the number of processors. The original decision was to use ten times the number of processors. Unfortunately, due to the fact that many leaves are being simultaneously expanded, the actual number of leaves generated can only be estimated using an estimated branching factor.

To avoid large communication overhead, it is necessary that the solves do a fair amount of work. Early observations indicated that a solve depth of at least 2 was needed. However, solve depths of 0 and 1 were retained in the program to allow a larger range of strength of performance.

7. Modifications

The above Othello program played correctly but contained several performance flaws. The major performance flaw was that very few alpha-beta cutoffs were actually obtained. There were two major contributors to this problem. Because a number of leaves were being solved at the same time, by the time a solve returned with a value sufficient to cutoff a leaf, that leaf had almost certainly already been sent out to be solved. No attempt to terminate solves early had been implemented. Similarly, when a leaf was sent out to be solved, no context information was sent with it. In general, a solve should include a **window** of the highest and lowest values which currently exist on the path back to the root. This window might allow significant cutoffs during the solve process.

Other problems included the following. The program made no attempt to think off the move. It waited passively for the opponent to input a move. The program had no time control capability. At the beginning of the game the opponent set the depth of search in the solve tasks and then the program took whatever time was needed. This is insufficient in a tournament environment in which 25 minutes are allowed to finish the game. The program used integer indices into arrays as pointers. Since huge model c was not available, this limited the size of the structure holding the tree to 64K bytes, which was much less than the available memory.

A second version of the Othello program was written. It was intended to solve all of the above problems but not all of the changes were implemented. The new program used c pointer to maintain the tree so that more memory could be accessed (using malloc). The semantics of the tree were changed slightly. Each treenode maintained a movelist and an updated position. Each treenode also stored the number of its move in its parent's list. This saved significant storage since the leaves of the Node0 tree were now represented only as an element of a

movelist.   Each treenode also had integer fields hi and lo which
maintained the highest and lowest value on its path back to the root.
These values were updated as necessary by the parallel alpha-beta
procedure and they were sent (along with the position and move) when
a solve task was sent out.   Finally, to increase the likelihood that
siblings were solve sequentially (so that the hi and lo values were
up to date) the order in which solve were sent out was modified.
Each real leaf of the Node0 tree now represented a whole movelist of
solves to be computed.   These leaves were kept in a queue and one
move was sent out to be solved each time the leaf got to the front
of the queue.

It was intended to control time by controlling the number of leaves
in Node0 tree.   Currently, this is not implemented.   The number of
leaves in the Node0 tree (that is, how many build tasks are done) is
set in the program.   The current number is two times the number of
processors.   Thinking off the move was going to be implemented by
rotating the role of Node0 (renamed **manager**).   The current manager
would send the result of an opponent's possible move to another
processor.   That processor would catch it and take over the task of
manager.   If it finished, the current manager would send the opponent's next move to another processor.   When the opponent actually
moved, the current manager would promote one of the potential managers
and demote the others.   The purpose of rotating the managers was to
avoid running out of memory while thinking off the move.   This is not
completely implemented.

8.   Chess

If chess is implemented on the iPSC, it is becoming clear that it
will not use the same distributed tree structure that the Othello
program uses.   The primary reason for this is a common occurrence in
chess which is very rare in Othello.   For most games, the game tree
is not really a tree.   The same position may occur in many places in
the tree.   If these positions are coalesced into one node, the resulting structure is a graph instead of a tree.   In Othello, it is very
rare for the same position to occur twice and it is not worth checking for.   In chess, on the other hand, a depth 6 tree may contain the
same position 50 or more times.   To evaluate each position separately
is fatal to the efficiency of the program.   Unfortunately, in the
distributed Othello tree, these positions are spread out among the
processors.   There is no central location to do this position checking (in most chess programs this is accomplished by a hash table
which contains all the positions which have been seen).

A lesser problem (which is true even in the Othello program) is that
the subtrees which are solved are not saved.   This requires that
certain positions be recomputed and, more importantly, means that
their previous values have been lost.   Correct ordering of siblings
in the chess tree is even more important than in the Othello tree

because the average branching factor is much larger (about 10 for Othello and about 40 for chess).

It is expected that the chess program will maintain the structure of the tree in one processor but that the actual positions will be stored in the other processors. The master processor can check for repeated positions and control which nodes are expanded, while the remaining processors can do the actual move generation, position updating, and position evaluation. This will also allow for implementing other chess program techniques, such as the killer move heuristic [1].

[1] Frey, Peter W., "Chess Skill in Man and Machines",
          Springer-Verlag, New York, Inc., 1978

[2] Moler, Cleve, "Multiprocessor Matrix Computation",
          in "Proceedings of the Conference on Hypercube
          Multiprocessors", ed. Michael Heath, SIAM press,
          to appear.

[3] "Problem-heap: A Paradigm for Multiprocessor Algorithms",
          Moller-Nielsen, Peter and Jorgen Stunstrup Technical
          Report, Computer Science Dept., Aarhus University,
          Aarhus, DENMARK

CHAPTER 3

DOMINO: A Transportable System for Parallel Processing*

D. P. O'Leary[†]
G. W. Stewart[†]
Robert van de Geijn[†]

ABSTRACT

DOMINO is a system for coordinating processes running on a network of computers. A DOMINO program has the property of determinacy; it produces the same results to matter how its processes are assigned to processors and how they are scheduled for execution. In particular, this means that a DOMINO program can be debugged on a single processor with the assurance that it will work when it is distributed on a network. The system dependent parts of DOMINO have been isolated in two interfaces, so that it should be relatively easy to transport between systems.

1 Determinacy in Parallel Computations

DOMINO programs take place in a *computational network*, of which Figure 1 is a very simple example. It consists of four *nodes* represented by the square boxes. These nodes may thought of as programs that communicate with each other. The communication is through the lines indicated by the arrows. At the end of each arrow is a queue to store unconsumed messages.

Figure 2 contains a simple C program to pass the numbers $1, 2, \ldots, n$ from the first node to the last. Each node has its own copy of the program, which is divided into two parts. In the first part the node gets the number in mes. This part may be further subdivided. If the node is the first in the array, it generates

† Department of Computer Science, University of Maryland, College Park. * This work was supported in part by the Air Force Office of Sponsored Research under Grant AFOSR-82-0078.

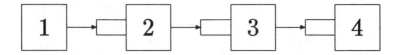

Figure 1: A Linear Computational Network

```
for (k=1; k<=n; k++){
    if (NODENO == 1)
        mes = k;
    else{
        request(&LEFT, &mes);
        pause();
    }
    if (NODENO != 4)
        sendn(&RIGHT, 1, &mes);
    else
        printf("%d", mes);
}
```

Figure 2: Message Passing Program

the message. Otherwise, it requests the message from its queue and pauses to allow the message to arrive.

In the second part, the node does something with the message. If it is not the last node, it passes the message to the queue of the node on the left; otherwise it prints the message.

Note the sequence by which information is transferred between nodes. The function sendn places a message on the queue of the node named by the first argument. A node may place as many messages on a queue as it likes. To get a message off a queue, a node must request it and then pause to allow the message to be delivered. The queues insure that messages cannot be delivered in the wrong order.

The sendn-request protocol gives DOMINO programs the property of determinacy. To see what this means, consider the two *execution sequences* in Figure 3. The first column contains the number of a node that is to be executed. The remaining columns contain the contents of the queues (or the output) immediately after the execution of the node. Node 1 must be executed first, since

Node	Q1	Q2	Q3	OUT
N1	4321			
N2	432	1		
N3	432		1	
N4	432			1
N2	43	2		
N3	43		2	
N4	43			2
N2	4	3		

Node	Q1	Q2	Q3	OUT
N1	1234			
N2	432	1		
N2	43	21		
N2	4	321		
N2		4321		
N3		432	1	
N3		43	21	
N3		4	321	

Figure 3: Two Execution Sequences

P1	P2	Q2	Q3	Q4	OUT
N1		4321			
N2		432	1		
N2	N3	43	2	1	
N2	N4	4	32		1
N2	N3		43	2	
	N4		43		2
	N3		4	3	

Figure 4: Parallel Execution Sequence

all the other nodes pause requesting input. When node 1 executes, it places the numbers 4321 on the input queue for node 2.

Thereafter the execution sequences diverge, and so do the contents of the queues. However, if we focus our attention on an individual node, say node 2, we see that at each execution in both sequences it receives the same input and produces the same output. This is what we mean by determinacy.

The two execution sequences in Figure 3 correspond to executing the program on a single processor using different algorithms to schedule the nodes. Figure 4 displays an execution sequence for two processors, the first running nodes 1 and 2 and the second nodes 3 and 4. Again determinacy is maintained; the nodes see the same input and generate the same output as in the other two execution sequences.

It should not be thought that determinacy is a consequence of the fact that our nodes are arranged in a linear array. Determinacy holds for arbitrary networks of nodes, provided only that there is a queue at the end of each connection between two nodes to preserve the order in which messages are passed.

Determinacy has the important consequence that a DOMINO program can be debugged on a single processor. For if the program runs correctly on one processor, it must run correctly when its nodes are distributed over a network of processors.[2] This is not to say that it will run well; just that it will somehow work its way to the end, each node producing the same output as it did on the single processor. This ability to debug on one processor is one of the more attractive features of the DOMINO system.

Actually, DOMINO has two levels—a deterministic core and nondeterministic extensions, which have been added for efficiency. In the next section we will describe the features of core DOMINO and in §3 we will describe the extension. The paper concludes with a discussion of how a DOMINO program is set up for execution.

2   Core DOMINO

A core DOMINO program consists of nodes running on a network of processors and communicating by the sendn-request protocol introduced in §1. In this section we shall give an overview of nodes and their implementation. For reasons of space, we can only sketch the outlines. The reader is referred to the DOMINO documentation for further details.

2.1   Nodes

In the language of operating systems, a DOMINO node is a process assigned to a processor; that is, it is a task that is scheduled for execution by a resident operating system. We shall discuss the operating system in §2.3.

It is important to distinguish between a node and the code that implements it. In many DOMINO programs, the individual nodes will be performing essentially the same functions and can be represented by a single piece of code, which we call a *node program*. The program in Figure 2 is an example. DOMINO allows nodes to share programs.

A node can be in three states: READY, ACTIVE, and DETACHED. A READY node is one that is ready for execution, but has not yet been awakened by the system. An ACTIVE node is one that is currently executing. A DETACHED node is one that is finished executing. A node can detach itself by invoking the function finis.

Nodes have two kinds of variables: internal and auxiliary. The variable k in Figure 2 is an example of an internal variable. The internal variables of a node are maintained on a stack associated with the node.

---

[2] Here we assume that communicating nodes are assigned to processors that can communicate and that the scheduling algorithms on the processors allow each node its chance to execute.

The internal variables of a node cannot be initialized by other nodes. To circumvent this problem, nodes are provided with auxiliary storage which can be accessed by other nodes. An example might be the variable LEFT in Figure 2, which would presumably be initialized to identify the node to the left of the node being executed.

A node is uniquely specified by the processor that it is on and by its position in the *node table*, a table of all the nodes on the processor. This way of identifying nodes is economical; but since nodes can be created and destroyed (see §4 for more details), it can be risky. DOMINO therefore provides an alternative by which a node can be assigned a name, which serves to identify it.

There are three kinds of nodes: USER, UTILITY, and EXECUTIVE. USER nodes are the garden variety node that would be created by the typical user. UTILITY nodes are built into the system and perform special functions—for example initializing the system to the user's specification. EXECUTIVE nodes were included to enhance DOMINO's value as a research tool. On the reception of a special control message, DOMINO will stop executing USER nodes and start executing EXECUTIVE nodes, which might compile a report on the status of the user nodes. Another control message toggles the system back to executing USER nodes. In this way one can take snapshots of a DOMINO program as it is executing.

2.2   Communication

Communication between nodes in core DOMINO is managed by **sendn-request** sequences of the kind illustrated in Figure 2. The **sendn** function causes the following to happen.

1. The message is wrapped in a packet containing identifiers of the source node and the destination node.

2. The packet is transmitted to the processor on which the destination node resides.

3. The packet (less the destination node identifier) is placed on a queue, called the *inqueue*. Each node has its own inqueue.

The **request** function causes a request for a message from the source node to be placed on a queue, called the *wantqueue*. As with the inqueues, each node has its own wantqueue.

After a **sendn-request** pair has been issued, the destination node has a message on its inqueue and a request for that message on its wantqueue.[3] The

---

[3] Actually it may have several entries on both queues, depending who has sent it messages and what messages it has requested

problem is to get them together and deliver the message. To do this the destination node must invoke the function pause, which returns control to the system where the matching and delivering is done. It is now time to examine the system in greater detail.

2.3   Control

Figure 5 contains a block diagram of the control system that is resident on each processor. We call this system DOMINA to distinguish it from DOMINO, which refers to the entire system as it exists on all the processors.

DOMINA consists of three parts: data structures, system dependent interfaces, and control functions. We have already encountered the data structures—the node table, the inqueues, and the wantqueues. We will now discuss the interfaces and the control functions.

DOMINA uses two interfaces, one to awaken nodes and one to communicate between processors. Each depends on the system on which DOMINO runs and must be coded specially.

CONOFACE (for *control node interface*) mediates between DOMINA's control program and the node programs. It has the responsibility for retrieving the stack pointer for a node as it is awakened by DOMINA and saving it when the node returns control to DOMINA. It also saves the location where the node paused. If the node finished with a finis(), it sets the node's status to DETACHED.

PROFACE (for *processor interface*) is used by the data transmission function sendn to transfer messages between processors. It also invokes the function accept to place information from other processors on the queue.

The isolation of system dependent features into these two interfaces is deliberate. The hope is that it will make DOMINO relatively transportable. Certainly this is true of CONOFACE; we have coded versions for a VAX, a SUN workstation, an IBM PC, and the ZMOB, a parallel computer at the University of Maryland. Since a PROFACE need only be written for a multiprocessor system, our only experience here is with the ZMOB. However, this experience suggests that PROFACES should not be too difficult to code.

Perhaps the best way of understanding control functions of DOMINA is to follow it as it awakens a node and then follow the node until it returns control to DOMINA. The reader should consult Figure 5 during this discussion.

The story begins in control, just after a node has returned control to DOMINA. The first task control faces is finding another node to awaken. This is the function of *schedule*, which proceeds through the node table in an order that depends on the particular implementation of DOMINO examining each node to see if it is ready for execution. The actual determination is done by the function ready, which tries to satisfy the requests on the node's wantqueue with entries

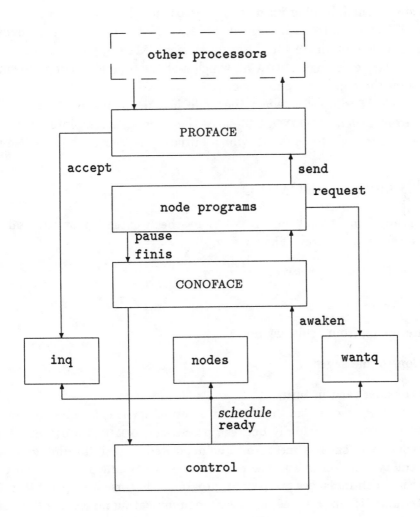

Figure 5: DOMINA

on its inqueue. In doing so **ready** transfers messages from the inqueue to their final destinations. If the node wants nothing when **ready** is finished with it, **ready** tells *schedule* that the node is ready to execute, and *schedule* passes the news back to **control**, which awakens the node. If not, *schedule* passes another node to **ready**.

When DOMINA receives a node from *schedule*, it invokes its node program using the CONOFACE awaken function. This causes the node to begin executing at the statement following its most recent pause. The node can compute and send and receive data as described in §2.2. Note that function **sendn** uses PROFACE to communicate with other processors. Messages from nodes on other processors arrive through PROFACE, which uses the function **accept** to enter the message on the appropriate inqueue.

The cycle is completed when the node invokes **pause** or **finis** to return control from DOMINA. CONOFACE saves the node's stack pointer, restores the old one, and returns to **control**, which initiates another round of scheduling.

3   Extended DOMINO

We mentioned in §1 that core DOMINO has been extended by the addition of nondeterministic features. They are

1. Message passing between processors.

2. DATA nodes.

3. Receiving from arbitrary nodes.

4. Control messages.

Let us consider each in turn.

The queuing mechanism that insures determinacy is expensive to implement. In order to move data rapidly between processors, DOMINO provides a function **sendp** which will cause a message to be deposited directly beginning at a specified memory location in another processor. Since DOMINO has no control over what order such messages are passed, programs that use **sendp** are in principle nondeterministic. In practice, however, communicating nodes will use **sendn** to synchronize such messages and thereby retain determinacy.

In some applications it is desirable for different nodes to manipulate the same data. For example, one computational network may compute a matrix decomposition, while another may apply the decomposition. To accommodate the need for common data, DOMINO provides DATA nodes that consist entirely of auxiliary storage. Special functions allow a node the access this data. Although data sharing is a nondeterministic construction, DATA nodes, like `sendp`, are usually used in such a way that there is no loss of determinacy.

If DOMINO programs are identified with computational networks, it should be possible for one network to use another as a subprogram. Unfortunately, we cannot use the `sendn-request` protocol to send parameters to a subnetwork, since that network will not in general know who is going to call it. To get around this problem, DOMINO allows a node to request a message from anyone. Such requests will will be satisfied by the first item on the inqueue that does not match previous requests on the wantqueue.

Finally, DOMINO provides a mechanism for handling asynchronous control messages from a master processor. We have seen one use of this in §2.1, where we discussed the use of EXECUTIVE nodes.

4 Setting Things Up

A DOMINO program is executed by linking its node programs with DOMINA and downloading it to the processors of the system. On each processor, the following operations occur.

1. DOMINA performs some system independent initialization and then awakens a UTILITY node whose program is named `boot`.

2. The boot node, which will differ from system to system, initializes storage pools, perhaps requesting information from the user on how to allocate storage. It then creates a USER node whose program name is go. This program is provided by the user, and is the DOMINO equivalent of the main program. The boot node may initialize the auxiliary storage of the go-node; e.g. setting up identifiers of go-nodes on neighboring processors. The boot-node then quits with a `finis`.

3. DOMINA now awakens the go-node. From here on it is the user's responsibility to create any further nodes that may be needed by the program and initialize their auxiliary storage.

There are two things to observe about this procedure. First, the boot node is the link between the system and the DOMINO program. Since the boot node knows the geometry of the network of processors, it is in a position to initialize identifiers in the go node. Eventually, we may hope that standard boot nodes will emerge for the various geometries of processors.

The fact that nodes can create other nodes increases the flexibility of DOMINO programs. In our typical applications, the go node does little more than create and initialize the nodes that actually do the work. It may also control the action of several computational networks, all manipulating DATA nodes which the go-node has created and initialized.

A Word on Availability

Preliminary documentation for DOMINO will be released as a University of Maryland Computer Science Technical Report, and should be available by the time this article appears.

CHAPTER 4

Statistical Methodologies for the Control of Dynamic Remapping*

Joel H. Saltz[†]
David M. Nicol[†]

Abstract. Following an initial mapping of a problem onto a multiprocessor machine or computer network, system performance often deteriorates with time. In order to maintain high performance, it may be necessary to remap the problem. The decision to remap must take into account measurements of performance deterioration, the cost of remapping, and the estimated benefits achieved by remapping. We examine the tradeoff between the costs and the benefits of remapping two qualitatively different kinds of problems. One problem assumes that performance deteriorates gradually, the other assumes that performance deteriorates suddenly. We consider a variety of policies for governing when to remap. In order to evaluate these policies, statistical models of problem behaviors are developed. Simulation results are presented which compare simple policies with computationally expensive optimal decision policies; these results demonstrate that for each problem type, the proposed simple policies are effective and robust.

1. Introduction. The performance of message passing multiprocessors and of distributed systems often hinges on the way in which data is distributed throughout the memories of the individual processors in the system or network. In many computational problems a discrete model of a physical system is assumed, and a set of values is calculated for every domain point in the model. Portions of a domain are assigned to the memory of each processor, and each processor assumes responsibility for calculations that relate to the subdomain assigned to its memory. As the problem proceeds, for reasons to be discussed later, changes may occur in the amount of work required for the calculations and communications pertaining to the portion of the problem assigned to a processor. Due to the coupling between subdomains, the rate at which progress is made in solving the problem is limited by the maximally loaded processor. System performance deteriorates

---

*This research was supported by the National Aeronautics and Space Administration under NASA Contract Numbers NAS1- 17070, NAS1-18107.
[†]ICASE, NASA Langley Research Center, Hampton VA 23665.

in time, often in a relatively gradual way, and at some point a remapping of the problem onto the processors may be advantageous. We shall call these types of problems *varying demand distribution problems*. Statistical models are developed of the behavior of this kind of problem and through the use of these models, policies are evaluated for deciding when remapping should occur.

In a wide variety of applications, the patterns of processor use and memory access are determined directly or indirectly by a population of users or programs whose requirements are difficult to anticipate. Database management systems are examples of such applications. When a database management system is mapped onto computer systems so that responsibility for computations and communications pertaining to subsets of the stored information is assigned to a given processor, the distribution of work among the processors is highly dependent on the nature of the queries received. A related problem occurs in the parallel simulation of digital circuitry. When responsibility for computations concerning particular circuit elements are assigned to each processor, the distribution of work among processors becomes highly dependent on the portions of the circuit currently undergoing testing. The system performance is closely linked to the distribution of work among the processors, and this distribution depends on often unpredictable inputs to the program.

Once a partition is chosen, it is necessary to monitor the performance of the system to determine whether changes in the nature of the inputs have caused a statistically demonstrable deterioration in system performance. The repartitioning of these applications may cost substantial overhead and consequently should be undertaken only when an overall benefit can be anticipated. If deterioration in system performance has taken place, it needs to be determined whether repartitioning might be worthwhile. A period of time in which a program exhibits no statistically demonstrable change in behavior will be called a *phase*. Problems which consist of a number of consecutive phases will be called *multiphase* problems. In this paper we shall discuss probabilistic models that describe varying demand distribution problems and problems exhibiting multiphase behavior. Policies for weighing the costs and benefits of partitioning for both types of problems will be evaluated.

2. Varying Demand Distribution Problems. Varying demand distribution problems assume a discrete model of a physical system, and calculate a set of values for every domain point in the model. These values are often functions of time, so that it is intuitive to think of the computation as marching through time. When such a problem is mapped onto a message passing multiprocessor machine, or a shared memory machine with fast local memories, regions of the model domain are assigned to each processor. The running behavior of such a system is often characterized as a sequence of steps, or iterations. During a step, a processor computes the appropriate values for its domain points. At the step's end, it communicates any newly computed results required by other processors. Finally, it waits for other processors to complete their computation step, and send it data required for the next step's computation.

The computational work associated with each portion of a problem's subdomain may change over the course of solving the problem. This may be true if the behavior of the modeled physical system changes with time. The distribution of computational work over a domain may also change in problems without explicit time dependence because during the course of solving a problem, for example, more work may be required to resolve features of the emerging solution. Since time stepping is often used as a means for obtaining a steady state solution, there is considerable overlap between the above mentioned categories. Because of the synchronization between steps, the system execution time during a step is effectively determined by the execution time of the slowest, or most heavily loaded processor. We can then expect system performance to deteriorate in time, as the changing resource demand causes some processor to become proportionally overloaded. One way of dealing with this problem is to periodically redistribute, or remap load among processors.

Changing distributions of computational work over a domain arise through the use of adaptive methods in the solution of hyperbolic partial differential equations in which extra grid points are placed in some regions of the problem domain in order to resolve all features of the solution to the same accuracy [1],[2],[3],[4], [5],[6]. A number of studies have investigated methods for redistributing load in message passing processors for this type of problem [7],[8],[9]. Vortex methods may be applied to the numerical simulation of incompressible flow fields. In these methods, invicid fluid dynamics is modeled by parcels of vorticity which induce motion in one another [10], [11]. The number of vortices corresponding to a given region in the domain varies during the course of the solution of a problem. Methods for dynamically redistributing work in this problem have been investigated [12].

In multirate methods for the solution of systems of ordinary differential equations[13], different variables in the system of equations are stepped forward with different timesteps. The size of the timesteps in the system is generally equal to that of a globally defined largest timestep divided by an integer. The size of the different timesteps utilized may vary during the course of solving the problem, and hence the computational work associated with the integration of a given set of variables may change. Methods for solving elliptic partial differential equations have been developed where iterations on a sequence of adaptively defined meshes are carried out [14],[15],[16],[17],[18] Generally both the total amount of computational work required by each of the meshes and the distribution of work within the domain changes as one moves from one mesh to the next. In time driven discrete event simulations [19], one simulates the interactions over time of a set of objects. Responsibility for a subset of objects is assigned to each processor. Over the course of the simulation, subsets of objects may differ in activity, and hence in their computational requirements. This problem may also arise in parallel simulations which synchronize asynchronously, such as those described in [20], [21], [22], [23], [24], [25].

There are two fundamentally different approaches to such remapping. The decentralized load balancing approach is usually studied in the context of a queueing network [26],[27],[28],[29],[30],[31], [32]. Load balancing questions are then focused on "transfer policies", and "location policies"[26]. A transfer policy governs whether a job arriving at a service center is kept or is routed elsewhere for processing. A location policy determines which service center receives a transferred job. Decentralized balancing seems to be the natural approach when jobs are independent, and when a global view of balancing would not yield substantially better load distributions.

However, a large class of computations is not well characterized by a job arrival model, and it may be advantageous to take a global, or centralized perspective when balancing. We will call a global balancing mechanism "mapping" to distinguish it from the localized connotations of the term load balancing. A centralized mapping mechanism can exploit full knowledge of the computation and its behavior. Furthermore, dependencies between different parts of a computation can be complex, making it difficult to dynamically move small pieces of the computation from processor to processor in a decentralized way. Global mapping is natural in an computational environment where other decisions are already made globally, e.g. convergence checking in an iterative numerical method. Yet the execution of a global mapping algorithm may be costly, as may the subsequent implementation of the new workload distribution. A number of authors have considered global mapping algorithms policies under varying model assumptions, for example, see [33], [34], [35], [36], [37], [38], and a comparison between global and static mapping strategies is reported in [39].

For the types of problems we describe, *remapping* the load with a global mechanism is tantamount to repartitioning the set of model domain points in regions, and assigning the newly defined regions to processors. A mapping algorithm of this sort is studied in [7] and the performance of this mapping algorithm in the context of vortex methods is investigated in [12]. Decision policies determining *when* a load should be remapped become quite important. The overhead associated with remapping can be high, so it is important to balance the overhead cost of remapping with the expected performance gain achieved by remapping. While this is a generic problem, the details of load evolution, of the remapping mechanism, and of various overhead costs are system and computation dependent. In order to study general properties of remapping decision policies, it is necessary to *model* the behavior of interest, and evaluate the performance of decision policies on those models. In the present paper we consider remapping of varying demand distribution problems using three different stochastic models.

The evaluation of policies for memory management in multiprogrammed uniprocessor systems has successfully employed a number of stochastic models to reflect the memory requirements of typical programs [40],[41]. In these models, the principal of memory reference locality plays a central role. Evaluating policies for scheduling a remapping in message passing machines is somewhat similar in spirit to the evaluation of paging algorithms in multiprogrammed uniprocessor systems. The principal of locality that we attempt to capture here is the locality of resource demand. The computational work corresponding to the problem region assigned to a given processor will often vary in a gradual fashion. In this paper we consider two models which describe this evolution probabilistically. The first model assumes that the computational requirements of each partition region behaves as a Markov chain, independently of any other region; this is called the Multiple Markov chain (MUM) model. The MUM model has the advantage of being analytically tractable in several ways. However, for many problems it may not be reasonable to assume independence in load evolution between partition regions. We address this issue with a second, less tractable model, the Load Dependency (LD) model. These models attempt to capture the dynamics by which the distribution of computational load changes in time, and are characterized by a small number of important parameters. Through the use of these load evolution models, we are able to evaluate policies for deciding when load should be remapped.

3. The Multiple Markov Chain Load Model. We describe both the drifting load and synchronization aspects of varying demand distribution problems with the Multiple Markov chain (MUM) model. MUM characterizes a processor's changing load by a discrete Markovian birth-death process. The state s of the chain is a positive integer describing the execution time of the processor at a step. We also assume that $s \leq L$ for some L. The transition probabilities out of s reflect the principle of locality, where all one step transitions are to neighboring states. When s is between 2 and $L-1$, the probability that the chain will make a one step transition to state $s+1$ is $p/2$, the probability of a one step transition to $s-1$ is $p/2$ and the probability that the chain will not make a transition is $1-p$. For $s = 1$ or $s = L$, the state remains the same with probability $1 - p/2$, and moves to the single neighboring state with probability $p/2$.

A system of N parallel processors is modeled by an independent and identically distributed collection of birth-death processes. We let $T_j(n)$ represent the time required by the jth processor to complete the nth step. The time required for the system as a whole to complete the nth step is given by

$$T_{max}(n) = \max_{1 \leq j \leq N}\{T_j(n)\}.$$

We thus model synchronization by requiring the system to wait for the longest running processor. The average processor execution time during the nth step is simply

$$\bar{T}(n) = \frac{1}{N}\sum_{j=1}^{N}T_j(n).$$

One measure of system performance during the nth step is the difference between the system execution time and average processor execution time at that step. In fact, this difference plays a key role in our remapping decision policy. Another parameter playing a key role is the cost of remapping once, denoted by C. This cost includes both the communication costs and the computational overhead required for performing a remapping operation. Note that for the sake of tractability, the cost of remapping is assumed here to be independent of the way in which load is distributed at the time remapping occurs. The cost of remapping may be affected in a problem and machine dependent way by the distribution of load prior to balancing.

Figure 1a depicts the behavior of the MUM model for varying numbers of chains. The performance shown is the average (per step) processor utilization as a function of step, taken over 500 simulations or sample paths, where $p = 0.5$ and each chain has 19 states. Performance declines more quickly and to a lower level as one simulates a problem with an increasingly large number of independent processors. For a given number of chains, the performance decline arises from the fact that the expected value of $\bar{T}(n)$ remains relatively constant as n increases, while the expected value of $T_{max}(n)$ increases in n. Figure 1b depicts the performance of single sample paths of the MUM model using varying numbers of chains, where as before $p = 0.5$ and each chain has 19 states. Note that the decline in performance as a function of step is true only in the sense of comprising a long term trend; each curve has many local maxima and minima. This point is particularly important, because any dynamic real time remapping policy mechanism is concerned with the current single sample path defined by the computation's execution.

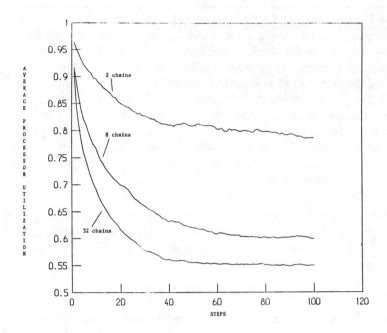

Figure 1a. MUM Model: Expected Average Processor Utilization as a
          Function of Step Estimated from 500 Sample Paths.   Each
          chain has 19 states, p = 0.5.

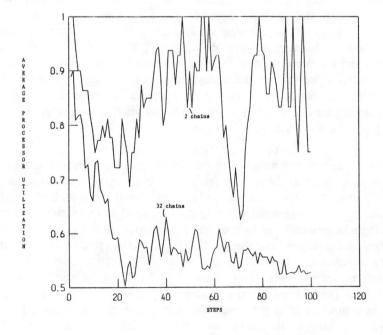

Figure 1b. MUM Model: Average Processor Utilization as a Function
          of Step–Single Sample Path. Each chain has 19 states,
          p = 0.5.

In considering the performance of the MUM model, both C and the difference $T_{max}(n) - \overline{T}(n)$ are viewed as costs; if the computation is first remapped at step n, then the average cost per step is denoted $W(n)$, and is given by

$$W(n) = \frac{\sum\limits_{j=1}^{n}(T_{max}(j) - \overline{T}(j)) + C}{n}.$$

In [42] we show that that for the MUM model, as long as the Markov chains are not extremely active, $E[T_{max}(n)] - E[\overline{T}(n)]$ is an increasing function of n. It is also shown there that if $E[T_{max}(n)] - E[\overline{T}(n)]$ is an increasing function of n, then $E[W(n)]$ has at most one local minimum. Furthermore, if that minimum exists at $\hat{n}$, and if remapping "resets" the behavior of $E[T_{max}(n)] - E[\overline{T}(n)]$, then the optimal fixed-interval remapping policy (which includes never remapping) is to remap every $\hat{n}$ steps.

An intuitively appealing remapping decision policy is to monitor system performance and to remap when the experimentally measured $W(n)$ is minimized. Even though the expected value of $W(n)$ may have at most one minimum, we have no such guarantee for a given simulation or sample path. The Stop at Rise (SAR) remapping policy chooses to remap when the first local minimum m of $W(n)$ is detected. Note that we cannot know that a local minimum of $W(n)$ was achieved at step m until step $m+1$, consequently we must remap at $m+1$ and achieve average cost $W(m+1)$.

Figure 2 shows the values of $W(n)$ achieved by simulation runs based on the MUM model when $p = 0.5$, $L = 19$, and $C = 8$. It is interesting to note that the value of $W(n)$ at its first local minimum tends to be quite close to the minimum value of $W(n)$. For a variety of MUM model parameter values, simulations were carried out comparing the expected value of the global minimum of $W(n)$ to the expected value of the local minimum of $W(n)$. The differences between the global and the local minima were observed to quite minor.

We studied the performance of the SAR policy by comparing it to three other policies: the optimal policy, the "remap every m steps" policy, and the policy which never remaps. It is possible to compute the expected time required to complete small sized problems when the optimal Markov decision policy is utilized to decide when to remap. Figure 3 compares a performance metric for the Markov decision policy, SAR, and a non-remapped system for three chains, 100 steps, and various remapping costs. The SAR data is the average of 500 simulation runs for each value of C. As the remapping cost increases, the discrepancy between the performance obtained through the optimal decision policy and SAR increases. With increasing remapping cost, both the performance of the optimal decision policy and of SAR approach the performance obtained when no remapping is performed.

The performance metric used in figure 3 for all policies depicted in that figure is an estimate of processor utilization: the *ratio* of the *expected* $\sum\limits_{j=1}^{n}\overline{T}(j)$ to the *expected* total time

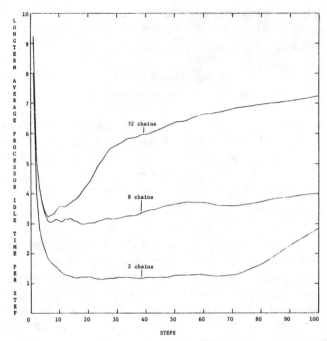

Figure 2.   Longterm Average Processor Idle Time per Step w(n) from
Single Sample Path.   Each chain has 19 states, p = 0.5,
load balancing cost = 8.

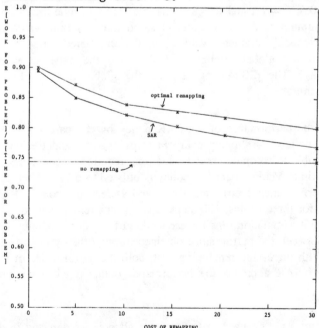

Figure 3.   MUM Model: Performance of Optimal Remapping Decision
Policy Compared with Performance of SAR.   Three chains,
100 steps, each chain has 19 states, p = 0.5, SAR
performance calculated from 500 sample paths.

spent by the system to solve the problem, including the cost of all remappings. This measure is useful in figure 3 as it is straightforward in the case of the optimal policy to calculate the expected time required to complete a problem as well as the expected $\sum_{j=1}^{n}\overline{T}(j)$. For
all subsequent figures, performance data is obtained by simulation, and the easily computed
average performance over all simulations is utilized, i.e. the *mean* of the *ratio* of the
$\sum_{j=1}^{n}\overline{T}(j)$ to the total time spent by the system to solve the problem, including the cost of all
remappings. Both performance measures were computed for all simulations, and found to
differ from each other by less than one percent.

One simple but intuitive remapping policy is the "remap every *m* steps" policy, or
fixed interval policy. This policy is insensitive to statistical variations in a system's performance, and requires pre-run-time analysis to determine an effective value of *m*. However,
we might well choose to employ a fixed interval policy if it is costly to measure system
performance at every step. In this case, we would attempt to choose *m* to optimize the
system's *expected* performance. In figure 4, we compare the performance obtained through
the use of: (1) SAR , (2) the fixed interval policy for a wide range of values of *m*, and (3)
not remapping at all. The performance obtained in a system using the MUM model with
eight independent processors is depicted. Each problem consists of 400 steps, each data
point is obtained through 200 simulations, and remapping costs of 2 and 8 are assumed.
For the SAR policy, we plotted performance against the calculated average number of steps
between consecutive remappings. In the fixed interval policy, we plotted performance
against *m*, the fixed number of steps between remappings. The number of steps between
remappings has no meaning when no remapping is done, the performance obtained when
no remapping occurs is plotted as a straight horizontal line to facilitate comparison with the
other results. The calculation of the performance obtained through the use of the optimal
Markov decision policy is not practical in this case due to the long run times and large
memory requirements that would be required.

It is notable that SAR's performance was comparable and in fact slightly higher than
that obtained by remapping at the optimal fixed interval. The average number of elapsed
steps between SAR remappings corresponds closely to the optimal fixed interval remapping
policy. Similar results were obtained in other cases using the MUM load model. These
results are encouraging for two reasons. Since SAR adapts to statistical variations in the
system's behavior, we would hope that it can outperform a non-adaptive policy. Our data
shows that SAR outperforms the **optimal** fixed interval policy. Secondly, SAR appears to
find the "natural frequency" of remapping for a given remapping cost. While the exact
number of steps between remappings may vary with the system's sample path, the average
number of steps between remappings is close to that of the optimal fixed interval policy.
Note also that the performance obtained by SAR is markedly superior to the performance
obtained when no remapping is performed. From extensive simulation results not
presented here, we found that the difference between the performance obtained by SAR
and the performance obtained when no remapping is performed increases with the number
of chains. This is consistent with the observed results in figures 3 and 4.

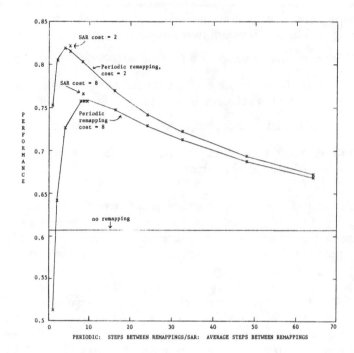

Figure 4.   MUM Model: Performance of SAR Compared with Performance
of Periodic Remapping.   Eight chains, 400 steps, each
chain has 19 states, p = 0.5, each data point calculated
from 200 sample paths.

In the face of uncertainty about future problem behavior, it is reasonable to design a
remapping decision policy which optimizes performance locally in time. The SAR policy
does this by attempting to minimize $W(n)$, a statistic which measures performance since the
last remapping. Performance experiments show that the SAR policy effectively finds the
"natural frequency" of remapping as a function of the rate at which resource demand
changes, and the cost of remapping. As such, SAR is a promising policy for real remapping situations. We will next demonstrate that the SAR policy can also be effectively
employed with computational models other than the MUM model.

4. Load Dependency Model. While the MUM model is analytically tractable, some of
its assumptions may not be realized in practice. For example, MUM assumes that a
processor's load drift is stochastically independent of any other processor's load drift. It is
easy to construct examples where this assumption is violated. This flaw could be corrected
by allowing correlation between chains' transitions, but then an appropriate model of correlation would have to be determined. MUM also assumes homogeneous Markov chains;
there is no problem in allowing heterogeneous chains, but the analysis we have developed
does not apply to such a model. More seriously, the MUM model implicitly assumes that
the transitional behavior of a processor's computational load is determined by the processor, rather than the load. This flaw is corrected in a model where the distinction between a
processor and its load is clearly drawn. We call this the Load Dependency (LD) model.

The LD model directly simulates the spatial distribution of computational load in a domain. We consider a two dimensional plane in which activity occurs, for example, a factory floor. To simulate this activity we impose a dense regular grid upon the plane; each square of the grid defines an *activity point*. We suppose that activity in the plane is discretized in simulation time, and model the behavior of activity as follows. Each time step a certain amount of activity may occur at an activity point. This activity is simulated (for example, arrival of parts to a manufacturing assembly station), causing a certain amount of computation. By the next time step some of that activity may have moved to neighboring activity points. This movement of activity simulates the movement of physical objects in a physical domain, and is modeled by the movement of *work units*. A work unit is always positioned at some activity point, and has a weight describing its computational demand at that activity point. From one time step to the next, a work unit may move from an activity point to a neighboring activity point; this movement is governed probabilistically. In the LD model, the probability that a work unit will move from one activity point to another, as the problem goes from one time step to the next is called the *transition probability* linking the two activity points.

We employ binary dissection [7] to partition the activity points into N *activity regions*, where the points in an activity region form a rectangular mass. The weight of an activity point is taken to be the sum of the weights of work units at the point, at the time that the partitioning is performed. The computational load on a processor during a time step is found by adding the weights of all work units resident on activity points assigned to that processor.

In a wide variety of problems, including those mentioned in section 1 as examples of varying demand distribution problems, data dependencies are quite local. Decomposition of a domain into contiguous regions with a relatively small perimeter to area ratio is thus generally desirable for reducing the quantity of information that must be exchanged between partitions. Furthermore, due to the local nature of the data dependencies, the communication required between partitions in a binary dissection will generally be greatest in partitions that are in physical proximity. The analysis in [7] shows that this type of partition is effective for static remapping, and is easily mapped onto various types of parallel architectures. Estimates are also obtained of the communication costs incurred when binary dissection is used to partition a problem's domain, and the resulting partitions are mapped onto a given architecture. The communication cost estimates obtained by such analysis are inevitably problem, mapping and architecture dependent.

A processor's load changes from one time step to the next when a work unit either moves to an activity point assigned to another processor, or similarly moves from an activity point in a different processor. This explicit modeling of work unit movement removes the most serious flaw with the MUM model. Unlike the MUM model, the change in a processor's computational load from one time step to the next is explicitly dependent on its own load, and on the loads of processors with neighboring activity regions.

To ensure the correctness of the simulation, we require that all computation associated with a time step be completed before the simulation advances to the next time step.

Thus, as in the MUM model, the time required to complete a time step is the maximum computation time among all processors. Again like the MUM model, as time progresses any initial balance will disappear, and average processor utilization will drop. This is particularly true if the work unit movement probabilities are anisotropic, i.e. work movement probabilities vary with the direction of movement.

The SAR policy can also be used with the LD model, since the $W(n)$ statistic requires only the mean processor execution time, the maximum processor execution time per time step, and the remapping cost C. The performance of SAR on the LD model was examined by once again comparing SAR to the performance of fixed interval polices. Figure 5 plots expected processor utilization as a function of time for remapping costs of 50 and 100 work units, when a 64 by 64 mesh of activity points is initialized with one work unit per activity point, and 16 processors are employed. The transition probabilities are anisotropic (given in the figure legend), so that the work tends to drift to the upper right portion of the mesh over time. Not taken into account here is the cost of the interprocessor communication that occurs at the end of each step when partitions exchange newly computed results. As was observed in the MUM model the the performance of the SAR rule and the average number of elapsed steps between SAR remappings corresponded closely to that of the fixed interval leading to the optimal performance. In figure 5, the performance of SAR for a given cost is superior to that obtained from fixed load balancing at the optimal frequency. In other simulations, the performance obtained from SAR was comparable to, but slightly below that obtained from the optimal fixed load balancing method. Note that the performance obtained by SAR in figure 5 is markedly greater than that obtained when no remapping is performed. We shall now shift attention to the other type of multiprocessor performance pattern we are considering here. In this case we will also describe a probabilistic model for this type of problem and propose and evaluate policies for weighing partitioning costs and benefits.

5. <u>Multiphase Problems.</u> The patterns of computation and memory access of many programs are highly dependent on data that become available only at run-time. The effective partitioning of a database between a number of communicating processes is a function of the information stored in the database as well as the transactions that are to be executed. Methods for partitioning logical objects or relations among processors involve deciding how to partition the relation and how to assign the resulting partitions to processors [43],[44]. A related area of active research has involved finding the optimal distribution of files among processors in a message passing machine or computer network, given a set of transactions involving the files. For a review of this work see [45].

A similar problem occurs during the computer aided design and design testing of VLSI components. Testing is generally performed using computer simulation, for which the time costs often grow exponentially with the number of components to be simulated. A logic network can be characterized as a collection of functional units whose executions are constrained by precedence relations defined by input and output lines. Examples of such functional units are AND and OR gates, a more complex functional unit might be an instruction decoder. Typical logic simulators will simulate a functional unit only when at least one of its input values change. Hence in this case as well, the performance achievable by any given problem partitioning is sensitive to the probabilistic distribution of input values [25].

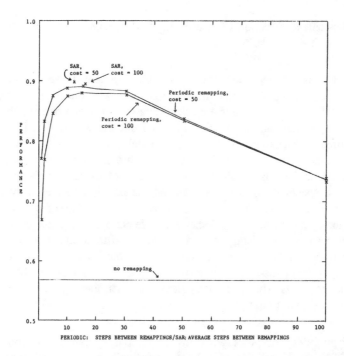

Figure 5.   LD Model: Performance of SAR Compared with Performance
of Periodic Remapping.   64 by 64 activity array
initialized with one work unit per activity point.   Work
unit transition probabilities: up – 0.1, right – 0.1,
down – 0.05, left – 0.05.   Each data point calculated
from 50 sample points.

Once a partition is chosen, monitoring the performance of the system to determine
whether a phase change has occurred may be essential for the efficient functioning of the
multiprocessor system. If a computation mapped onto a parallel computer experiences a
phase change, the computation's mapping may no longer effectively exploit parallelism,
particularly if the mapping was chosen to optimize performance during a previous phase.
It may then be desirable to remap the computation when a phase change occurs. However,
it is generally unreasonable to assume that phase changes can be predicted and identified a
priori. It is necessary then to detect and react to phase changes as they occur. However,
several problems exist which must be considered. The phase change detection mechanism
may not be completely reliable; it may report a phase change when none has occurred, or
fail to report a true phase change. Furthermore, the delay cost of remapping the computation may be high; the cost of remapping must be balanced against the resulting expected
performance gains. We have treated these problems in the framework of a Markov Decision Process. Within this framework, we are able to demonstrate the structure of a decision policy which minimizes the computation's expected execution time. One of our major
results is that the optimal decision policy is a threshold policy: we remap when the probability that a phase change has occurred is high enough. Our second major result is that
optimal performance is relatively insensitive to precise estimation of the parameters which
determine the optimal policy. Our empirical work suggests that the dominant issue in this

problem is the accurate detection of phase changes. We next describe our model of the problem, and present these results.

6. Phase Change Model. Our model of the problem makes several simplifying assumptions. First, we suppose that the computation will undergo at most one phase change. We will later argue that our empirical data shows that further mathematical detail is unnecessary. Note that this assumption differs from the MUM or LD models of load drift we have already discussed. In the current model, a change in behavior is assumed to occur abruptly, rather than gradually. A significant assumption is that the computation's behavior can be described as consisting of a number of *cycles*. For a given problem, a cycle represents a specified unit of work, and at the beginning of each cycle we assume that a measurement of system performance is available. We assume the existence of a phase change detection mechanism. Because the detection of a phase change is likely to be problem and system dependent, we do not attempt to treat change detection other than to assume that the mechanism is not completely reliable. We model its unreliability by assuming that every invocation of the detection mechanism has a probability α of reporting that a phase change exists when it actually does not exist, and a probability β of it failing to report an existing phase change.

Our remapping decision process will invoke the phase change detection mechanism at the beginning of every cycle. To model the uncertainty in the occurrence of the phase change, we assume that the probability of a phase change having occurred since the last change test is ϕ. When invoked, the change detection mechanism attempts to determine whether the phase has changed any time in the past, presumably on the basis of the computation's recent behavior. Upon receiving the mechanism's report, the decision process will update the probability of a phase change having already occurred. This probability is a function of the mechanism's report, α, β, ϕ, and a prior probability of change. The decision process then decides whether to remap on the basis of the calculated probability. For this reason, we call the sequence of change test and decision a *decision step*. We will let p_n denote the probability of change which is calculated by the *nth* decision step.

We intuitively understand that the decision to remap should be a function of the costs and benefits of remapping. We next define model parameters which capture these costs and benefits. We make the reasonable assumption that the time required for the system to execute a cycle depends on the mapping, and whether the mapping was designed to exploit parallelism during that cycle's phase. We let e_O denote the mean time to execute a cycle before a phase change. We let e_B denote the mean time to execute a cycle after a phase change, but before a remapping. We let e_R denote the mean time to execute a cycle after a phase change, and after a remapping. We suppose that $e_R < e_B$, which simply says that remapping after a phase change leads to higher performance during the new phase. In fact, the difference $e_B - e_R$ is interpreted as the per cycle cost of not remapping after a phase change. We also explicitly identify the costs of remapping. We let D_d be the expected time delay of calculating and testing a new mapping. For reasons which will become apparent later, we separate this cost from the cost D_r of actually implementing the new mapping.

We also contend that the decision to remap should consider the remaining length of the computation. If the remaining computation is quite short, then it is likely that the benefits of remapping after a phase change cannot outweigh remapping's overhead costs; conversely, a long computation may admit remapping early in the computation even if the per cycle performance gain is small. We model our uncertainity in the duration of the computation by supposing that the computation requires a random number of cycles, denoted M. For tractability reasons, we assume that M is bounded from above by some constant, and that M has an increasing failure rate function. The latter requirement simply means that the longer the computation runs, it becomes more likely that the computation will terminate with the next cycle. Table I below summarizes our model parameter definitions. After the *nth* cycle, the decision process invokes the phase change detection mechanism and calculates a new probability p_n of the phase change having occurred. Our model does not attempt to capture the cost of invoking the mechanism. On the basis of the value of p_n, the decision process decides whether to generate a new mapping (based on the computation's post-change behavior). The decision to retain the current mapping causes no further activity until the end of the next cycle. If the phase change has not occurred, the expected execution time of the next cycle is e_O; if the phase change has occurred, then the expected execution time of the next cycle is e_B. The decision to remap initially has two components. A new mapping is calculated on the basis of the computation's recent behavior. We then suppose that it is possible to estimate the performance of the computation under the new mapping (this issue is discussed in [46]). We can then compare the

Table I

Model Parameter Definitions

Notation	Definition
n	Decision Step Number
M	Random number of decision steps
e_O	Decision Interval Pre-Change Execution Time, Original Partition
e_B	Decision Interval Post-Change Execution Time, Original Partition
e_R	Decision Interval Post-Change Execution Time, New Partition
D_d	Delay to Calculate and Test New Partition
D_r	Delay to Implement New Partition
α	Change Test False Positive Error
β	Change Test False Negative Error
ϕ	Time of Change Failure Rate Probability

performance of the new mapping with the performance of the old, and implicitly verify whether the phase change has occurred. The delay associated with calculating and testing a new mapping is D_d. If the testing phase reveals that the phase change has not occurred, then the new mapping is rejected, the probability of a phase change having already occurred is set to zero, and the decision process continues as before. If the new mapping is accepted, then a delay D_r is required to implement it. The decision process then stops, with the expectation that every remaining cycle has a mean execution time of e_R.

We place the remapping decision problem in the context of a Markov decision process [47] by defining the state of the process at the nth decision step to be $<p_n,n>$, the probability of the phase change having already occurred coupled with the decision step identifier n. The immediate costs of the possible decisions have been identified as mean per cycle execution costs, and remapping overhead costs. The cost of a decision policy is the expected sum of its decision costs; in our formulation that sum is the expected execution time of the computation (including any remapping overhead). An optimal decision policy is one which minimizes that expected sum. The optimal decision policy is determined by the *optimal cost function* $V(<p_n,n>)$, which expresses the expected future costs of using the optimal decision policy. By the principle of optimality, the optimal cost function is expressed by

$$V(<p_n,n>) \;=\; \min \begin{cases} ER(<p_n,n>) \\ EC(<p_n,n>) \end{cases}$$

where $ER(<p_n,n>)$ is the minimized expected future costs given that remapping is chosen from state $<p_n,n>$ and $EC(<p_n,n>)$ is the minimized expected future costs given that remapping is not chosen from state $<p_n,n>$. The optimal decision to make from state $<p_n,n>$ is the decision with the minimum value of the expected future costs function. In [46] it is shown that the optimal decision policy for our problem has a particularly nice form. This result is stated as Theorem 1.

Theorem 1 : For every decision step n, there exists a threshold π_n such that the optimal decision at step n is to choose remapping if and only if $p_n > \pi_n$.

Theorem 1 appeals to our intuition: to remap, we must be sufficiently certain that a phase change has occurred. The magnitude of our required confidence is reflected in the value of the thresholds $\{\pi_n\}$, which are a function of all the model parameters we have identified.

While Theorem 1 gives a nice form for the optimal decision policy, there are severe problems which prohibit its general use. In [46] we show that solving for the $\{\pi_n\}$ is computationally intractable. Furthermore, that solution depends on the quantification of model parameters we may not be certain of. In particular, it may be unreasonable to expect a good estimate of the per cycle gain from remapping. We addressed these concerns by conducting an empirical study which showed that optimal performance can be nearly achieved without explicitly calculating the $\{\pi_n\}$, and without precisely estimating model parameters. This study focused on a simple decision heuristic whose performance is close to that of the optimal policy. We now outline the details of the heuristic.

Like the optimal decision policy, the decision heuristic maintains the probability of change, and reacts to high values of this probability. A threshold ρ is chosen so that ρ is approximately equal to the probability of change which would occur after three successive phase change tests report a change. When the probability of change exceeds ρ, a new mapping is computed. However, this mapping is not necessarily adopted immediately. The parameters e_B and e_R are estimated to determine the gain from remapping. Then, as a function of these and all other model parameters, a time threshold n_0 is computed as outlined in [46]. n_0 represents a "break-even" point, $\pi_n = 1$ for all $n \geq n_0$, and $\pi_n < 1$ for $n < n_0$. This means that if the computation is close enough to termination, the optimal decision policy will not remap even if the probability of change is 1. Likewise, our heuristic will not adopt a remapping if $m \geq n_0$, m being the current step. Supposing that $m < n_0$, our heuristic calculates pseudo-optimal thresholds $\{\tau_n\}$ for the steps between m and n_0. These thresholds are found by a linear interpolation between $\tau_m = 0.8$ and $\tau_{n_0} = 1.0$. The decision process then proceeds as though the $\{\tau_n\}$ are the optimal decision thresholds $\{\pi_n\}$.

Our study of the heuristic's performance assumed relatively small values of change test error probabilities ($\alpha = 0.05$, $\beta = 0.2$). It used $\phi = 1/E[M]$, which says (approximately) that we expect that it is as likely as not that a phase change occurs during the computation. We used remapping overhead values of $D_d = D_r = 100$; and we used $e_B = 200$. We therefore implicitly assume that the remapping overhead costs are essentially the same as a single post-change cycle under the original mapping. Our cost structure only takes into account computational costs after a phase change, hence we assumed that $e_0 = 0$. The gain from a new mapping is $G = e_B - e_R$. The study varied G, and it varied the length of the computation. For simplicity, we assumed M to be a degenerate, constant random variable.

The empirical study accurately estimated the optimal thresholds $\{\pi_n\}$ using a method described in [46]. It also calculated the performance obtained if a new mapping is never chosen. Comparing the performance of these two extreme policies, we calculated the percentage $\%_n$ improvement possible using the optimal policy. Using a simulation of our model, we measured the percentage of this gain which is achieved by the heuristic, denoted $\%_H$. Table II gives the values of $\%_n$ and $\%_H$ for varying values of G and M.

Table II

$\%_n$ and $\%_H$ for varying values of G and M.

M	G	$\%_n$	$\%_H$	G	$\%_n$	$\%_H$	G	$\%_n$	$\%_H$
10	5	0.0		50	4.7	55.2	100	19.2	75.3
50	5	0.48	54.8	50	11.3	93.4	100	32.4	95.5
100	5	0.5	82.9	50	12.2	95.1	100	33.9	97.1
1000	5	0.94	98.3	50	12.5	99.5	100	34.3	99.5

Obviously, when the gain achievable by remapping is small, there is very little difference between using the optimal policy, and the policy which does nothing at all. If G is larger, the possible performance gains are larger, and most of those gains are captured by our heuristic. It is also clear that the length of the computation affects performance. As the length grows, our heuristic's performance approaches that of the optimal decision policy.

The data given above assumed that the decision heuristic knew precisely what the value of G was. Because this is unrealistic, we re-examined performance under the assumption that the heuristic grossly under or over estimates the value of G. For each pair of G and M, we caused the heuristic to under-estimate G by factors of 10^{-1}, 10^{-2}, and 10^{-3}. We also caused it to over-estimate G by factors of 10, 10^2, and 10^3. Table III lists the resulting $\%_H$ as a function of G, M, and the estimation error factor. This table clearly shows that the heuristic's performance becomes insensitive to estimation error as the length of the computation increases. When the length of the computation is small and the gain G is not estimated correctly, remapping can lead to a degradation in performance. The negative percentages depicted in table III demonstrate this phenomenon. This data suggests the following conclusion, which is quite important if model parameters cannot be estimated:

If remapping costs are the same order of magnitude as a cycle execution time, and if the number of cycles in a computation is modestly large, then most of the gain possible from remapping is achieved if the phase change is detected relatively accurately.

In particular, when the number of cycles in a computation is reasonably large, it is not critically important to be able to estimate what the remapping gain will be. This observation also supports our decision to model only one phase change. Not only would the explicit modeling of multiple phase changes require more difficult analysis, but our data suggests the extra detail is not important. Good performance depends on the relative costs of remapping, the length of the computation, and the accuracy of phase change detection. Since a high cost of remapping can be amortized over a long enough computation, the dominant concern (for long computations) is accurate detection of a phase change.

Table III

$\%_H$ as a function of G, M, and the estimation error factor.

G	M	10^{-3}	10^{-2}	10^{-1}	10	10^2	10^3
50	10	-7.1	-16.7	-19.4	44.5	48.3	44.1
100	10	5.2	-3.5	0	77.0	77.1	74.3
5	50	35.2	35.1	34.6	-67.1	-97.7	-108.2
50	50	10.0	23.1	33.8	93.9	94.2	92.4
100	50	14.1	27.0	82.0	95.6	96.4	95.1
5	100	11.4	21.7	22.3	49.6	42.9	42.6
50	100	53.1	50.5	86.9	95.2	96.4	96.1
100	100	55.7	53.2	95.7	97.2	97.5	97.6
5	1000	92.7	92.6	95.3	98.4	98.3	98.4
50	1000	94.8	98.0	99.6	99.7	99.7	99.7
100	1000	95.2	99.2	99.6	99.7	99.7	99.7

6. Summary. The tradeoff between the costs and the benefits of remapping a variety of different kinds of problems are examined. In one case, the time-variant behavior of many scientific computations is characterized by gradual changes in each processor's computational load. Coupled with the computation's synchronization needs, performance declines gradually. Good processor utilization requires that the computational load be balanced between processors, yet a good balance can't be sustained without periodic, possibly expensive remappings. To treat this type of problem, we need to both model the phenomenon of performance degradation, and develop remapping decision policies which effectively determine when the computational load should be remapped onto the parallel machine. We have done so using two different models of gradual load evolution. We have developed and studied an adaptive remapping decision policy SAR which proves to be effective on both models. SAR does not depend on the details of the model structure; rather, it attempts to minimize a statistic which measures the long-term average system degradation (including that due to remapping) as a function of time. For both load evolution models, the performance obtained through the use of SAR is compared to a variety of policies for scheduling remappings.

We have also considered strategies for deciding when to remap problems whose behavior undergoes unpredictable and sudden phase changes. We treat the problem of determining when and if the stochastic behavior of the workload has changed enough to warrant the calculation of a new partition. The problem is modeled as a Markov decision process, the solution to which is intractable. A heuristic is proposed which triggers a remapping when a phase change has been detected and when it is possible to estimate that the duration of the remaining computation duration is sufficiently large to allow performance gains to outweigh remapping overhead. Simulation studies suggest that most of the possible gains in performance that can be obtained through remapping can be captured by the heuristic. The key conclusion of this study is that the timely detection of phase change is the most important issue in achieving good performance. If phases tend to be long-lived, then the accurate estimation of performance gains and performance overheads is not critical. If phases are short-lived, then the heuristic we describe provides good performance if our model parameters can be accurately quantified.

The two types of remapping problems discussed here share common features. Both problems arise due to the fact that a computation is distributed across a parallel computation, and that the computation's stochastic behavior is not constant. In both problems a global remapping can temporarily restore good system performance, but the decision to remap must weigh the performance gains against the remapping overhead. The differences in these problems' behavior cause their respective treatments to differ; however, these treatments are similar in that they both are adaptive, and they both explicitly consider the appropriate costs and benefits involved in the decision. For both problems, empirical studies of the proposed policies prove their effectiveness.

Acknowledgments. We thank Bob Voigt for his continuing support. We also thank Roger Smith, Paul Reynolds, Dan Reed and Merrell Patrick for helpful discussions.

REFERENCES

[1]   M. J. BERGER and A. JAMESON, Automatic adaptive grid refinement for the euler equations, AIAA Journal, 23 (1985), pp. 561-568.

[2]   M. J. BERGER and J. OLIGER, Adaptive mesh refinement for hyperbolic partial differential equations, J. Comp. Phys., 53 (1984), pp. 484-512.

[3]   W. D. GROPP, Local uniform mesh refinement with moving grids, Yale Technical Report YALEU/DCS/RR-313, April 1984.

[4]   M. M. RAI and T. L. ANDERSON, The use of adaptive grid generation method for transonic airfoil flow calculations, AIAA Paper 81-1012, June 1981.

[5]   A. HARTEN and J. M. HYMAN, Self-adjusting grid methods for one-dimensional hyperbolic conservation laws, Los Alamos Report LA-9105, 1981.

[6]   W. USAB and E. M. MURMAN, Embedded mesh solutions of the euler equation using a multiple-grid method, Proceedings of the AIAA Computational Fluid Dynamics Conference, Danvers, Mass., Paper 83-1946, July 1983.

[7]   M. J. BERGER and S. BOKHARI, The partitioning of non-uniform problems, ICASE Report No. 85-55, November 1985.

[8]   W. D. GROPP, Local uniform mesh refinement on loosely-coupled parallel processors, Yale Technical Report YALEU/DCS/RR-352, December 1984.

[9]   W. D. GROPP, Dynamic grid manipulation for PDEs on hypercube parallel processors, Yale Technical Report YALEU/DCS/RR-458, March 1986.

[10]   C. ANDERSON and C. GREENGARD, On vortex methods, SIAM J. Numer. Anal., 22 (1985), pp. 413-440.

[11]   A. LEONARD, Vortex methods for flow simulation, J. Comp. Phys., 37 (1980), pp. 289-335.

[12]   S. BADEN, Dynamic load balancing of a vortex calculation running on multiprocessors, Computer Science Technical Report, University of California Berkley, 1986.

[13]   D. R. WELLS, Multirate linear multistep methods for the solution of systems of ordinary differential equations, Report No. UIUCDCS-R-82-1093, University of Illinois, July 1982.

[14] D. BAI and A. BRANDT, Local mesh refinement multilevel techniques, Dept. of Appl. Math., Weizmann Institute of Science Report, 1984.

[15] S. McCORMICK and J. THOMAS, The fast adaptive composite grid method for elliptic equations, Math. Comp., 46 (1986), pp. 439–456.

[16] A. BRANDT, Multilevel adaptive solutions to boundary value problems, Math. Comp., 31 (1977), pp. 333–390.

[17] R. E. BANK, A multi-level iterative method for nonlinear elliptic equations, in Elliptic Problem Solvers (Martin Schultz, ed.), Academic Press, New York, 1981.

[18] O. C. ZIENKIEWICZ and A. W. CRAIG, Adaptive mesh refinement and a posteriori error estimation for the p-version of the finite element method, in Adaptive Computational Methods for Partial Differential Equations (Ivo Babuska, ed.), SIAM, Philadelphia, 1983.

[19] G. S. FISHMAN, Principles of Discrete Event Simulation, Wiley & Sons, New York, 1978.

[20] K. M. CHANDY and J. MISRA, Distributed simulation: A case study in design and verification of distributed programs, IEEE Trans. on Software Engineering, SE-5, 5 (September 1979), pp. 440–452.

[21] A. I. CONCEPCION, Distributed simulation on multi-processors: Specification, design, and architecture, Ph.D. Dissertation, Wayne State University, January 1985.

[22] D. R. JEFFERSON and H. SOWIZRAL, Fast concurrent simulation using the time warp mechanism, Rand Report to the Air Force, FN-1906-AFFR, December 1982.

[23] J. K. PEACOCK, E. MANNING, and J. W. WONG, Synchronization of distributed simulation using broadcast algorithms, Computer Networks, 4 (1980), pp. 3–10.

[24] P. F. REYNOLDS, Jr., A shared resource algorithm for distributed simulation, Proceedings of the Ninth Annual International Computer Architecture Conference, Austin, Texas (1982), pp. 259–266. Distributed Comp.

[25] D. M. NICOL and P. F. REYNOLDS, Jr., The automated partitioning of simulations for parallel execution, Technical Report No. TR-85-15, Department of Computer Science, University of Virginia, August 1985.

[26] D. L. EAGER, E. D. LAZOWSKA, and J. ZAHORJAN, Adaptive load
      sharing in homogeneous distributed systems, IEEE Trans. on
      Software Eng., SE-12 (May 1986), pp. 662-675.

[27] G. J. FOSCHINI, On Heavy Traffic Diffusion Analysis and
      Dynamic Routing in Packet Switched Networks, Computer
      Performance (K. M. Chandy and M. Reiser, eds.), New York:
      North-Holland.

[28] L. M. NI, C. XU, and T. B. GENDREAU, A distributed drafting
      algorithm for load balancing, IEEE Trans. on Software
      Engineering (October 1985), pp. 1153-1161.

[29] J. A. STANKOVIC, An application of Bayesian decision theory to
      decentralized control of job scheduling, IEEE Trans. on
      Computers, C-34, 2 (February 1985), pp. 117-130.

[30] J. A. STANKOVIC, K. RAMAMRITHAM, and S. CHENG, Evaluation of a
      flexible task scheduling algorithm for distributed hard real-
      time systems, IEEE Trans. on Computers, C-34, 12 (December
      1985), pp. 1130-1143.

[31] D. TOWSLEY, Queueing network models with state-dependent
      routing, Journal of the ACM, 27, 2 (April 1980), pp. 323-337.

[32] A. N. TANTAWI and D. TOWSLEY, Optimal static load balancing,
      Journal of the ACM, 32, 2 (April 1985), pp. 445-465.

[33] W. W. CHU, L. J. HOLLOWAY, M. LAN, and K. EFE, Task allocation
      in distributed data processing, Computer, 13, 11 (November
      1980), pp. 57-69.

[34] A. DUTTA, G. KOEHLER and A. WHINSTON, On optimal allocation in
      a distributed processing environment, Management Science, 28,
      8 (August 1982), pp. 839-853.

[35] D. GUSFIELD, Parametric combinatorial computing and a problem
      of program module distribution, Journal of the ACM, 30, 3
      (July 1983), pp. 551-563.

[36] H. S. STONE, Critical load factors in distributed computer
      systems, IEEE Trans. on Software Engineering, SE-4, 3 (May
      1978), pp. 254-258.

[37] J. A. BANNISTER and K. S. TRIVEDI, Task allocation in fault-
      tolerant distributed systems, Acta Informatica, 20 (1983), pp.
      261-281.

[38] S. BOKHARI, Partitioning problems in parallel, pipelined, and
      distributed computing, ICASE Report No. 85-54, November 1985.

[39] M. A. IQBAL, J. H. SALTZ, and S. H. BOKHARI, Performance
      tradeoffs in static and dynamic load balancing strategies, to
      appear in the Proceedings of the 1986 International Conference
      on Parallel Processing.

[40] P. J. DENNING, Working sets past and present, IEEE Trans. on
      Software Engineering, SE-6, 1 (January 1980), pp. 64-84.

[41] J. R. SPIRN, Program Behavior: Models and Measurement,
      Elsevier North-Holland Inc., New York, 1977.

[42] D. M. NICOL and J. H. SALTZ, Dynamic remapping of parallel
      computations with varying resource demands, ICASE Report 86-
      45, June 1986.

[43] D. SACCA and G. WIEDERHOLD, Database partitioning in a cluster
      of processors, ACM Transactions on Database Systems, 10
      (1983), pp. 29-56.

[44] S. NAVATHE, S. CERI, G. WIEDERHOLD, and J. DOU, Vertical
      partitioning algorithms for database design, ACM Database, 9
      (1984), pp. 680-710.

[45] L. W. DOWDY and D. V. FOSTER, Comparative models of the file
      assignment problem, ACM Surveys, 14 (1982), pp. 287-313.

[46] D. M. NICOL and P. F. REYNOLDS, Jr., An optimal repartitioning
      decision policy, ICASE Report 86-7, February 1986.

[47] S. ROSS, Applied Probability Models with Optimization
      Applications, Holden and Day, San Francisco, 1971.

CHAPTER 5

Sparse Cholesky Factorization on a Local-Memory Multiprocessor*

Alan George[†]
Michael T. Heath[†]
Joseph Liu[‡]
Esmond Ng[†]

Abstract. This article deals with the problem of factoring a large sparse positive definite matrix on a multiprocessor system. The processors are assumed to have substantial local memory but no globally shared memory. They communicate among themselves and with a host processor through message passing. Our primary interest is in designing an algorithm which exploits parallelism, rather than in exploiting features of the underlying topology of the hardware. However, part of our study is aimed at determining, for certain sparse matrix problems, whether hardware based on the binary hypercube topology adequately supports the communication requirements for such problems. Numerical results from experiments running on a multiprocessor simulator are included.

1. Introduction. This article deals with the problem of factoring a large sparse positive definite matrix A on a multiprocessor system. It is assumed that the system supports message passing among individual processors, and that each processor has a substantial amount of local memory. We assume also that there is no globally shared memory. These assumptions are appropriate for a number of recent commercially available machines, such as the binary

* Research was supported by the Applied Mathematical Sciences Research Program of the Office of Energy Research, U.S. Department of Energy under contract DE-AC05-84OR21400 with Martin Marietta Energy Systems, Inc., by the U.S. Air Force Office of Scientific Research under contract AFOSR-ISSA-85-00083, and by the Canadian Natural Sciences and Engineering Research Council under grants A8111 and A5509.

† Mathematical Sciences Section, Oak Ridge National Laboratory, Oak Ridge, Tennessee 37912. The first author is also with Departments of Mathematics and Computer Science, University of Tennessee, Knoxville, Tennessee.

‡ Department of Computer Science, York University, Downsview, Ontario, Canada M3J 1P3.

hypercube multiprocessors marketed by Ametek, Intel and NCUBE corporations. In [8], a parallel algorithm was developed for solving dense positive definite systems on such machines, so this article can be regarded as a sequel to that work, in which the sparsity of the problem is addressed and exploited.

The process of solving large sparse positive definite systems typically involves four distinct steps:

1. (*Ordering*)   Find a good ordering P for A. That is, a permutation matrix P so that PAP^T has a sparse Cholesky factor L. This is usually referred to as the *ordering problem*.

2. (*Symbolic factorization*)   Determine the structure of the Cholesky factor L of PAP^T, and set up a data structure for this factor.

3. (*Numerical factorization*)   Place the elements of A into the data structure, and then compute L.

4. (*Triangular solution*)   Using the computed L, solve the triangular systems $Ly = Pb$, $L^T z = y$, and then set $x = P^T z$.

The problems of implementing an ordering algorithm and performing the symbolic factorization procedure on a multiprocessor machine are major projects that will be considered in a subsequent article. In this paper we develop and test a parallel algorithm for step 3 only.

Before proceeding with the description and details of the algorithm, some general remarks about the design and implementation of parallel algorithms should be made. First, it should be kept in mind that the objective is *speed-up*. That is, given a p-processor machine, we would like to solve our problem in time that is as close as possible to a factor of p less than that needed to solve the same problem on a single processor version of the machine, using the best serial algorithm available. Of course in the latter case we assume that the single processor machine has adequate memory, presumably much more than the amount available to a single processor in the multiprocessor configuration.

There is a tendency to focus on *processor utilization* in studying parallel algorithms. However, while high processor utilization is a *necessary* condition for good speed-up, it is clearly not sufficient; the processors have to be doing *useful work*. Thus, in order to achieve our objective, it is necessary to be able to distribute the computation approximately uniformly across the processors, to identify sufficient parallelism so that most of the computations can be performed simultaneously, and to reduce the amount of communication among the processors.

Let us assume that we are able to achieve this distribution. Except in unusual circumstances, some communication among the processors will be required during the computation. This leads us to an important point about *communication traffic*.

Ideally, every processor in the system should be able to send a message *directly* to any other processor. However, for large p, economics make building machines with such a capability infeasible, so most local-memory multiprocessors provide physical communication links among only a few nearest neighbors in some geometric layout. (Common topologies include the ring, the two-dimensional regular grid and the binary hypercube.) A consequence is that a message to be sent from processor i to processor j may have to traverse several physical links, and be *forwarded* by processors along the transmission path.

It is therefore useful to distinguish between *logical* and *physical* data traffic. By the logical traffic from processor i to processor j, we mean the amount of data originated from processor i that must be received and utilized by processor j. On the other hand, we use physical traffic from i to j to refer to the total amount of data traffic that actually flows on the physical link (assuming it exists) from processor i to j in the multiprocessor network. If there is no direct link between processors i and j, the amount of physical traffic will always be zero even if there is some logical data traffic between them. In this case, data originated from processor i and required by processor j has to travel through one or more intermediate processors in some transmission path before reaching j.

It is clear that logical traffic is determined by the way in which the total computation has been distributed across the processors, and physical traffic further depends on the underlying hardware topology and routing strategies. Loosely speaking, logical traffic is a function of the algorithm only, while physical traffic is a function of both the algorithm and the hardware.

An outline of the paper is as follows. In Section 2, we review the basic Cholesky algorithm for the dense matrix case, and examine the effect of ordering for the sparse case. Although we defer the discussion of a parallel algorithm for computing an ordering until a later paper, the choice of the ordering can have a drastic effect on both the sparsity of the triangular factor and the degree of parallelism that can be exploited in computing it. For the numerical experiments reported in this paper, the ordering is computed by a standard sequential algorithm. The design and implementation of the parallel algorithm for sparse numerical factorization are presented in Section 3, and the results of our numerical experiments in Section 4.

2. Sparse Cholesky Factorization.

2.1. Dense Case: the Basic Algorithm. We begin by providing a column-oriented version of the basic Cholesky factorization algorithm, described in the following algorithmic form.

```
for j := 1 to n do
begin
      for k := 1 to j −1 do
            for i := j to n do
                  a_ij := a_ij − a_ik * a_jk
      a_jj := √a_jj
      for k := j +1 to n do
            a_kj := a_kj / a_jj
end
```

$$a_{ij} := a_{ij} - a_{ik}*a_{jk}$$
$$a_{jj} := \sqrt{a_{jj}}$$
$$a_{kj} := a_{kj} / a_{jj}$$

It is shown in [9] that this form of Cholesky factorization, the so-called column-Cholesky formulation, is particularly well suited to medium- to coarse-grain parallel implementation. It was found to have the best combination of work-load balance and overlapped execution in the outer loop sub-tasks. This version is implemented for shared-memory multiprocessors in [9], and for various local-memory architectures supporting message passing in [8,13].

Following [9], we let $Tcol(j)$ be the *task* that computes the j-th column of the Cholesky factor. Each such task consists of the following two types of subtasks:

1. $cmod(j,k)$: modification of column j by column k ($k < j$);
2. $cdiv(j)$: division of column j by a scalar.

Thus, in terms of these sub-tasks, the basic algorithm can be expressed in the following condensed form.

```
for j := 1 to n do
begin
      for k := 1 to j −1 do
            cmod (j ,k )

      cdiv (j )
end
```

We now consider the potential for parallelism in the above formulation of the algorithm. We implicitly assume throughout this paper that the *cmod* and *cdiv* operations are atomic in the sense that we do not attempt to exploit parallelism within them, although such exploitation is clearly possible.

Note first that $cdiv(j)$ cannot begin until $cmod(j,k)$ has been completed for all $k < j$, and column j can be used to modify subsequent columns only after $cdiv(j)$ has been completed. However, there is no restriction on the order in which the $cmod$ operations are executed, and $cmod$ operations for different columns can be performed concurrently. For example, after $cdiv(1)$ has completed, $cmod(2,1)$ and $cmod(3,1)$ could execute in parallel. These precedence relations are depicted in Fig. 1.

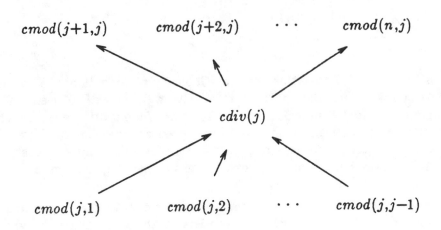

Fig. 1: Subtask precedence graph for column–Cholesky.

2.2. Parallel Sparse Column–Cholesky and the Effect of Ordering. The main difference between the sparse and dense versions of the algorithm stems from the fact that for sparse A, column j may no longer need to be modified by *all* columns $k < j$. Specifically, column j is modified *only* by columns k for which $l_{jk} \neq 0$, and after $cdiv(j)$ has been executed, column j needs to be made available only to tasks $Tcol(r)$ for which $l_{rj} \neq 0$. This can be understood easily by examining the basic form of the algorithm displayed at the beginning of section 2.1. If $a_{jk} = 0$, it is obviously unnecessary to execute the loop on i, since it has no effect.

Ideally, we would like to choose an ordering for the matrix A which achieves a number of objectives. First, just as in the use of serial machines, we would like to preserve sparsity and obtain a low arithmetic operation count. In addition, the ordering should allow a high degree of parallelism, and allow the distribution of the computation across the processors in a way that allows the parallelism to be exploited without requiring an inordinate amount of communication.

Fortunately, these objectives turn out to be mutually complementary. In order to gain insight into this problem, it is useful to introduce the notion of elimination trees for sparse Cholesky factors [3,16].

Consider the structure of the Cholesky factor L. For each column $j \leqslant n$, if column j has off-diagonal nonzeros, define $\gamma[j]$ by

$$\gamma[j] = \min\{ i \mid l_{ij} \neq 0,\ i > j \} \quad ;$$

that is, $\gamma[j]$ is the row subscript of the first off-diagonal nonzero in column j of L. If column j has no off-diagonal nonzero, we set $\gamma[j] = j$. (Hence $\gamma[n] = n$.)

We now define an *elimination tree* corresponding to the structure of L. The tree has n nodes, labelled from 1 to n. For each j, if $\gamma[j] > j$, then node $\gamma[j]$ is the *parent* of node j in the elimination tree, and node j is one of possibly several *child* nodes of node $\gamma[j]$. We assume that the matrix A is *irreducible*, so that n is the only node with $\gamma[j] = j$ and it is the *root* of the tree. Thus, for $1 \leqslant j < n$, $\gamma[j] > j$. (If A is reducible, then the elimination tree defined above is actually a forest which consists of several trees.) There is exactly one *path* from each node to the root of the tree. If node i lies on the path from node j to the root, then node i is an *ancestor* of node j, and node j is a *descendant* of node i.

An example to illustrate the notion of elimination trees is provided by the structure of the Cholesky factor shown in Fig. 2, with the associated elimination tree being shown in Fig. 3. Elimination trees have been used either implicitly or explicitly in numerous articles dealing with sparse symmetric factorization [1,2,3,6,7,12,14,16,17,18,19,20]. In particular, the paper [18] uses the elimination tree as a model to study the parallel sparse Cholesky factorization algorithm in a shared-memory multiprocessor. In addition, Duff [2] is exploring the use of elimination trees in the parallel implementation of multifrontal methods.

$$
L = \begin{pmatrix}
\text{x} & & & & & \\
 & \text{x} & & & & \\
\text{x} & \text{x} & & & & \\
 & & \text{x} & \text{x} & & \\
\text{x} & \text{x} & \text{x} & \text{x} & \text{x} & \\
 & \text{x} & & \text{x} & \text{x} & \text{x}
\end{pmatrix} .
$$

Fig. 2: Structure of a Cholesky factor.

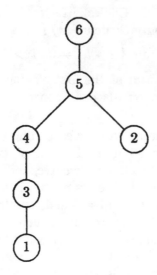

Fig. 3: The elimination tree associated with the Cholesky factor in Fig. 2.

The elimination tree provides precise information about the column dependencies. Specifically, $cdiv(i)$ cannot be executed until $cdiv(j)$ has completed for all descendant nodes j of node i.

The elimination tree has simple structure that can be economically represented using γ, as shown in Fig. 4. Thus, the representation requires only a single vector of size n.

j	1	2	3	4	5	6
$\gamma[j]$	3	5	4	5	6	6

Fig. 4: Computer representation of the tree of Fig. 3.

In order to see the role that elimination trees might play in identifying parallelism, we now consider two different orderings of the same problem, and study their corresponding elimination trees. Consider a 3 by 3 grid problem, where the 9 vertices of the grid are numbered in some manner, and the associated matrix A has the property that $a_{ij} \neq 0$ if and only if vertex i and vertex j are associated with the same small square in the grid. Two different orderings of the grid are given in Fig. 5, the associated Cholesky factors are displayed in Fig. 6, and their corresponding elimination trees are shown in Fig. 7.

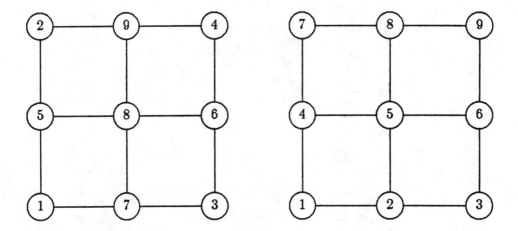

Fig. 5: Two orderings of a 3 by 3 grid.

$$\begin{pmatrix} x & & & & & & & & \\ & x & & & & & & & \\ & & x & & & & & & \\ & & & x & & & & & \\ x & x & & & x & & & & \\ & & x & x & & x & & & \\ x & & x & & x & x & x & & \\ x & x & x & x & x & x & x & x & \\ & x & & x & x & x & x & x & x \end{pmatrix} \quad \begin{pmatrix} x & & & & & & & & \\ x & x & & & & & & & \\ & x & x & & & & & & \\ x & x & x & x & & & & & \\ x & x & x & x & x & & & & \\ & x & x & x & x & x & & & \\ & & & x & x & x & x & & \\ & & & x & x & x & x & x & \\ & & & & x & x & x & x & x \end{pmatrix}$$

Fig. 6: Structure of the Cholesky factors for the orderings of Fig. 5.

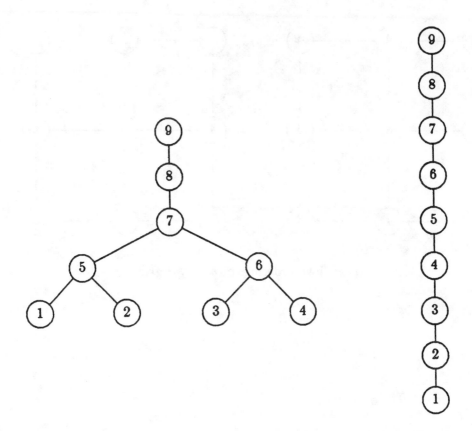

Fig. 7: The elimination trees associated with the matrices in Fig. 6.

The elimination tree on the left is typical of those generated by orderings that are good in the sense of yielding low fill and low operation counts. Its tree structure is short and wide, and such trees and their associated orderings lend themselves well to parallel computation. For example, it should be clear that $Tcol(1)$, $Tcol(2)$, $Tcol(3)$, and $Tcol(4)$ can start immediately in parallel. Moreover, when they have completed execution, $Tcol(5)$ and $Tcol(6)$ may proceed independently. The remaining tasks are no different than those for a dense matrix, and the findings in [8] apply equally well here.

On the other hand, the band-oriented ordering shown above is undesirable because it imposes the same serial execution on the *cdiv* operations that is imposed in the dense case (note, however, that even in the dense case, some *cmod* operations can still be carried out concurrently [9]). Moreover, the operation counts and fill-in are inferior to that of the first ordering.

In the elimination tree, if node i and node j belong to the same level of the tree, it is clear that the tasks $Tcol(i)$ and $Tcol(j)$ can be performed independently so long as the tasks associated with their descendant nodes have all been completed. In order to gain high processor utilization, it is therefore desirable to assign, if possible, nodes on the same level of the tree to different processors. An overall task assignment scheme will then correspond to assigning the $Tcol(i)$ tasks to successive processors in a breadth-first bottom-up manner from nodes of the elimination tree.

It should be pointed out that some of the practical fill-reducing orderings will already order the nodes of the elimination tree in this desirable sequence. They include the recent implementation of the minimum degree ordering using multiple elimination [15] and a version of the nested dissection ordering [10]. In such cases, the task assignment scheme corresponds to the straightforward wrap-around assignment, where task $Tcol(i)$ will be assigned to the processor s, given by $s = (i-1)\ mod\ p$.

3. Design and Implementation. In this section, we consider the design and implementation of a sparse Cholesky factorization algorithm appropriate for a parallel multiprocessor with local memory. Let A be the given n by n sparse symmetric positive definite matrix with Cholesky factor L. We assume that the matrix has already been permuted by some fill-reducing ordering appropriate for parallel elimination.

As before, we let $Tcol(j)$ be the task of computing the j-th column of the sparse Cholesky factor L. This task consists of the two types of subtasks: $cmod(j,k)$ and $cdiv(j)$.

In the sparse case, the task $Tcol(j)$ can be expressed in the following algorithmic form:

> for each k with nonzero l_{jk} and $j > k$ do
> $cmod(j,k)$
> $cdiv(j)$

It should be clear that the number of $cmod$ operations required in the task $Tcol(j)$ is given by the number of off-diagonal nonzeros in the j-th row of L. To facilitate our discussion, we introduce the vector $nmod[*]$, where the value $nmod[j]$ is the number of column modifications $cmod$ required in the execution of $Tcol(j)$. This vector can be obtained by simply counting the number of off-diagonal nonzeros in each row of L.

Consider the symmetric factorization of A in a given parallel message-passing multiprocessor environment. Let p be the number of processors in the parallel machine. We assume that an assignment of the column tasks $Tcol(*)$ to the computational nodes of the multiprocessor has been given. For definiteness, let $map[*]$ be the mapping of these n tasks into the p processors. That is, $map[j]$ will be the processor that is responsible for the performance of the task $Tcol(j)$, and hence the computation of column j of L. It should be pointed out that the effect of task-to-processor assignment on load balancing and communication cost can be studied by choosing different $map[*]$ functions.

In the parallel environment, we further assume that there are two primitives: *send* and *await*. Execution of a *send* does not cause the sending process to wait for a reply. On the other hand, execution of an *await* causes the process executing it to be suspended until the message is received. Messages that arrive at the destination process before the execution of the receiving *await* are placed in a queue until needed.

We shall now describe, in an algorithmic form, the work to be performed by the host and node processors. Each node processor uses a *multisend* routine, which will be discussed later in detail.

HOST processor:

Determine the mapping function $map[*]$
for $s := 1$ to p do   /* broadcast $map[*]$ */
    send $map[*]$ to processor s

Determine the $nmod[*]$ function
for $j := 1$ to n do
    send column j of A and $nmod[j]$ to processor $map[j]$

repeat n times do
    await a column of L and store it into the data structure

NODE processor s:

await $map[*]$ from the host
compute $ncol$ (using map), the number of columns to be
        processed by processor s

/* obtain columns from the host and eliminate if possible */
repeat $ncol$ times do
begin
    await a column j of A and $nmod[j]$ from the host
    if $nmod[j] = 0$ then
    begin
        $cdiv(j)$
        $multisend(j, L_{*j})$
    end
end

$ncol := ncol -$ number of columns received with zero $nmod$

```
/*  main loop: driven by the incoming columns  */
while ncol >0 do
begin
      await a column of L, say L*k
      for each offdiagonal nonzero ljk with map [j ]= s do
      begin
            cmod (j ,k )
            nmod [j ] := nmod [j ]−1
            if nmod [j ] = 0 then
            begin
                  cdiv (j )
                  multisend (j , L*j )
                  ncol := ncol −1
            end
      end
end
```

It is clear that the host processor is merely responsible for the initiation of the tasks by sending the relevant information to each node processor, and then for the collection of the computed columns of the factor matrix L. In each node processor, a routine called *multisend* is used. Its function is to send the column L_{*j} to the host processor and also to all the node processors that require this column for performing modifications. Specifically, this routine can be formulated as follows.

Subroutine *multisend* (j , L_{*j}):

    for each processor d such that
            for some $i > j$, $l_{ij} \neq 0$ and $map [i]= d$ do
    send L_{*j} to processor d

    send L_{*j} to the host

It should be emphasized that the routine *multisend* should only send one copy of the column L_{*j} to a processor even though the processor may use this column to modify more than one column in this processor. Furthermore, the routing strategy in the distribution of the column L_{*j} to the processors concerned can be changed by simply coding a new version of *multisend* .

There are a few points worth mentioning in the scheme for each node processor. As soon as a column L_{*j} of L is completely formed, it is immediately sent to the other processors that need this column, including the node processor that computed L_{*j} if that node processor also needs L_{*j}. A node's sending messages to itself in such circumstances makes the logic and programming much cleaner. This should not result in a significant performance penalty in any reasonable multiprocessor design since it should involve merely an internal movement of data. The immediate transmission of completely formed columns allows an overlapping of column elimination and column input from the host in the *repeat* loop in the algorithm. More importantly, by making columns of L immediately available, this will reduce wait time on node processors.

Note also that the main loop is driven by the incoming columns of L. This implies that the parallel algorithm is working at the granularity level of the subtasks *cmod* (j,k) and *cdiv* (j), rather than at the level of the tasks *Tcol* (j). This is in direct contrast to the serial implementation of the sparse Cholesky method (for example, SPARSPAK [11] or YSMP [5]), where each *Tcol* (j) is executed and completed in succession.

Another important characteristic of this formulation is that it is independent of the interconnection network topology. In other words, the parallel algorithm as formulated is applicable to any parallel multiprocessor in a message–passing environment. For different processor interconnections, it may be desirable to choose a different task-to-processor mapping function *map* [*] or a different message routing strategy. But the basic algorithm remains unchanged.

4. Experiments and Conclusions. In the previous sections our discussion has been independent of the interconnection topology of the multiprocessor. Our objective has been to distribute the workload uniformly and to reduce the amount of communication that must be performed. In this section we report some experimental results obtained from an implementation of our algorithm running on a binary hypercube multiprocessor. For background information about hypercube multiprocessors, see [8] and the references contained therein.

In order to test our implementation, and to gain some information on communication traffic, we solved some finite element problems derived from a sequence of L–shaped triangular meshes described in [10]. The ordering used for these problems was an automatic nested dissection ordering produced by the algorithm described in [10]. The *Tcol* (i) tasks were assigned to the processors in a simple serial wrap–around manner, with no account whatsoever being taken of the underlying topology of the hypercube multiprocessor. Both the ordering and the symbolic factorization phases were done in serial mode. Parallel versions of these algorithms are under development.

Our experiments were conducted using a binary hypercube simulator written by T. H. Dunigan of the Oak Ridge National Laboratory. For details about the simulator, see [4].

Statistics on both the logical and physical communication for one of the problems were collected, as shown in the tables that follow. The results reported are typical of those found in experiments for other problems in the set of nine problems in [10]. The entry in row r and column c of each table is the amount of data traffic from the processor corresponding to row r to the one corresponding to column c. Thus, the entries in the last row of the tables represent traffic from the host processor to the individual node processors.

We have included both communication counts and volume in the statistics. Communication count simply refers to the number of messages sent. Note that a message associated with the nonzeros of a column includes the number of nonzeros, the subscript information and the actual nonzero values. The volumes reported are the total number of bytes transmitted. In the experiments, an integer requires 4 bytes, and a floating point number requires 8 bytes.

	0	1	2	3	4	5	6	7	Host
0	106	121	115	107	111	106	106	100	126
1	108	100	120	108	107	100	100	101	127
2	108	102	99	118	112	105	100	98	126
3	105	105	104	99	120	112	109	104	126
4	99	103	102	99	93	120	113	103	126
5	110	106	98	97	90	95	118	106	126
6	116	112	107	102	100	97	94	117	126
7	118	116	113	101	110	103	98	97	126
Host	127	128	127	127	127	127	127	127	0

Table 1: Logical communication counts among 8 processors for $n = 1009$.

	0	1	2	3	4	5	6	7	Host
0	31692	33576	32916	31656	32412	31776	31716	30972	34116
1	30504	29232	32040	30408	30540	29748	29724	29748	32724
2	30864	30048	29484	32088	31524	30552	29868	29676	33096
3	30768	30828	30720	30072	32640	31500	31260	30528	33420
4	29664	30180	30108	29628	28884	32160	31248	29988	32928
5	30552	30060	29076	28944	27996	28536	31464	30024	32364
6	32028	31656	31032	30252	30216	29688	29100	32088	33240
7	32496	32244	31848	30336	31536	30600	29832	29856	33372
Host	42224	40832	41204	41528	41036	40472	41348	41480	0

Table 2: Logical communication volume among 8 processors for $n = 1009$.

	0	1	2	3	4	5	6	7	Host
0	106	438	423	0	423	0	0	0	126
1	441	100	0	423	0	408	0	0	127
2	438	0	99	426	0	0	415	0	126
3	0	444	435	99	0	0	0	445	126
4	403	0	0	0	93	428	422	0	126
5	0	411	0	0	427	95	0	425	126
6	0	0	437	0	414	0	94	418	126
7	0	0	0	448	0	445	425	97	126
Host	127	128	127	127	127	127	127	127	0

Table 3: Physical communication counts for 8 processors and $n = 1009$.

	0	1	2	3	4	5	6	7	Host
0	31692	125460	124308	0	126876	0	0	0	34116
1	124320	29232	0	120468	0	119760	0	0	32724
2	124596	0	29484	123624	0	0	121620	0	33096
3	0	126336	123684	30072	0	0	0	125928	33420
4	119580	0	0	0	28884	124176	123924	0	32928
5	0	118632	0	0	122712	28536	0	120960	32364
6	0	0	124968	0	121980	0	29100	122724	33240
7	0	0	0	126924	0	126276	122280	29856	33372
Host	42224	40832	41204	41528	41036	40472	41348	41480	0

Table 4: Physical communication volume among 8 processors for $n = 1009$.

There are several noteworthy aspects of the numbers in Tables 1-4. First, observe that the logical communication is quite evenly distributed among all the processors. That is, the algorithm generates about the same amount of traffic between any and every pair of processors.

Entries in the logical communication tables associated with the processor nodes are all nonzero. However, there are a number of zero entries in the physical communication table. Indeed, each zero in the tables (except for the "Host" row and column) means that a physical link does not exist between the two associated processors. For example, there is no direct link between processors 0 and 3. The messages from processor 0 to 3 must be directed through an intermediate processor, processor 1. This will have the effect of increasing the physical traffic from processor 0 to 1 and from processor 1 to 3. This explains why the nonzero entries in the physical communication tables are much larger than the corresponding entries in the logical communication tables.

Furthermore, it is interesting to observe that the actual physical links in the hypercube topology all carry about the same amount of traffic. Thus, it would appear that this particular topology adequately supports the actual (logical) traffic generated by the algorithm, at least for this class of sparse problems.

In order to determine what our implementation achieved in actual speed-up, we ran our code using one processor and eight processors, and in addition we ran the *best* serial code we have available.

A comparison of the times for the serial code and the parallel code with one processor was done to assess the cost incurred in the parallel implementation per se. It is noteworthy that the penalty is quite substantial, in the neighborhood of 25 percent. This is different from experience with solving dense systems on multiprocessors, where the performance of the best serial code and the parallel code running on one processor are comparable [8]. This is to be expected for the dense case, since the parts of the codes where the majority of the computation is done are *identical*. However, serial codes for sparse Cholesky factorization gain important performance advantages through heavy use of *context*. For example, efficient processing and storage of a column depend on rapid and direct access to information about certain selected previous columns. This context is inevitably lost in a parallel implementation, since the columns are distributed among many processors, and the use of such context would almost certainly require prohibitive amounts of communication. Thus, the data structures and computational schemes used in the serial and parallel implementations are quite different.

Another aspect of parallel sparse matrix computations that tends to make them less efficient than their dense counterparts is that the associated messages in sparse parallel implementations tend to be shorter. The time required to transmit a message from one processor to another typically involves a fixed startup time plus a cost proportional to the message length. It is therefore desirable to have a few large messages rather than many small ones in parallel computations, but this is difficult to achieve for sparse matrix computations.

The results of our experiments are contained in Table 5. Note that the "time" reported is artificial. The simulator measures time simply as the number of machine instructions executed, with no distinction being made between the relative cost of executing instructions of different types.

n	serial	one processor		eight processors	
RESULTS ON SPEED-UP					
	time	time	speed-up	time	speed-up
265	719606	1027215	.70	285614	2.52
406	1462056	2005731	.73	484443	3.02
577	2567430	3454271	.74	776278	3.31
778	4022592	5357658	.75	1120536	3.59
1009	6112334	8060091	.76	1591583	3.84

Table 5: Speed-up for one processor and 8-processor configurations.

REFERENCES

[1] I. S. Duff, *Full matrix techniques in sparse Gaussian elimination*, in Lecture Notes in Mathematics (912), G.A. Watson, ed., Springer-Verlag (1982).

[2] I. S. Duff, *Parallel implementation of multifrontal schemes*, Technical Memorandum No. 49, Mathematics and Computer Science Division, Argonne National Laboratory, Argonne, IL (March 1985).

[3] I. S. Duff and J. K. Reid, *The multifrontal solution of indefinite sparse symmetric linear equations*, ACM Trans. on Math. Software, 9 (1983), pp. 302-325.

[4] T. H. Dunigan, *A message-passing multiprocessor simulator*, Technical report ORNL/TM-9966, Mathematical Sciences Section, Oak Ridge National Laboratory, Oak Ridge, TN (1986).

[5] S. C. Eisenstat, M. C. Gursky, M. H. Schultz, and A. H. Sherman, *The Yale sparse matrix package, I. the symmetric codes*, Internat. J. Numer. Meth. Engrg., 18 (1982), pp. 1145-1151.

[6] S. C. Eisenstat, M. H. Schultz, and A. H. Sherman, *Applications of an element model for Gaussian elimination*, in Sparse Matrix Computations, J. E. Bunch and D. J. Rose, eds., Academic Press, New York, NY, 1976, pp. 85-96.

[7] S. C. Eisenstat, M. H. Schultz, and A. H. Sherman, *Software for sparse Gaussian elimination with limited core storage*, in Sparse Matrix Proceedings 1978, I. S. Duff and G. W. Stewart, eds., SIAM, Philadelphia, Pennsylvania, 1979, pp. 135-153.

[8] G. A. Geist and M. T. Heath, *Parallel Cholesky factorization on a hypercube multiprocessor*, Technical Report ORNL-6190, Mathematical Sciences Section, Oak Ridge National Laboratory, Oak Ridge, Tennessee (1985).

[9] J. A. George, M. T. Heath, and J. W-H. Liu, *Parallel Cholesky factorization on a multiprocessor*, Research Report CS-84-49, Department of Computer

Science, University of Waterloo, Waterloo, Ontario, Canada (1984).

[10] J. A. George and J. W-H. Liu, *An automatic nested dissection algorithm for irregular finite element problems*, SIAM J. Numer. Anal., 15 (1978), pp. 1053-1069.

[11] J. A. George and J. W-H. Liu, *The design of a user interface for a sparse matrix package*, ACM Trans. on Math. Software, 5 (1979), pp. 134-162.

[12] J. A. George and J. W-H. Liu, *An optimal algorithm for symbolic factorization of symmetric matrices*, SIAM J. Comput., 9 (1980), pp. 583-593.

[13] M. T. Heath, *Parallel Cholesky factorization in message passing multiprocessor environments*, Technical Report ORNL-6150, Mathematical Sciences Section, Oak Ridge National Laboratory, Oak Ridge, Tennessee (1985).

[14] J. A. G. Jess and H. G. M. Kees, *A data structure for parallel L/U decomposition*, IEEE Trans. Comput., C-31 (1982), pp. 231-239.

[15] J. W-H. Liu, *Modification of the minimum degree algorithm by multiple elimination*, ACM Trans. on Math. Software, 11 (1985), pp. 141-153.

[16] J. W-H. Liu, *A compact row storage scheme for sparse Cholesky factors using elimination trees*, to appear in ACM Trans. on Math. Software (1986).

[17] J. W-H. Liu, *On general row merging schemes for sparse Givens transformations*, to appear in SIAM J. Sci. Stat. Comput. (1986).

[18] J. W-H. Liu, *Computational models and task scheduling for parallel sparse Cholesky factorization*, to appear in Parallel Computing (1986).

[19] F. J. Peters, *Sparse matrices and substructures*, Mathematical Centre Tracts 119, Mathematisch Centrum, Amsterdam, The Netherlands (1980).

[20] R. Schreiber, *A new implementation of sparse Gaussian elimination*, ACM Trans. on Math. Software, 8 (1982), pp. 256-276.

CHAPTER 6

Concurrent Global Optimization on a Network of Computers

Richard H. Byrd*
Cornelius L. Dert†
Alexander H. G. Rinnooy Kan‡
Robert B. Schnabel*

Abstract. This paper presents a new parallel algorithm for the global optimization problem, which is to find the lowest minimizer of a nonlinear function of several variables that has multiple local minimizers. The algorithm is a stochastic method related to the multi-level single-linkage methods of Rinnooy Kan and Timmer for sequential computers. Concurrency is achieved by partitioning the work of each of the three main parts of the algorithm, sampling, start point selection, and multiple local minimizations, among the processors. This parallelism is of a coarse grain type and is especially well suited to a local memory multiprocessing environment. Test results of an implementation of this algorithm on a local area network of computer workstations are presented.

1. *Introduction.* This paper presents a parallel algorithm for the global optimization problem. The algorithm is a stochastic method related to the multi-level single-linkage methods of Rinnooy Kan and Timmer [1984] for sequential computers. The parallelism is of a coarse grain type and is especially well suited to a local memory multiprocessing environment. The paper presents test results of a distributed implementation of this algorithm on a local area network of computer workstations.

The global optimization problem is to find the lowest function value of a function that may have multiple local minimizers. We denote the problem by

$$\text{given } f(x): R^n \rightarrow R \quad \text{and} \quad S \subseteq R^n$$

$$\text{find } x_* \in S \text{ for which } f(x_*) \le f(x) \text{ for all } x \in S . \tag{1.1}$$

---

* Department of Computer Science, University of Colorado, Boulder, Colorado, USA
† Econometric Institute, Erasmus University Rotterdam, The Netherlands and Department of Computer Science, University of Colorado, Boulder, Colorado USA
‡ Econometric Institute, Erasmus University Rotterdam, The Netherlands

We refer to x_* as the *global minimizer* of $f(x)$ and $f(x_*)$ as the *global minimum*. The term "global" contrasts with a *local minimizer* of $f(x)$, which is the lowest value of $f(x)$ in some open neighborhood in S. Thus a function may have multiple local minima but it can have only one global minimum value. In this paper we assume that $f(x)$ is a nonlinear, twice continuously differentiable function. We also assume that the feasible region S is given by a set of lower and upper bounds on each variable, i.e.

$$S = \{ x \mid l_i \leq x_i \leq u_i , \; i=1, \cdots ,n \} .$$

and that the global minimizer lies in the interior of S.

Global optimization problems of the above form occur in many practical applications. Most optimization software, however, only is constructed to find local minimizers. (See e.g. Gill, Murray, and Wright [1981] or Dennis and Schnabel [1983].) One reason is that it is difficult to construct reliable algorithms for finding the global minimizer of general nonlinear functions. A second reason is that it often is very expensive to reliably solve the global optimization problem, requiring many evaluations of $f(x)$ and many iterations and arithmetic operations within the optimization code itself. In many practical optimization applications, the evaluation of $f(x)$ is very expensive so that the large number of function evaluations is the main expense.

There has been a moderate amount of work done in developing global optimization algorithms for sequential computers. Among these approaches, we favor *stochastic* methods, which include some component of random sampling of the function space, because these methods provide some guarantee of their reliability while still appearing at least as efficient as other approaches. Thus we also use a stochastic approach in our parallel algorithm. The main costs of such an approach are the evaluation of $f(x)$ at the sample points, combinatorial algorithms such as sorting or nearest-neighbor calculations involving these sample points, and the application of local minimization algorithms starting from some subset of the sample points. A modern sequential stochastic global optimization algorithm of Rinnooy Kan and Timmer [1984] is reviewed in more detail in Section 2.

Due to the expensive nature of global optimization and the practical need to solve such problems, there is ample incentive to devise parallel global optimization methods if they can lead to significantly faster solution of this problem. It appears that the global optimization problem is well suited to parallel solution in a number of ways.

In this paper we concentrate on the high level, coarse grain concurrency available in the global optimization algorithm itself. Obvious opportunities for high level parallelism include conducting multiple local minimizations concurrently, or evaluating $f(x)$ at multiple random sample points concurrently. Such an approach is intended to efficiently utilize multiple processors in solving the global optimization problem whether or not the evaluation of $f(x)$ is expensive.

An alternative, lower level use of parallelism in global optimization would be to apply a parallel algorithm to evaluate $f(x)$. In cases where the function evaluation is very expensive this approach might be very effective. We do not take this approach for several reasons. First, parallelization of $f(x)$ is problem dependent and outside the realm of the optimization algorithm designer. Second, this approach would be effective only for expensive functions, whereas our approach is effective regardless of the cost of evaluating $f(x)$. Third, if one has an efficient parallel code for evaluating $f(x)$, then it can be used in conjunction with the approach presented here. For example, if $f(x)$ vectorizes well, then the appropriate computational environment would be a multiprocessor where each node is a vector processor. In this environment the function evaluations could be performed on individual vector processors while the higher level parallelism in our algorithm could still go on among the processors. Indeed, we believe that this computational environment (currently embodied by machines including the Cray X-MP and the Alliant) will be a very important one in the future, and that it will be suitable to many optimization problems with expensive functions, as the computation of $f(x)$ often does vectorize well in these cases. In other cases where the computation of $f(x)$ requires multiple processors, it would be possible to divide the processors into clumps, with each clump of processors used to evaluate $f(x)$ and the multiple clumps used to implement the high level parallelism of our algorithm.

The implementation of the type of coarse grain parallel algorithm we develop requires a computer capable of executing multiple independent instruction streams at the same time. In the taxonomy of Flynn these are known as *Multiple Instruction Multiple Data* (MIMD) computers. The class of MIMD computers includes both shared and local memory multiprocessors.

Shared memory multiprocessors are computers with multiple processors all connected, via a switching network or global bus, to a shared memory which they all can access. *Local memory multiprocessors* are computers with multiple processors, each with its own local memory, connected by some sort of interconnection network. Examples currently in use include the hypercube computers pioneered at Caltech (Seitz [1985]) and local area networks of computers. On these machines, synchronization or communication between processors is achieved by passing messages between the processors. Generally message throughput rates are several orders of magnitude slower than the arithmetic operation rate. Thus local memory multiprocessors are best suited to parallel algorithms where, on the average, many instructions (say 1000 or more) are executed on individual processors in between synchronization or communication points with other processors. Such algorithms are generally referred to as *medium grain* or *coarse grain* parallel algorithms.

Since the global optimization problem appears amenable to solution by a coarse grain parallel algorithm, a local memory multiprocessor appears to be an appropriate parallel environment for this problem. For this reason, we have chosen to implement our parallel algorithm on the local area network of workstations that is being used for parallel computation at the University of Colorado. This environment is discussed in Section 4.1.

The goal of this research, therefore, is to develop an efficient and reliable parallel algorithm for the global optimization problem that is well suited to implementation in a local memory multiprocessing environment. By reliable, we mean that the algorithm should be successful in finding the global minimum and preferably that there be some theoretical guarantee of this reliability. By efficient, ideally we mean that our parallel algorithm, when implemented on P identical processors, should require $1/P$ of the time that the best sequential algorithm would on one of these processors to solve the same problem.

The remainder of the paper discusses our algorithm, parallel computing environment, and our theoretical and experimental results. In Section 2 we briefly describe sequential methods for global optimization, concentrating on the approach from which our parallel algorithm is derived. Section 3 presents our parallel global optimization method. In Section 4 we first describe the multiprocessing environment, a network of computer workstations, used in our experiments. Then we present our computational results in this environment. Some comments on future directions for this work are presented in Section 5.

2. *Sequential global optimization methods.* The methods that have been developed to solve the global optimization problem for general nonlinear functions $f(x)$ can be divided into two main classes, *deterministic* methods and *stochastic* methods (Dixon and Szego, [1978]). Deterministic methods do not incorporate any random or stochastic features. A wide variety of approaches are contained in this class, including trajectory methods (Branin [1972], Branin and Hoo [1972]), deflation methods (Goldstein and Price [1971], Levy and Gomez [1985], Levy and Montalvo [1985]), piecewise approximation methods (Shubert [1972]), and interval arithmetic methods (Hansen [1980], Hansen and Sengupta [1980], Walster, Hansen, and Sengupta [1985]). Most of these methods either do not provide a guarantee that they will find the global minimizer, or do so only at the expense of making additional assumptions about $f(x)$ which are difficult to verify in practice. Stochastic methods differ in that they incorporate stochastic features, generally sampling of $f(x)$ at randomly selected points in the feasible region. This enables them to provide a probabilistic guarantee that the global minimizer will be found, assuming only that $f(x)$ is continuously differentiable. Generally, these methods combine the random sampling phase with a phase where local minimization algorithms are performed from some of the sample points.

Recent stochastic methods, such as those of Zielinski [1981], Boender, Rinnooy Kan, Stougie, and Timmer [1982], and Rinnooy Kan and Timmer [1984, 1985a, b, c], combine random search and local minimization carefully and appear to be quite efficient in computational experiments. In addition, the most recent methods (Boender and Rinnooy Kan [1983], Rinnooy Kan and Timmer [1985c]) also provide probabilistic guarantees of their computational efficiency. Thus, they appear to provide an attractive choice from both the theoretical and computational points of view. For these reasons, we have chosen to base our concurrent global optimization algorithms on a stochastic approach.

In particular, our concurrent methods are most closely related to the recent *multi-level single linkage* methods of Rinnooy Kan and Timmer [1984]. This method appears to combine state-of-the-art computational performance with strong theoretical properties. The remainder of this section briefly reviews sequential multi-level single linkage methods, with emphasis on aspects that will have importance for our concurrent methods.

The multi-level single linkage method is an iterative algorithm. Each iteration consists of a sampling phase, in which the function is evaluated at a number of randomly sampled points, followed by a minimization phase, in which a local minimization procedure is applied to $f(x)$ starting from a subset of the sample points. Finally a probabilistic stopping rule is applied to determine whether the algorithm should be continued, and if it should, the next iteration is begun. An outline of the algorithm is given in Algorithm 2.1.

Several portions of Algorithm 2.1 require further elaboration. Most important to the practical and theoretical success of the method is the selection of start points for local minimizations in step 2. At iteration k, each sample point x is selected as a start point for a local minimization if it has not been used as a start point at a previous iteration, and if there is no lower sample point y within the *critical distance* $r(k)$ of x with a lower function value, i.e with

$$\|x \_ y\| \le r(k) \quad \text{and} \quad f(x) < f(y).$$

The critical distance is given by

$$r(k) = \pi^{-\frac{1}{2}} [\; \Gamma(1+\tfrac{n}{2})\, m(S)\, \sigma\; \frac{\log kN}{kN}\;]^{1/n} \tag{2.1}$$

where $m(S)$ denotes the Lebesque measure of S, Γ denotes the gamma function, σ is a positive constant, and N is the sample size per iteration.

The local minimizations are performed by any standard unconstrained minimization code. The theoretical analysis of the multi-level single linkage method simply assumes that the unconstrained minimization code will find a local minimizer x^* when started within the "basin" of x^*, the set of points x from which all strictly descent paths converge only to x^*.

Algorithm 2.1 -- Multi-Level Single Linkage Method for Global Optimization

Given $f : R^n \rightarrow R$, feasible region S

At iteration number k:

1. **Generate sample points and function values**
   Add N points, drawn from a uniform distribution over S, to the (initially empty) set of sample points, and evaluate $f(x)$ at each new sample point.

2. **Select start points for local searches**
   Determine a (possibly empty) subset of the sample points from which to start local searches.

3. **Perform local minimizations from all start points**

4. **Decide whether to stop**
   If stopping rule is satisfied, regard the lowest local minimizer found as the global minimizer, otherwise go to step 1.

The methods of Rinnooy Kan and Timmer [1985a,c] use the VA10AD variable metric subroutine from the Harwell Subroutine Library, while the methods reported in this paper use the line-search BFGS code in the UNCMIN package of Schnabel, Koontz, and Weiss [1985]. Both are well-tested and widely used codes.

A Bayesian stopping rule of Boender and Rinnooy Kan [1983] is applied at step 4. The algorithm is terminated after the kth iteration if and only if the number of local minimizers found is within 0.5 of a Bayesian estimate of the total number of local minimizers, and a Bayesian estimate of the portion of S covered by the regions of attraction of the local minimizers found so far is $\geq .995$.

Strong theoretical properties of the multi-level single linkage algorithm have been proven in Boender [1984]. If the critical distance is given by (2.1) with $\sigma > 0$, then with probability 1, all the isolated local minimizers of $f(x)$ will be found within a finite number of iterations. If $\sigma > 4$ in (2.1), then, even if the sampling continues forever, the total number of local searches started by the algorithm will be finite with probability 1. Thus both the accuracy and the efficiency of the method are guaranteed in a probabilistic sense.

Test results for the multi-level linkage algorithm are reported in Rinnooy Kan and Timmer [1985a,c]. The algorithm has been tested on a standard set of test problems, and compared with a number of other stochastic approaches for global optimization. Overall, it seemed to offer the best combination of efficiency and reliability of the methods tested. Computational comparisons with recent deterministic methods, such as the tunneling method, have not yet been made.

3. *A concurrent algorithm for stochastic global optimization.* We can readily identify three sources of high level parallelism in the multi level single linkage method. In the first phase of each iteration, sampling, each processor can generate $1/P$ of the sample points (P the number of processors) and evaluate the function at each of them. In the second phase, start point selection, each processor can select start points from its own subsample. (Some checking with other subsamples may be required; this is discussed later.) Finally in the third phase, local minimization, each processor can be responsible for one or more of the local searches.

An obvious mechanism for achieving this concurrency is to divide the feasible region into P subregions of equal size, and assign each subregion to a different processor. Then the sampling phase can be implemented concurrently simply by having each processor sample its subregion, and the major part of the start point selection can be accomplished by having all the processors concurrently generate the start points for their subregions based on their own samples. It is possible, however, that the number of start points for local searches may vary widely between subregions, and the lengths of local searches also may vary widely. Thus it may not be advantageous to have each processor simply handle the local searches for the start points from its own region. Instead, in our algorithm a master process collects all the start points from all the subregions and then distributes them back to the processors as evenly as possible. This is discussed in more detail below. The master process also coordinates the small amount of synchronization and communication that is required.

At this point it may be useful to point out a basic difference between the second source of parallelism described above and the other two sources. The first and the third phases of the algorithm, sampling and local minimization, generally are dominated by the costs of the evaluations of $f(x)$. Thus our concurrent algorithm essentially is distributing these function evaluations among the processors. In the second phase, start point selection, however, there are no function evaluations, and our concurrent algorithm is carrying out part of the global optimization algorithm itself in parallel. The impact of the latter type of concurrency relative to the former on the overall speedup of the algorithm clearly will be determined by the percentage of time spent in various phases of the algorithm; this in turn will depend on the cost per function evaluation and the number of function evaluations required to solve a particular problem. The more time spent on function evaluations, the more important the concurrency from the sampling and local minimization phases of the algorithm. In fact, if function evaluations are sufficiently expensive it may be profitable to also exploit a lower level of parallelism, performing parallel function evaluations within the individual local minimizations. This is not done in the main algorithm described in this paper, but this possibility is discussed briefly in Section 5.

A concurrent multi level single linkage algorithm employing P processors and making use of all three high level sources of parallelism is outlined in Algorithm 3.1. The four basic steps of this algorithm are identical to those of the sequential multi level single linkage algorithm, Algorithm 2.1. Concurrency is achieved in the implementation of each of these steps, with the exception of step 4, which hardly contributes to the algorithm's running time. The remainder of this section consists of a more detailed discussion of Algorithm 3.1. In subsections 3.1 - 3.3 we focus on the aspects where the concurrent algorithm differs from the sequential method in steps 1, 2, and 3, respectively. In subsection 3.4 we make some comments on how the concurrent algorithm is expected to meet the goals of reliability and efficient utilization of a local memory multiprocessing environment that were mentioned in the introductory section.

3.1 *The generation of sample points and function values.* In the sampling phase, each processor i extends its set of sample points by N/P new points and evaluates $f(x)$ at each of them. Whereas the random sampling was done from a uniform distribution over the entire region S in the sequential method, in the concurrent algorithm each processor generates a random sample from a uniform distribution over its own subregion S_i. This necessitates that the theoretical analysis of the algorithm be modified but does not alter the theoretical properties of the method.

3.2 *The selection of start points for local searches.* The selection of start points for local minimizations is carried out in two phases. The first, local, phase is performed independently and concurrently by each processor. Processor i selects the points in its own subregion S_i which locally satisfy the multi-level single linkage start point selection rule described in Section 2. That is, at iteration k each sample point $x \in S_i$ is selected as a candidate start point if it has not been used as a start point in a previous iteration, and if there is no sample point $y \in S_i$ within the critical distance $r(k)$ of x given by equation (2.1) with a smaller function value.

For a given sample over the entire region S, any sample point that would be selected as

**Algorithm 3.1 -- A Concurrent Multi-Level Single Linkage Method
for Global Optimization**

Given $f : R^n \to R$, feasible region S and P processors

0. Partition S

Subdivide S into P equal size, regular shaped subregions S_i, $i = 1,...P$, and assign subregion S_i to processor i for $i = 1,...,P$.

At iteration number k:

1. Generate sample points and function values

For $i = 1,...,P$

Add N/P points, drawn from a uniform distribution over subregion i, to the (initially empty) set of sample points, and evaluate $f(x)$ at each new sample point.

2. Select start points for local searches

For $i = 1,...,P$

Determine a (possible empty) set of start points in subregion i, disregarding sample information from all other subregions.

Resolve start points near borders between subregions (some start points selected above may be eliminated).

3. Perform local minimizations from all start points

Collect all start points and distribute one to each processor, which performs a minimization from that point. Issue a processor a new start point as soon as it terminates its current local search, until local searches from all start points have been completed.

4. Decide whether to stop

If stopping rule is satisfied, regard the lowest local minimizer found as the global minimizer, otherwise go to step 1.

---

a start point by the sequential algorithm will also be selected as a candidate start point by this first start point selection phase of the concurrent algorithm. This is because the sequential algorithm selects a sample point x as a start point if there is no lower sample point within the critical distance from it, whereas the first phase of the concurrent algorithm will select x as a start point if there is no lower sample point within the *same* critical distance from x *and* within the same subregion as x. Thus, if x is within the critical distance of any border of its subregion, it is possible that it will be selected as a candidate start point by the first phase of the concurrent algorithm but not by the sequential algorithm, because some sample point in another subregion but within the critical distance has a smaller function value. To prevent the initiation of unnecessary local searches from these points, the local selection phase of the concurrent algorithm is followed by a second, global selection step. First, all candidate start points within the critical distance of a border between subregions are distributed to all processors. Then, each processor determines whether its sample contains a point within the critical distance of one of these candidate start points with a lower function value. If so, this candidate point is not used as a start point for a local minimization. The remaining start points will be the same ones that would have been selected from the same sample by the sequential method.

3.3 *The local minimizations.* The distribution of the computational effort in the local minimization phase is fairly straightforward. After all the local search start points have been identified in the previous step, all these points are reported to the master process. The master process then distributes one start point to each processor, and if there are more start points than processors, a processor that completes one local search it is given another start point until all start points have been processed.

As discussed in the beginning of this section, this phase may not keep all the processors equally busy. The remaining issue is in what order to assign the local minimizations in order to keep processor idle time as small as possible. If we knew in advance how long each local search would take, we could use a scheduling heuristic to minimize the total time, and thus the idle time, needed to complete all minimizations. A well known, simple heuristic with attractive theoretical properties for similar scheduling problems is the *longest processing time* rule, which states that the jobs should be scheduled in order of descending processing time.

In the case of local minimizations we do not know in advance how long each minimization will take, so we cannot order the start points according to processing time. One crude way to estimate these times is to guess that the higher the function value at the start point, the longer the minimization will take. Our computational experiments indicate using this heuristic, i.e. dispatching start points to processors by highest function value first, has given slightly better results than using an arbitrary ordering and at least as good results as any other heuristics we have attempted.

3.4 *Some comments on the concurrent global optimization algorithm.* In this subsection we make some general remarks concerning the expected efficiency and reliability of the concurrent global optimization algorithm we have just described. We will also examine how effectively the algorithm is likely to utilize a local memory multiprocessing environment.

From the point of view of the sample points that are used, the local minimizations that are performed, and the answer that is found, the concurrent algorithm differs from the sequential one only in that it samples from a slightly different distribution. Therefore we expect that, the number of sample points, function evaluations, and local searches that are used by the sequential and concurrent methods on any particular problem will be very similar. Furthermore we expect that the number of minimizers found by the two methods will be roughly the same, and that they usually will find the same global minimizer. This similarity between in two algorithms is reinforced by the theoretical analysis in Dert [1986].

Now we turn to the parallel characteristics of Algorithm 3.1. Notice that Algorithm 3.1 requires very little synchronization of processes or communication or sharing of information between them. Information is exchanged at three places in the algorithm : after the local phase of step 2 is completed the candidate start points within the critical distance of the subregion border must be collected and sent to the other subregions; after the border resolution phase of step 2 is completed the final start points must be collected and distributed to the processors; after the local minimizations are completed in step 3 each process must report the minimizers found to the process making the stopping test. The only synchronization requirements are inherent in these actions : the local phase of step 2 must be completed by all subregions before the global phase is begun, and all the local searches must be completed before the stopping test is made and the next iteration is started if required.

In our implementation, a master process, which resides on the same processor as one of the subregion processes, takes care of the coordinating activities described above. It collects the candidate start points that are near subregion borders and distributed them to the subregion processes when it has all of them; it collects the start points and distributes them to the processors using the heuristic discussed in Section 3.3; and when all local searches are completed, it performs the stopping test (two simple equations) and starts the next iteration if required.

This organization makes it clear that our concurrent algorithm requires very little shared information, and therefore is well suited for implementation on a local memory multiprocessor. If a local memory multiprocessor is used, at each iteration the number of messages received, and sent, by each subregion process will be two plus the number of local searches conducted by that processor. At each iteration the master process will receive, and send, $2P$ messages plus the total number of local searches for that iteration. The messages all are short, containing either one number, one n-vector, or a small number of n-vectors. Thus the total interprocess communication requirements are quite small.

Finally, we will examine how much overhead is introduced by the parallelization of the algorithm at steps 1, 2, and 3 of Algorithm 3.1, and how fully we expect all processors to be utilized.

In step 1 each processor samples N/P points and evaluates the function at each one of them. This step requires no interprocess communication or parallel overhead, and is expected to achieve equal utilization of all processors as long as the time required to evaluate $f(x)$ at different points x is (nearly) uniform.

Now consider the start point selection step. Since the selection of candidate start points requires each processer to consider the same number of points (kN/P), we expect equal utilization of all processors during this portion of step 2. In our experience, the second part of the step, in which the border points are resolved, requires very little running time in comparison. So in step 2 we introduce little parallel overhead or interprocess communication (each process has to send and read 1 message), and as in step 1 we expect all processors to do the same amount of work. In fact, we will see in Section 4 that step 2 has the interesting effect of applying a divide and conquer strategy that actually causes greater than linear speedup in comparison to some standard sequential implementations.

Finally consider step 3, the local minimization phase. Again, the cost of interprocessor communication in this phase is small (one message sent and received for each local search) and no other parallel overhead is introduced. As we have discussed previously, however, this step will probably not utilize all processors evenly due to the uneven lengths of local searches, and the fact that the number of searches may be less than the number of processors. This is one of the main effects that we will examine in Section 4. We will also present some results about improving the efficiency of the local minimization phase by introducing concurrency into the individual local minimizations.

In summary, the concurrent global optimization algorithm adds fairly few new costs, either new operations or interprocess communication, to those present in the sequential algorithm. In the sampling phase and the start point selection phase, it appears to readily allow full utilization of all processors. In the local minimization phase, the synchronization requirements may cause some processors to be idle at some times. In problems where function evaluation is expensive, the expense of the algorithm is dominated by the sampling and local minimization steps, so that the efficiency of these steps is most important and the start point selection step becomes relatively unimportant.

4. *Computational testing.* We have implemented and tested the concurrent global optimization algorithm described in Section 3 on a network of computer workstations. This section reports the results of these tests. First, we briefly describe our parallel computing environment.

4.1 *The Testing Environment.* The University of Colorado is engaged in a large research project on the use of a network of computer workstations for concurrent computation. This project includes developing and implementing numerical algorithms for important practical problems that are well suited to this loosely coupled multiprocessing environment. It also includes the development of systems and software support that will make a network of computers easier to use for distributed concurrent computation. This project is supported by a Coordinated Experimental Research grant from the National Science Foundation as well as individual research grants.

The concurrent global optimization algorithm described in Section 3 appears to be an excellent candidate for solution in this environment. As discussed in section 3.4, the algorithm divides the problem into large chunks that can be executed concurrently, and requires relatively infrequent communication between processes and little shared data. For these reasons we chose to implement our concurrent global optimization algorithm on our network of workstations.

Our current test environment consists of a network of Sun workstations, connected on an ethernet and sharing several file servers. The experiments reported in Section 4.2 were conducted on a dedicated subnet consisting of four or eight Sun-3 workstations. That is, when we conducted these experiments we were the only users of these workstations and the subnet was physically disconnected from the remainder of our computer network. Thus the subnet functioned as a stand alone local memory multiprocessor.

Our ability to use the network of workstations for distributed concurrent processing is based upon the Sun version of the Berkeley Unix 4.2 operating system, which each workstation runs. The Berkeley Unix 4.2 operating system provides the basic interprocessor communication facility, the ability to send messages between processes on different machines, that is needed to use a network of computers as a multi-processor. In Berkeley Unix 4.2, this capability is provided by stream sockets, reliable point to point connections between two processors, as well as datagram sockets. When combined with the Unix *fork* and *exec* commands, these facilities allow a process on one computer to start a process on another computer and subsequently communicate with it.

Researchers in the Computer Science Department at the University of Colorado have built a distributed processing utilities package, called DPUP, that makes a network of computers running the Berkeley Unix 4.2 operating system easier to use for distributed concurrent processing (Gardner et al [1986]). DPUP builds upon the interprocessor communication facilities in Berkeley 4.2 to provide two models of concurrent computation. The first is a master-slave model where all processes are linked to one master in a "spokes of a wheel" arrangement and all communication is through the master. The second is a broadcast model where each process is an equal member of a ring of processes and can send messages to all of the processes at once. For both models, DPUP provides several basic concurrency capabilities including the creation and termination of remote processes (with required communication connection automatically established) and various means to send and receive messages. Our concurrent global optimization software uses the master-slave model of DPUP.

4.2 *Computational results.* Both the sequential and the concurrent global optimization algorithms have been run on the test problems given in Dixon and Szego [1978]. At present these seem to be the only widely accepted global optimization test problems. The characteristics of these problems are summarized in Table 4.1. The problems are low dimensional (up to 6 variables) with only few minimizers (up to 10). In addition, evaluation of the test functions is very cheap. These characteristics limit what one can determine from the test set, and how one should interpret the computational results, in several ways.

The small number of variables and local minimizers limits the amount of parallelism that can be obtained in solving the global optimization problem. The number of sample points required, the number of local searches required, and often the number of iterations required would all be significantly higher for more difficult problems, which in turn would enable the use of more concurrency. We currently are attempting to obtain and construct more difficult test problems; we discuss this topic briefly in Section 5.

The fact that the evaluation of the test functions themselves is very cheap (sometimes requiring only a few floating point operations) means that our timing results are not indicative of performance on many real world problems where function evaluation is the dominant cost.

Therefore we will report two speedup measures. The first measure is the actual timed speedup, the time required by the sequential algorithm to solve a problem divided by the time required by the concurrent algorithm to solve the same problem, i.e.

$$speedup_{timed} = \frac{elapsed \times sequential \ algorithm}{elapsed \times concurrent \ algorithm} \qquad (4.1)$$

In many of our experiments this measure is dominated by the start point selection phase, which in fact requires no function evaluations. Thus this measure is an interesting indication of how well we have sped up the overhead calculations of the algorithm, and also gives some indication of how practical our approach would be on small problems with very inexpensive function evaluations.

In many practical optimization problems, however, the evaluation of the objective function $f(x)$ is very expensive. The computational effort then will consist mainly of computing function values. So in this case one is primarily interested in the distribution of function evaluations among the processors. To use our test results to indicate the speedup our concurrent algorithm would achieve on this type of problem, we introduce a second speedup measure. Let $funevals_{i,j}$ denote the number of function evaluations done by the ith processor at the jth iteration, and let the total number of processors and iterations be P and $ITNS$, respectively. Then the speedup for expensive function evaluations may be approximated by

$$speedup_{expensive\_func} = \frac{\sum\limits_{j=1}^{ITNS} \sum\limits_{i=1}^{P} funevals_{i,j}}{\sum\limits_{j=1}^{ITNS} \max_{(k=1,...,P)} funevals_{k,j}} \qquad (4.2)$$

This measure is the limit of the timed speedup ratio we would obtain on our test problems if the function values were unchanged but the cost of each function evaluation was increased without bound. As opposed to the first measure, it is independent of the speedup achieved during the start point selection phase.

Our test results are presented for two different modes of operation of the sequential and concurrent algorithms, using 200 or 1000 sample points per iteration. The parameter σ was set to 4 in both cases. Since the algorithm is stochastic, the results are influenced to some extent by the random sample that is generated. To dampen the effect of the variation in random samples, 10 independent runs were performed for each problem/algorithm combination.

The reliability of each algorithm on each problem is summarized in Table 4.2, and the average costs in function evaluations are given in Table 4.3. (These data are given for the 8 processor concurrent algorithm but are very similar when using different numbers of processors.) On these simple test problems, using 200 sample points per iteration usually led the algorithm to require fewer total function evaluations, although the reliability of the algorithm was somewhat better with 1000 points per iteration. (The reliability results are similar to those reported in Rinnooy Kan and Timmer [1985a] and no attempt was made to change the algorithm to improve upon them.) We consider the 1000 point per iteration size, however, to be far more indicative of what would be required on problems with more variables or more local minimizers. Therefore we consider the test results with 1000 sample points per iteration to be the more important ones.

When we first timed our concurrent global optimization algorithm on a network of 3 Sun-2 workstations, the speedups in comparson to the sequential algorithm on a Sun-2 were consistently *greater than* 3. In fact, they generally ranged from about 3 to about 8. The reason for this was fairly easy to see. A large portion of the time was being spent in the start point selection phase, which in the sequential case used an $O(N^2)$ algorithm, where N is the number of sample points. The concurrent algorithm was essentially applying one stage of divide and conquer to this algorithm, first dividing the process into 3 equal parts (which reduces the *total* work of an $O(N^2)$ algorithm by a factor of 3 and thus would induce a speedup of 9 in our situation), and then applying the border resolution strategy to "patch together" the 3 regions. But since the border resolution strategy is only applied to a small portion of the original sample, its cost is small and the total speedup for the start point phase was still close to 9. Indeed, when we modified the sequential algorithm to use the identical strategy, that is divide the feasible region into 3 equal parts, do the start point selection in each separately, and then do border resolution, the sequential algorithm times dropped significantly and the speedups by the concurrent algorithm no longer were greater than 3. Instead, then ranged from about 2 to 3.

From a theoretical point of view, it is known that one can do better than the straightforward $O(N^2)$ algorithm for start point selection. Timmer [1984] shows that the *spiral search* technique of Bentley, Weide and Yao [1980] can be applied so that the expected running time of the start point selection phase, when totaled over all the iterations of the algorithm, is linear in the total number of sample points used. We subsequently implemented this technique in the manner suggested by Timmer. We found that it is more efficient than the one stage divide and conquer strategy described above only for very small dimension problems. For example, with sample size 1000 and $n=4$, the time required by a 16 subdivision divide and conquer algorithm is roughly equivalent to that required by spiral search, while when $n=6$ a 4 subdivision divide and conquer algorithm already is about as efficient as spiral search and a 16 subdivision divide and conquer is about 4 times more efficient. Thus for our computational results on sequential machines, we have chosen to use the one stage divide and conquer approach : when comparing to a P processor concurrent algorithm, we use a sequential algorithm that also subdivides into P subregions in the start point selection phase. (This accounts for the different times for the same sequential algorithms in Tables 4.4 and 4.5.) Note that from a computational point of view, our research into concurrent global optimization algorithm seems to have led to an improved sequential algorithm as well.

Tables 4.4 and 4.5 give the timed speedups of our concurrent global optimization algorithm using 4 and 8 processors, respectively. The differences between the times for the same sequential algorithms in the two tables shows that the times are dominated by the start point selection phase. There often is almost a factor of two difference in the sequential times between Table 4.4 and 4.5. This is accounted for by the nearly factor of 2 reduction in the start point selection phase when switching from the 4 subdivision to 8 subdivision sequential algorithm, as discussed above; the times required by all other phases of the sequential algorithm are identical in the two cases but take a small portion of the total time.

The times for 4 processors show good speedup. This is especially true with sample size 1000 where the speedups average about 3.6. In this case the start point selection phase is dominant and is parallelized almost fully. Recall that this sample size is more indicative of the sample size that would be used on most real-world problems. For sample size 200 the speedups are somewhat less good, averaging about 2.8. Here the total running time has become small enough that the idle time in the search phase and the small communications overhead begins to have an effect. Recall that since the start point selection phase requires no function evaluations, the algorithmic aspects that mainly determine these timing results will be irrelevant in the expensive function results.

The speedups for 8 processors are still quite good with 1000 sample points, averaging about 6.2. By comparing to the 8 processor line for this algorithm in Table 4.6, it is seen that these speedups are fairly close to the expensive function limits. The reason is that with 8 processors, the start point selection time per processor has become relatively small and the sampling and search phases are beginning to dominate. The limit in the parallelism is caused by the small total number of local searches (usually there are fewer than 8) and the unequal lengths of the searches.

The speedups for 8 processors with 200 sample point are not very good, averaging about 3.0. The main reason for these poorer results is that the run times are so small that the interprocessor communication overhead and the idle times in the search phase have a large effect. This demonstrates the limit to the grain of parallelism that is effective in our multi-computer multiprocessing environment, and is simply a consequence of the very inexpensive function evaluations.

The expensive function evaluation speedups for each algorithm are given in Table 4.6. Note that once we have run our global optimization algorithm on a particular problem with any particular number of processors, we know the total number of iterations it will use, the total number of sample points it will use, and the number and length of local searches it will perform at each iteration, regardless of the number of processors. (There can be slight variations due to the stochastic effects and the effect of requiring an equal number of sample points per subregion.) Thus, given the rule for ordering and distributing local searches in the concurrent algorithm, we can calculate the expensive function speedup on this problem for any other number of processors from equation (4.2). We use this flexibility to calculate expensive function speedups, for each problem and sample size, for 2, 4, 8, 16, 32, and 64 processors. (The data from the 8 processor concurrent algorithm is used.) In addition, the speedup with the number of processors equal to the number of sample points per iteration, 200 or 1000, is given. Since the number of local searches per iteration is always far less than 200, the cost of an iteration of the concurrent algorithm in this case is 1 (for the sampling phase) plus the number of function evaluations in the longest local search. This is the limiting speedup for this algorithm; i.e. if more processors were available the expensive function speedup would not change.

For the algorithm with 1000 sample points per iteration, the expensive function speed-ups are reasonably high. With 8 processors most problems make at least 80% utilization of the processors, with 16 processors the utilization is generally at least 60%, and even with 32 processors the utilization is often around 50%. The limiting speedups (for 1000 processors) are over 20 in most cases. Since the maximum parallelism in the local search phase is generally between 5 and 10, the sampling phase is having a large effect; in the problem with the longest searches, Hartman 6, the speedups are lower.

When 200 sample points per iteration are used, the expensive function speedups are much lower, with limiting speedups between 5 and 10. In this case the sampling phase is a much smaller portion of the algorithm and the local search phase dominates. The speedups are simply a reflection of the small number of local searches. The concurrency in this case could be improved by parallelizing the individual local searches; this is discussed briefly in Section 5.

Taken together, these results confirm that our concurrent global optimization algorithm is able to exploit parallelism reasonably well, to the extent that it is available in the problem. The parallelism that is possible is limited by the number of variables, the number of local minimizers, and the expense of the function evaluations. It appears that it is possible to obtain good utilization of a moderate number of processors even for problems with inexpensive function evaluations, and that quite effective use of multiple processors can be made for problems with expensive function evaluations. Besides the inherent limitations of the problem, the main deterrent from achieving even higher speedups with the current algorithm is the sequential nature of the individual local searches. In the next section we briefly discuss several techniques for introducing additional concurrency into the global optimization algorithm that deal with this problem.

Table 4.1 -- Test Problem Data

Name	Abbreviation	Problem Variables	Local Minimizers
Goldstein-Price	GP	2	4
Branin	BR	2	3
Hartman 3	H3	3	4
Hartman 6	H6	6	4
Shekel 5	S5	4	5
Shekel 7	S7	4	7
Shekel 10	S10	4	10

Table 4.2 -- Number Times Global Minimizer Found in 10 Runs
(8 processors)

	Problem						
	GP	BR	H3	H6	S5	S7	S10
200 points per iteration	10	10	10	10	8	6	6
1000 points per iteration	10	10	10	10	10	7	7

Table 4.3 -- Number of Function Evaluations, Averaged over 10 Runs
(8 Processors)

	GP	BR	H3	H6	S5	S7	S10
				Problem			
200 points per iteration	412	306	380	1522	487	469	447
1000 points per iteration	1420	1150	1213	3104	1395	1346	1375

Table 4.4 -- Times and Speedups on 4 Processors, Averaged over 10 Runs
(times in seconds)

	GP	BR	H3	H6	S5	S7	S10
				Problem			
200 points per iteration,							
Sequential Time	4.7	5.0	9.0	31.2	9.3	10.1	10.9
Concurrent Time	1.6	1.7	3.2	10.0	3.7	3.8	3.6
Speedup	2.9	3.0	2.8	3.1	2.5	2.7	3.0
1000 points per iteration,							
Sequential Time	142.2	152.1	184.0	339.0	186.1	189.0	188.0
Concurrent Time	38.0	40.9	55.8	98.8	51.3	51.2	51.1
Speedup	3.7	3.7	3.3	3.4	3.6	3.7	3.7

Table 4.5 -- Times and Speedups on 8 Processors, Averaged over 10 Runs
(times in seconds)

	GP	BR	H3	H6	S5	S7	S10
				Problem			
200 points per iteration,							
Sequential Time	2.7	3.1	5.1	27.7	6.0	6.5	6.9
Concurrent Time	1.2	1.2	1.7	5.8	2.2	2.3	2.2
Speedup	2.3	2.6	3.0	4.8	2.7	2.8	3.1
1000 points per iteration,							
Sequential Time	68.3	74.0	76.7	223.0	94.7	94.8	97.6
Concurrent Time	11.7	10.9	12.3	40.7	51.1	15.2	14.5
Speedup	5.8	6.8	6.2	5.5	6.3	6.2	6.7

**Table 4.6 -- Simulated Speedups for Expensive Function Evaluations
Averaged Over 10 Runs**

	Number of Processors	Problem						
		GP	BR	H3	H6	S5	S7	S10
200 points per iteration	2	1.9	1.9	1.9	2.0	1.8	1.8	1.9
	4	3.4	3.5	3.3	3.6	2.7	3.0	3.1
	8	4.6	5.0	4.8	6.1	3.5	3.9	4.1
	16	5.4	6.4	5.7	8.6	4.1	4.6	4.8
	32	5.9	7.4	6.3	9.6	4.4	5.1	5.3
	64	6.1	8.0	6.6	9.8	4.6	5.3	5.5
	200	6.3	8.4	6.9	10.0	4.8	5.5	5.7
1000 points per iteration	2	2.0	2.0	2.0	2.0	2.0	2.0	2.0
	4	3.9	3.9	3.8	3.8	3.6	3.6	3.7
	8	7.1	7.1	6.7	6.8	6.0	6.3	6.5
	16	11.0	11.2	10.3	11.7	8.9	9.4	9.5
	32	14.6	15.9	14.0	15.4	12.0	12.5	12.4
	64	17.5	20.2	17.3	16.7	14.6	15.2	14.9
	1000	21.4	27.0	21.6	18.1	18.3	18.7	17.9

5. *Future research directions.* The concurrent global optimization algorithm discussed in this paper appears to have two important limitations. First, the amount of parallelism is limited by the number of local minimizations at each iteration and possibly by the distribution of their lengths. Secondly, the sampling efforst is distributed uniformly over the entire feasible region regardless of the characteristics of the objective function. (This limitation is shared by the sequential algorithm.) We are working on ways to overcome both limitations.

When function evaluation is expensive, one way to introduce more parallelism into the local minimization phase of our algorithm is to distribute the gradient calculations (assuming they are done by finite differences as is often the case) among various processors. This has the potential to increase the parallelism obtained by up to a factor of n, although a speedup of about $n/2$ is the most one can expect if each gradient evaluation is preceded by a function evaluation that is performed sequentially. If there are not enough processors to evaluate n function values for each local search simultaneously, then a strategy for ordering function and gradient evaluations is required, and this strategy may also be used to attempt to give the longer local searches higher priority. We have conducted some preliminary tests of such a strategy on the test problems of Section 4. Our preliminary indications are that it can significantly increase the speedup of the local minimization phase of each iteration, if function evaluation is expensive and the number of processors significantly exceeds the number of local searches for that iteration. Further modifications, including conducting function and gradient evaluations simultaneously before it is known whether the gradient actually is needed, and using multiple gradient values at an iteration, are currently being investigated in the contexts of local and global minimization.

A second approach for obtaining more parallelism in global optimization is to move towards a more asynchronous algorithm. By this we mean that there are fewer synchronization points where a task on one processor cannot start until a task on another processor has completed. In our concurrent global optimization algorithm, these synchronization points occur at the end of the start point selection phase before the local minimization phase can begin, and at the end of the local minimization phase before the next iteration can begin. One way to do reduce synchronization within the framework of a concurrent multi-level single-linkage algorithm is to make each subregion autonomous, meaning that it decides on its own to conduct searches or whether to go on to the next iteration. In place of the synchronization in our present algorithm, in this approach a scheduler process distributes the local minimization tasks and sampling / start point selection tasks that are generated. This approach also naturally permits work to be concentrated in subregions of greatest interest. We currently are developing such an algorithm.

Finally, there is an important need for more difficult global optimization test problems. We have begun to construct such problems ourselves by subdividing n dimensional regions into a large number (say 2^n) of n dimensional subregions, and defining the objective function to be a separate function with one local minimizer in each of these subregions. The resultant, overall function is discontinuous at the boundaries of these subregions but this doesn't adversely affect the global optimization algorithm since local searches do not attempt to cross these boundaries. In our experience so far, the results of running the concurrent algorithm described in this paper on such functions are as expected. Since there are considerably more local searches than on the problems in Section 4, it is possible to achieve higher parallelism in the search phase and overall. The real need, however, is for more difficult test problems drawn from actual applications.

REFERENCES

G. Boender [1984], "The gernalized multinormial distribution: a Bayesian analysis and applications," Ph.D. thesis, Econometric Institute, Erasmus University, The Netherlands.

C.G.E. Boender and A.H.G. Rinnooy Kan [1983], "Bayesian stopping rules for a class of stochastic global optimization methods", Technical Report, Erasmus University Rotterdam, The Netherlands.

C. G. E. Boender, A. H. G. Rinnooy Kan, L. Stougie, and G. T. Timmer [1982], "A stochastic method for global optimization", *Mathematical Programming* 22, pp. 125-140.

F.H. Branin [1972], "Widely convergent methods for finding multiple solutions of simultaneous nonlinear equations", *IBM Journal of Research Developments* pp. 504-522.

F.H. Branin and S.K. Hoo [1972], "A method for finding multiple extreme of a function of n variables", in *Numerical Methods of Nonlinear Optimization*, F.A. Lootsma, ed., Academic Press, London.

J. E. Dennis Jr. and R. B. Schnabel [1983], *Numerical Methods for Nonlinear Equations and Unconstrained Optimization*, Prentice-Hall, Englewood Cliffs, New Jersey.

C. L. Dert [1986], "A parallel algorithm for global optimization", M.S. thesis, Econometric Institute, Erasmus University, The Netherlands.

L.C.W. Dixon and G.P. Szego (eds.) [1978], *Towards Global Optimization 2,* North-Holland, Amsterdam.

T. J. Gardner, I. M. Gerard, C. R. Mowers, E. Nemeth, and R. B. Schnabel [1986], "DPUP: A distributed processing utilities package", Technical Report CU-CS-337-86,

P. E. Gill, W. Murray, and M. H. Wright [1981], *Practical Optimization,* Academic Press, London.

A.A. Goldstein and J.F. Price [1971], "On descent from local minima", *Mathematics of Computation 25,* pp. 569-574.

E.R. Hansen [1980], "Global optimization using interval analysis -- The multidimensional case", *Numerical Math 34,* pp. 247-270.

E.R. Hansen and S. Sengupta [1980], "Global constrained optimization using interval analysis", in *Interval Mathematics*, K. Nickel, ed., Academic Press.

A.V. Levy and S. Gomez [1985], "The tunneling method applied to global optimization", in *Numerical Optimization 1984*, P.T. Boggs, R.H. Byrd and R.B. Schnabel, eds., SIAM, Philadelphia, pp. 213-244.

A.V. Levy and A. Montalvo [1985], "The tunneling algorithm for the global minimization of functions", i "SIAM Journal on Scientific and Statistical Computing" 6, pp. 15-29.

A.H.G. Rinnooy Kan and G.T. Timmer [1984], "Stochastic methods for global optimization", to appear in the *American Journal of Mathematical and Management Sciences.*

A.H.G. Rinnooy Kan and G.T. Timmer [1985a], "A stochastic approach to global optimization," in *Numerical Optimization 1984*, P. Boggs, R. Byrd and R.B. Schnabel, eds., SIAM, Philadelphia, pp. 245-262.

A.H.G. Rinnooy Kan and G.T. Timmer [1985b], "Stochastic global optimization methods -- Part I: clustering methods," Report 85391A, Econometric Institute, Erasmus University, The Netherlands.

A.H.G. Rinnooy Kan and G.T. Timmer [1985c], "Stochastic global optimization methods -- Part II: multi-level methods," Report 85401A, Econometric Institute, Erasmus University, The Netherlands.

G. Th. Timmer [1984], "Global optimization : a Bayesian approach," Ph.D. thesis, Econometric Institute, Erasmus University, The Netherlands.

C. L. Seitz [1985], "The cosmic cube", *Communications of the ACM* 28, pp. 22-33.

B.O. Shubert [1972], "A sequential method seeking the global maximum of function", *SIAM Journal on Numerical Analysis 9* pp. 379-388.

G.W. Walster, E.R. Hansen and S. Sengupta [1985], "Test Results for a global optimization algorithm", in *Numerical Optimization 1984*, P. Boggs, R.H. Byrd and R.B. Schnabel, eds., SIAM, Philadelphia, pp. 272-287.

R. Zielinski [1981], "A stochastic estimate of the structure of multi-external problems", *Mathematical Programming 22*, pp. 104-116.

CHAPTER 7

Heterogeneous Processes on Homogeneous Processors*

George Cybenko[†]
David W. Krumme[†]
K. N. Venkataraman[†]
A. Couch[†]

ABSTRACT

We study various aspects of mapping specific heterogeneous parallel programs onto a homogeneous hypercube multiprocessor system. The programs are implementations of the Lanczos and conjugate gradient algorithms for sparse matrix computations. We investigate some general characteristics of heterogeneous processes and the associated problems of optimizing process to processor allocation from the point of view of minimizing communication overhead and latency.

1. Introduction

Hypercubes are homogeneous multiprocessor networks in a natural sense - from the perspective of every processor, the interconnection network looks the same. This feature makes hypercubes appealing to the applications programmer in that every processor can be treated in the same way. Many important applications lead to homogeneous parallel programs when targeted for message passing multiprocessor systems. These include dense linear system solvers and many PDE solvers when the discretization is over a regular grid. In this paper, we explore some difficulties that arise when a heterogeneous parallel program is targeted for a homogeneous hypercube multiprocessor. The applications we consider are sparse matrix problems - eigenvalue and linear systems solving. We study algorithms well known in the sequential case, namely the Lanczos and conjugate gradient methods.

* The work of all four authors was partially supported by NSF grant DCR-8505634. The work of the first and fourth authors was partially supported by NSF grant DCR-8619103 and US-Spain Joint Committee for Scientific and Technological Cooperation grant 84-019.

† Department of Computer Science, Tufts University, Medford, Massachusetts, 02155.

We shall see that a natural approach to parallelizing these algorithms for sparse matrices leads to novel combinatorial problems involving optimal data allocation and communication strategies. Our results are negative in the case of optimally assigning data to processors to minimize communication latency - virtually all formulations of that problem are NP-complete. Optimal communication strategies for general networks have been greatly advanced but the hypercube case remains problematic.

We have discovered one moral from our study of the optimal data assignment problem for hypercubes. It goes roughly like this:

> If you are mapping a processes with essentially random interprocess communication requirements, then there is little if anything to be gained by using heuristics for improving the assignment.

Suppose we have processes that optimally map into a hypercube with at least one pair of processes that need to communicate being at a distance $d-k$ apart where d is the dimension (and hence diameter) of the hypercube. Suppose that a random assignment results in communications traversing paths of length d. If the optimal assignment results in paths of length $d-k$ then our effective speedup on the communications alone is $d/(d-k)$ if we use the optimal mapping (providing we can determine it!). If k is small relative to d, the effect on performance is marginal. Vendors of hypercube machines tout that the diameter of a hypercube is small enough that one can view it as a completely connected network. On the other hand, a quick survey of current technical reports and conference papers shows that most researchers are focusing on exact embeddings of applications problems. The point is that if it is possible to map a parallel algorithm exactly onto a hypercube, then the ratio between a sloppy, random allocation and the optimal one is d which can be significant. Thus the problems we consider are at the high end, where attempts to optimize allocations may be too costly given their benefits.

Section 2 describes the basic allocation and communication problems encountered in random sparse matrix operations on a hypercube, Section 3 discusses the allocation problems in depth while Section 4 describes results on inner product computation. Section 5 is a brief summary.

2. The Lanczos and Conjugate Gradient Algorithms

Computations involving large sparse matrices present an interesting challenge for parallel computing. While much of the work on parallel linear algebraic algorithms has focused on dense unstructured problems or highly structured sparse problems, few results are available for matrices with general sparsity patterns. The difficulty of course lies in the fact that vector or array type operations are no longer natural ways to parallelize such problems. In any case, just as in the context of serial computation, we suspect that both direct and iterative methods will play significant roles in sparse matrix parallel computation.

The Lanczos and conjugate gradient algorithms have recently gained wide popularity for solving sparse eigenvalue and linear equations problems on sequential machines. Among their virtues are that they rely solely on matrix-vector multiplies and vector inner products and so users need only supply routines for generating the matrix-vector multiplications. Accordingly, sparse matrices can be stored economically as linked lists or implicitly generated for computing the required products. The actual matrices are never modified so that whatever sparsity pattern exists at the beginning persists throughout the computation. Another major strength of these methods is that although they generate theoretically exact solutions, if viewed as iterative methods, they can compute excellent approximate solutions. Many applications problems that lead to large sparse problems require only approximate solutions or at least good estimates of the solutions.

In this paper, we will assume that the reader is familiar with the Lanczos and conjugate gradient algorithms. We will present only work relative to the Lanczos algorithm since this is the only method with which we have actually experimented. The conjugate gradient method consists of computations and communications so similar that there are only obvious modifications necessary in order to discuss and implement that method. Details and derivations of the Lanczos algorithm for symmetric matrices can be found in [1-3]. Details and derivations of the conjugate gradient method are in [1]. A separate paper deals with rearrangements of the Lanczos and conjugate gradient algorithms that lump together the matrix-vector and inner product computations at each iteration thereby minimizing the effects of communication. The rearrangements involve working with denormalized vectors temporarily within an iteration and are quite different from the classical versions of the algorithms.

Readers not interested in algorithmic details can work at a higher conceptual level by regarding both algorithms as consisting of some number of iterations of two basic computations:

a.   one (or more) matrix-vector multiply;

b.   two (or more) vector inner products.

Specifically, let A be an nk by nk matrix and suppose that

$$A = (B_{ij})$$

is a block matrix representation for A. Here the matrices B_{ij} are of size n by n and, in the sparse case we are considering, most of the B_{ij} are 0.

We shall write nk vectors as

$$x = \begin{bmatrix} x_1 \\ x_2 \\ \cdot \\ \cdot \\ \cdot \\ x_k \end{bmatrix}$$

with each x_i an n vector.

Our approach to distributing the iteration matrix and various vectors among the processors in a hypercube is to assign distinct rows of block matrices and block vectors to distinct processors. For simplicity we assume that $k = 2^d$ for d the dimension of the hypercube. Using the intrinsic numbering scheme for processors within a hypercube (whereby processors are assigned integer labels between 1 and k and processor i and j have a direct communication channel if the binary representations of $i-1$ and $j-1$ differ in precisely one bit), the assignment is completely captured by a permutation π:

$$\pi : \left\{ 1 , 2 , \ldots , k \right\} \xrightarrow{1-1} \left\{ 1 , 2 , \ldots , k \right\}$$

whereby block row i of A is mapped to processor $\pi(i)$. We will let Π denote the set of all $k!$ permutations of k elements. In order that the block matrix-vector product $y = Ax$ be computed with such a data distribution, it is evident that processor $\pi(i)$ must communicate with processor $\pi(j)$ whenever $B_{ij} \neq 0$. This is so because we require that y_i reside on node $\pi(i)$ and so the evaluation of

$$y_i = \sum_{j=1}^{k} B_{ij} x_j$$

necessitates such a communication.

On message passing systems such as the hypercubes manufactured by NCUBE and INTEL, communication can take place between nonadjacent processors but with a time delay penalty that results from the fact that intermediate processors must forward mail along the communications path. Ideally, we would like to arrange for all communications to occur only between adjacent processors but this can only be done for a small collection of special parallel programs. More typically, we are faced with a parallel program that requires an assignment of processes to processors with nonadjacent communications. Since there are as many such assignments as there are permutations, we must try to select an assignment that somehow matches the hypercube topology in some optimal sense. In the next section, we discuss some possible optimality criterion and present some results concerning the computation of optimal assignments using the simulated annealing approach.

Returning to the basic computations in the Lanczos algorithm, let us focus now on the inner product evaluation. Regardless of how block rows of the data are mapped onto a hypercube multiprocessor, we will need to solve problems of the form:

Given a value (floating point number) at each node in the hypercube, say α_i at node $\pi(i)$, compute

$$\mathbf{IP} = \sum_{i=1}^{2^d} \alpha_i$$

and arrange for the sum $\mathbf{IP}$ to be resident on all k processors.

This global operation is evidently independent of the data allocation mapping π.

In the next two sections, we will discuss aspects of implementing the matrix-vector multiplies and vector inner products on message passing multiprocessors with a hypercube topology.

3. Optimal Data Assignments for Matrix-Vector Multiplication

Recall that our matrices and vectors are block partitioned as:

$$A = (B_{ij}) \quad , \quad x = (x_i) \, .$$

Thus if we require storing the ith block row of A and x on processor $\pi(i)$, then for the ith block of Ax to also reside there, we must have communication from processor $\pi(j)$ to processor $\pi(i)$ whenever block $B_{ij} \neq 0$. We can simplify our discussion by considering the node adjacency graph induced by sparse block matrix and the underlying communications requirements for the partitioning as described above.

To be more specific, we consider the node adjacency matrix,

$$G = (g_{ij}) \left\{ \begin{array}{l} g_{ij} = 0 \text{ if } B_{ij} = 0 \\ g_{ij} = 1 \text{ otherwise} \end{array} \right.$$

It is important to note that under our proposed data distribution and computation/communication scheme, there is redundancy in the storing of nonzero off-diagonal blocks. There is clearly a complicated load-balancing/storage/communication tradeoff that at present we are not studying because consideration of this tradeoff would require a level of sophistication beyond our current understanding of parallel computation. Moreover, study of the admittedly simpler problem we describe already indicates the difficulty of optimal problem partitioning.

Under a particular assignment of block rows to processors, say π, we note that node $\pi(i)$ must communicate with node $\pi(j)$ if $g_{ij} \neq 0$. Using $H(i,j)$ to denote the Hamming distance between nodes i and j within a hypercube (namely the number of binary bits that have to be flipped to obtain the binary form of $i-1$ from the binary form of $j-1$), such a communication requires $H(\pi(i),\pi(j))$ message forwardings under the most efficient routing. The maximum delay resulting from such forwarding is thus

$$M_\pi = \max_{g_{ij} \neq 0} H(\pi(i), \pi(j)) \tag{1}$$

for a particular matrix G and assignment π. Thus in order to minimize the communication latency introduced by using a hypercube instead of complete interconnection network we must solve the combinatorial optimization problem

$$\min_{\pi \in \Pi} M_\pi.$$

Solving this minimax problem by enumeration is clearly infeasible except for the smallest sized hypercubes, since as already noted there are $k! = (2^d)!$ permutations for a d dimensional hypercube.

At this juncture, it is worth reviewing some related problems and their respective complexities.

3.1. Hypercube Embedding

The general question of subgraph isomorphism is well known to be NP-complete. Even the special case of embedding into hypercubes as target graphs is difficult. Consider the problem of deciding whether a given graph is a subgraph of *some* hypercube with no restriction on hypercube dimension. In [4], it was shown that this specialized problem is NP-complete. Moreover, it can be shown that if we allow edges to be expanded into paths of length no greater than 2, then all graphs are embeddable into hypercubes of some large dimension. This establishes is that finding an edge expansive embedding (that is, an embedding which maps edges to paths of length one or two) that is minimal in the sense of using the fewest number of paths with length 2 is NP-hard since it answers, as a by-product, the question of strict embeddability.

Deciding whether a given graph can be embedded into a hypercube of *fixed* dimension is shown to be NP-complete in [5]. In that paper, graphs with 2^d nodes are given that have the property that they are all embeddable into $d+1$ dimensional hypercubes but deciding whether they are embeddable into d dimensional hypercubes is NP-complete. This effectively shows that the optimization problem

$$\min_{\pi \in \Pi} M_\pi$$

is NP-hard. Precisely the same argument shows that the related problem

$$L_\pi = \sum_{g_{ij} \neq 0} H(\pi(i), \pi(j)) \tag{2}$$

$$\min_{\pi \in \Pi} L_\pi$$

is NP-hard as well. On the other hand, deciding if a graph is precisely a hypercube can be done in linear time (see [6]).

These results show that any attempt at allocating the blocks of a sparse matrix to processors in a hypercube with the goal of minimizing some measure of communication latency will involve an NP-hard problem and is therefore not likely something that can be done efficiently . Before becoming overly pessimistic about the use of hypercube machines for the general class of sparse matrix computations, it is appropriate to review some other results and our attempts at finding good allocations of blocks to processors.

3.2. Embedding into Other Target Graphs

If instead of a hypercube we use a linear array in the above optimization problem, the resulting problem remains NP-complete. More precisely, if L is a linear graph with k nodes labeled 1 through k in the natural way and $G = (V,E)$ is an arbitrary graph with k nodes numbered 1 through k as well, consider the minimization of

$$M_\pi = \max_{(i,j) \in E} \mid \pi(i) - \pi(j) \mid$$

where π is a permutation on k elements. Note that the difference between labels determines the length of the shortest path in a linear array. This problem is known as *bandwidth minimization* since it is equivalent to finding a simultaneous permutation of the rows and columns of a matrix that minimizes the bandwidth of the resultant matrix [7, papamiditriou bandwidth minimization Furthermore, replacing the objective function with the summation

$$\sum_{(i,j) \in E} \mid \pi(i) - \pi(j) \mid$$

and seeking to minimize this measure is also NP-complete [7]. If we replace the linear array with a circular array, namely a ring, the problems for both measures remain NP-complete (see [8]). Embedding graphs into grids of unbounded dimensions, bounded dimension and bounded extent, bounded dimension and unbounded extent are all NP-complete problems as well (the first result can be found in [4] while the others have recently been obtained and will be presented in forthcoming reports).

3.3. Computing Good Assignments Using Simulated Annealing

Simulated annealing has emerged as a promising technique for solving difficult optimization problems. The results of actual computational experiences with the method are only beginning to be publicized and one can view the experiments we have performed as contributing to this body of knowledge. We will now briefly describe the simulated annealing technique in a form suitable for discrete optimization problems (for more details and references, the reader can consult [9, 10]).

Suppose we have a discrete optimization problem involving an objective function, f , defined on some finite set, S . We seek to minimize f over S . In the context of sparse matrix computation using Lanczos or conjugate gradient methods, the function f is either M_π or L_π and we try to minimize f over the set of permutations on k elements.

On this finite set S we need to define transition probabilities that determine essentially a random walk within S. This allows the algorithm to stochastically visit different points in S. In the case we are studying where S is the set of permutations on k elements, a natural transition probability function is given by

$$\rho(\pi_1, \pi_2) = \begin{cases} 2(k(k-1))^{-1} & \text{if } \pi_1 \text{ and } \pi_2 \text{ differ in two positions} \\ 0 & \text{otherwise} \end{cases} \qquad (3)$$

The simulated annealing algorithm describes a selection process for moving from point to point within S. The basic selection is determined by the transition probability function ρ but a new point is not actually accepted unless an additional criterion is satisfied.

Suppose that at time t we are at permutation π_t. We select a neighboring permutation according to the probability function ρ. Call this permutation π_{temp}. Recall that our objective is to minimize f. If $f(\pi_t) \geq f(\pi_{temp})$ then we accept π_{temp} and let $\pi_{t+1} = \pi_{temp}$. In case $f(\pi_t) < f(\pi_{temp})$, we resort to the following acceptance criterion:

 - with probability

$$\exp((f(\pi_t) - f(\pi_{temp}))/T(t))$$

accept so that $\pi_{t+1} = \pi_{temp}$; otherwise reject and let $\pi_{t+1} = \pi_t$.

This process is repeated, incrementing t by one at every iteration. Here the function $T(t)$ is called the *temperature* and plays a crucial role in the behavior of the algorithm. Note that the larger the value of $T(t)$ the greater the probability of accepting a step moving to a larger value of the objective function. The key to the simulated annealing approach is to let $T(t)$ tend to zero as t increases. The specific rate at which T decreases is called a cooling schedule. We have only experimented with the schedule

$$T(t) = \frac{c}{\log(t)}$$

which is justified in the previously cited references. Here c is a sufficiently large constant.

The basic result concerning the behavior of this algorithm in this setting is that the probability that π_t is an optimal assignment with respect to the criterion f tends to 1 as t tends to infinity. Since this is purely an asymptotic result, the algorithm performs suboptimally when run for finite time - consequently fine tuning and considerable testing are necessary in order to discover good suboptimal implementations.

Our experiments indicated that the criterion given by (2) performed significantly better than (1) even when optimizing with respect to (1). This is the case because (2) rewards steps moving in the right direction more explicitly than under the minimax criterion (1).

For a 32 node problem, using randomly generated sparsity patterns, we used the logarithmic cooling schedule with c equal to 10. We ran the process for 10,000 iterations - this took about 30 minutes of VAX 11/780 CPU time. Our tests consisted of generating sparsity patterns where the probability of generating a nonzero block was independent of other blocks and had value λ, a variable parameter.

Our preliminary experiences with running a random allocation and comparing it with an optimized (but not optimal) allocation execution have mixed interpretations. In general, we were able to decrease total execution time for iterations of the Lanczos tridiagonalization process by about 20%. This can be taken positively and negatively.

First of all, a 20% reduction in execution time is rather small considering the 30 minutes of VAX 780 CPU time invested. This suggests that simulated annealing and perhaps other heuristics for optimal process allocation might reap modest benefits. Part of the explanation is that process allocation in this example only affects the matrix-vector multiply stage, not the inner product computation. The second reason for the disappointing speedup is that most graphs don't fit snuggly into a hypercube. Although we couldn't compute actual optimal allocations or statistics about random optimal assignments, we believe that most completely random graphs, in some unspecified sense, do not map well.

4. Optimal Inner Product Computation

Our formulation of the both the Lanczos and conjugate gradient algorithms requires an inner product computations distributed across all processors. The problem reduces to the following:

Each processor in an n-processor network has one component of an n-vector in its local memory. The components have to be summed and the sum must be communicated to all n processors.

All currently available loosely coupled multiprocessors of which we are aware require much more time for communicating a floating point number than to add two such numbers. Thus the model which we shall use to study this problem deems that the time cost of communication dwarfs and local computation used to combine partial results. This combination can be either addition or array catenation. Thus we are interested finding an algorithm that minimizes the number of communication steps within the network. Moreover, our model assumes that a processor can only be engaged in one communication activity at a time step - either a send or a receive along one of its channels. This also is a realistic model of the architectures currently being marketed.

Before considering the special case of a hypercube interconnection network, let us review some general results. In [11], it is shown that this problem requires at least

$$\frac{1}{\log_2((1+\sqrt{5})/2)}\log_2 n$$

steps on *any* interconnection network. Moreover, there exists a network on which this lower bound can be achieved so that the bound is tight. Thus, on an ideal complete interconnect graph the problem can be solved in no better than about $1.44\log_2 n$ communication steps. The paper [11] discusses a variety of other interconnect networks as well, establishing tight bounds for rings and grids. How does a hypercube compare?

Consider the following well known scheme - at the ith stage each processor exchanges its data with the neighboring processor that differs in the ith bit. Starting with $i = 0$, we increment i until all dimensions are done. The exchange requires two communication steps - one to and one from - so the total for this scheme is $2d = 2\log_2 n$ steps. Let us call this scheme *dimension exchange*. Recall the optimal network for this problem would require about $1.44\log_2 n$ steps. The dimension exchange is thus about a third worse than the optimal network algorithm independent of the hypercube size. This is an admirable property.

Is the complexity of dimension exchange optimal for the hypercube? The answer is a surprising *no*! In [12], Krumme has given a general construction for the hypercube that in the smallest case solves the 9-dimensional problem in only 17 as opposed to 18 steps! The lower bound the hypercubes is not known at present.

5. Summary

In this paper, we have shown that the Lanczos and conjugate gradient methods for eigenvalue and linear systems solving involve novel combinatorial questions when one considers optimal problem partitioning for sparse matrices on multiprocessor networks. We have surveyed work showing that the general problem of optimally mapping heterogeneous processes onto a homogeneous network such as a hypercube is in practical terms intractable. On the other hand, our experiments showed that for most *random* interprocess communication patterns there was only a marginal difference between a random process allocation and a partially optimized one. This lends credence to the vendors' claims that hypercubes are indeed general purpose and that the small diameter makes process allocation to some extent irrelevant. A number of results about distributed inner product computation were reviewed but the optimal algorithm for hypercubes is still not known.

References

1.   G.H. Golub and C.F. Van Loan, *Matrix Computations,* Johns Hopkins, Baltimore, 1983.

2.   B.N. Parlett, *The Symmetric Eigenvalue Problem,* Prentice-Hall, Englewood Cliffs, NJ, 1980.

3. J.K. Cullum and R.A. Willoughby, *Lanczos Algorithms for Large Symmetric Eigenvalue Computations Vol. I, Theory,* Birkhauser, Basel, 1985.

4. D.W. Krumme, N. Venkataraman, and G. Cybenko, "Hypercube embedding is NP-complete," *Proceedings of Hypercube Conference,* SIAM, Knoxville, TN, September, 1985.

5. G. Cybenko, K. N. Venkataraman, and D. W. Krumme, *Fixed Hypercube Embedding,* 1986. submitted to Information Processing Letters

6. K.V.S. Bhat, "On the complexity of testing a graph for N-cube," *Information Processing Letters,* vol. 11, pp. 16-19.

7. M.R. Garey and D.S. Johnson, *Computers and Intractability: A Guide to the Theory of NP-Completeness,* Freeman, San Francisco, CA, 1979.

8. J. Y-T. Leung, O. Vornberger, and J.D. Witthoff, "On some variants of the bandwidth minimization problem," *SIAM J. Comput.,* vol. 13, pp. 650-667, 1984.

9. B. Hajek, "A tutorial survey of theory and applications of simulated annealing," *Proc. 24th Conference on Decision and Control,* pp. 755-760, Fort Lauderdale, FL, 1985.

10. D.S. Johnson, *Simulated Annealing preprint.*

11. D. W. Krumme, K. N. Venkataraman, and G. Cybenko, *The Token Exchange Problem.* in preparation

12. D. W. Krumme, *Fast Algorithms for Token Exchange on a Hypercube.* to be submitted for publication

CHAPTER 8

Matrix Multiplication on Boolean Cubes Using Generic Communication Primitives*

S. Lennart Johnsson[†]
Ching-Tien Ho[†]

Abstract.   Generic primitives for matrix operations as defined by the level one, two and three of the BLAS are of great value in that they make user programs much simpler, and hide most of the architectural detail of importance for performance in the primitives. We describe generic shared memory primitives such as *one-to-all* and *all-to-all broadcasting*, and *one-to-all* and *all-to-all personalized communication*, and implementations thereof that are within a factor of two of the best known lower bounds. We describe algorithms for the multiplication of arbitrarily shaped matrices using these primitives. Of the three loops required for a standard matrix multiplication algorithm expressed in Fortran all three can be parallelized. We show that if one loop is parallelized, then the processors shall be aligned with the loop with the maximum number of matrix elements for the minimum arithmetic *and* communication time. In parallelizing two loops the processing plane shall be aligned with the loops having the most elements. Depending on the initial matrix allocation data permutations may be required to accomplish the processor/loop alignment. This permutation is included in our analysis. We show that in parallelizing two loops the optimum aspect ratio of the processing plane is equal to the ratio of the number of matrix elements in the two loops being parallelized.

1   Introduction

One of the most frequent operations in scientific and engineering computations is multiplication of matrices. We analyze this problem for arbitrary matrix shapes and Boolean n-cube configured *ensemble architectures* [22] and express the algorithms in generic communication primitives.

---

* This work has been supported in part by the Office of Naval Research under Contracts N00014-84-K-0043 and N00014-86-K-0564.

† Department of Computer Science, Yale University, New Haven, Connecticut 06520.

It is well known that for the classical multiplication algorithms requiring $PR(2Q-1)$ arithmetic operations for the multiplication of a $P \times Q$ matrix by a $Q \times R$ matrix, the access scheme has a significant influence on the actual running time for most architectures. Performance variations of up to one order of magnitude have been observed. Some access schemes make effective use of pipelining, while others do not. Some have locality of access, making good use of cache based architectures, others not. Some also result in accesses to the same storage bank at a rate causing the performance to be determined by storage bank bandwidth instead of the total storage or processor bandwidths.

In the Boolean n-cube architectures we consider, storage is uniformly distributed among nodes of identical architecture. The global architecture can be considered homogeneous. We also assume that the matrices to be multiplied are uniformly distributed throughout the machine. For a multiprocessor with few nodes relative to the total number of matrix elements, the time for the arithmetic operations, and local storage operations, are likely to dominate over the interprocessor communication times. If each processor holds a square block matrix of M elements of each of the operands, then $2M\sqrt{M}$ arithmetic operations are required per communication of two blocks, i.e., $2M$ elements. The number of arithmetic operations per element communication is $\sqrt{M}$. The ratio between elementary arithmetic operations and element communications approaches 1 as the aspect ratio of the blocks increases. As the number of processors increases relative to the matrix size, the importance of efficient communication increases.

The *granularity* is said to be *fine* if there are only a few elements per processor. Different data allocations and data movements may in such cases result in significantly different processor utilization and communication time. The emphasis of this paper is on the communication efficiency. The problem of efficient communication can be studied in the context of embedding one graph, the *guest graph*, in another, the *host graph*. The first graph captures the communication needs, or data dependencies, of the algorithm, the other models the processor ensemble. The communication needs of the classical matrix multiplication algorithms imply some form of broadcast operation. For instance, in computing $A \leftarrow C \times D + E$, every element of a column of C multiplies every element of the corresponding row of D. The guest graphs that implement some generic communication patterns that we consider are linear and multidimensional arrays, and a variety of spanning graphs that yield lower bound communication for different kinds of communication operations, or different capabilities of the hardware. The topological properties of the hardware is captured by the host graph.

The main feature of Boolean cube configured architectures, and other architectures designed to be scalable to a large number of processors, is that a high storage and communication bandwidth can be achieved at a relatively low cost. Similarly, the processing capability is obtained through replication, which, in VLSI technology, is cheap. The ensemble architecture can be operated with a single instruction stream, SIMD (Single Instruction Multiple Data) [18], or each node, or a subset thereof, may have their own instruction stream, resulting in a MIMD (Multiple Instruction Multiple Data). We present algorithms suitable for both kinds of architectures. In the Boolean cube configured architectures there is a nonuniformity in the distance from a processor to other processors, or storage modules. This nonuniformity offers the potential for performance enhancements through the exploitation of locality.

The outline of this paper is as follows. In the next section the notation and definitions used throughout the paper are introduced. Linear arrays and two-dimensional meshes can be simulated on Boolean cubes without a slow down. The embedding of such graphs are discussed in Section 3. Section 4 presents some spanning graphs and the complexity of *one-to-all broadcasting* and *all-to-all broadcasting* under various conditions. This section also contains a discussion of *one-to-all personalized communication* and *all-to-all personalized communication*. Section 5 presents matrix multiplication algorithms based on a few generic communication primitives both for one- and two-dimensional partitioning of the matrices, and a complexity analysis. Section 6 gives a summary and conclusions. Some of the estimated communication complexities have been verified through measurements on the Intel iPSC [13].

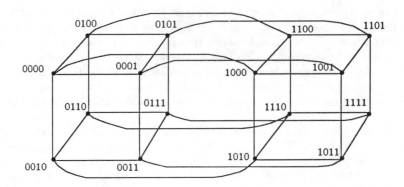

Figure 1: A recursive construction of Boolean cubes.

2   Notation and Definitions

Throughout the paper N denotes the number of processors. For a two-dimensional mesh $N = N_1 \times N_2$ and for a Boolean n-cube $N = 2^n$. We consider the multiplication of a dense matrix of size $P \times Q$ by a matrix of size $Q \times R$. The diameter of an $N_1 \times N_2$ mesh is $N_1 + N_2 - 2$, if there is no wrap-around, and is $\lfloor \frac{N_1}{2} \rfloor + \lfloor \frac{N_2}{2} \rfloor$ otherwise. There are 4 paths between any pair of "internal nodes" in a mesh. For i and j in different rows and columns, the length of two of these paths is $|i - j|_1$ for nodes i and j. $| \cdot |_1$ denotes the 1-norm. The other two paths are of length $|i - j|_1 + 4$.

A Boolean n-cube has diameter $n = \log N$, $\binom{n}{i}$ nodes at distance i from a given node, and n disjoint paths between any pair of nodes. The paths are either of the same length as the *Hamming* distance between the end points of the paths, or the *Hamming* distance plus two [21]. The fanout of every node is n, and the total number of communication links is $\frac{1}{2} N \log N$. The average distance between nodes is $\frac{1}{2} n$. A Boolean n-cube can be constructed recursively by joining corresponding nodes of two $(n-1)$-cubes. It follows that nodes can be given addresses such that adjacent nodes differ in precisely one bit, Figure 1. The distance between a pair of nodes i and j is equal to the *Hamming* distance between the nodes, where $Hamming(i, j) = |i \oplus j|$, and $\oplus$ is the bit-wise exclusive-or operator, and $|i|$ denotes the number of bits of i that is equal to one.

For the embedding of a *guest graph* in a *host graph*, an edge of the guest graph is, in general, mapped onto a path in the host graph. Let $p(i, j)$ be the path length between nodes i and j. Define the *edge dilation* of an edge (i, j) in the guest graph with respect to the mapping function ϕ to be $p(\phi(i), \phi(j))$. Hence, if the edge dilation is one for every edge in the guest graph, then the communication time for an algorithm on the host graph is the same as on the guest graph, assuming that $\phi(i) \neq \phi(j)$, if $i \neq j$. In many cases there is a trade-off between the maximum edge dilation, or average edge dilation, and the *expansion* = (*number of nodes in the host graph*) / (*the number of nodes in the guest graph*).

Different Boolean cube configured architectures are capable of supporting concurrent communication on a different number of ports. In *one-port* communication, communication can only take place on one port at a time for each processor. In *n-port* communication all ports on each processor can be used concurrently. The communication time is denoted $T(\cdot, \cdot)$, where the first argument refers to the number of ports used concurrently, and the second to the number of spanning graphs used concurrently, i.e., the number of source nodes for the broadcasting or personalized communication. The routing schemes are indexed similarly. T_{lb} denotes lower bound estimates.

In the following we also use the notions of *one-to-all broadcasting*, and *all-to-all broadcasting*. In *one-to-all broadcasting* a single node communicates the same information to every other node. In the *all-to-all* case every node performs *one-to-all broadcasting*. In *one-to-all personalized communication* a node sends a unique piece of information to every other node. In *all-to-all personalized communication* every node performs *one-to-all personalized communication*. When there is a need to distinguish between routing for broadcasting and routing for personalized communication, we do that by affixing -b, or -p to the name of the routing scheme.

The Yale version of the Intel iPSC is a 64 node multiprocessor usually configured as two 5-dimensional Boolean cubes. It has a message passing programming model. Up to $16k$ bytes can be passed in each communication, but the operating system subdivides messages of a size greater than $1k$ byte into $1k$ byte packets. We refer to the user defined packets as *external packets* and the operating system defined packets as *internal packets*. The size of the internal packets is denoted B_m. We denote the time for an arithmetic operation by t_a, the time for communication of a floating-point number (4 bytes) by t_c, and the start-up time for a communication by τ. With the initial operating system we recorded a start-up time of $\tau \approx 8$ *msec* for each external packet, and a start-up time of $\tau \approx 6$ *msec* for each internal packet. In a second version of the operating system the start-up time for external packets was reduced to $\tau \approx 5$ *msec*, and with the current operating systems, NX, the start-up time for external packets is reduced to $\tau \approx 1.5$ *msec*. Although there are n ports per processor in an n-cube, the storage bandwidth is only sufficient to support concurrent communication on $2 - 3$ ports. However, we have been unable to realize this potential effectively with any of the available operating systems. The concurrency in communication on different ports of the same processor amounts to an overlap of about 20%. The computational rate realized from FORTRAN is approximately 30 kflops.

3   Embedding of Arrays in Boolean Cubes

We assume that successive nodes of a path are labeled with successive integers with the least label being 0. Mapping the array nodes to processors according to the binary encoding of the integers does *not* preserve proximity. The binary encodings of $\frac{N}{2}$ and $\frac{N}{2} - 1$ differ in all bits and are assigned to processors at distance n. However, it is well known that the Boolean cube is Hamiltonian. The Gray code has the property that the binary codes of successive integers differ in precisely one bit. The *binary-reflected Gray code* can be defined recursively as shown below [19]. Let G_i^j be the j-bit Gray code of i, and $G(n)$ be the entire (cyclic) sequence of n-bit Gray code numbers (of length 2^n). Then, $G(n)$ can be represented in matrix form as

$$G(n) = \begin{pmatrix} G_0^n \\ G_1^n \\ \vdots \\ G_{2^n-2}^n \\ G_{2^n-1}^n \end{pmatrix}.$$

$$
\text{Then } G(n+1) = \begin{pmatrix} 0G_0^n \\ 0G_1^n \\ \vdots \\ 0G_{2^n-2}^n \\ 0G_{2^n-1}^n \\ 1G_{2^n-1}^n \\ 1G_{2^n-2}^n \\ \vdots \\ 1G_1^n \\ 1G_0^n \end{pmatrix}, \text{ or alternatively, } G(n+1) = \begin{pmatrix} G_0^n 0 \\ G_0^n 1 \\ G_1^n 1 \\ G_1^n 0 \\ G_2^n 0 \\ G_2^n 1 \\ \vdots \\ G_{2^n-1}^n 1 \\ G_{2^n-1}^n 0 \end{pmatrix}.
$$

Moreover, it is *cyclic* in that $Hamming(G_0^k, G_{2^k-1}^k) = 1$. The cyclic property means that loops with 2^n nodes can be embedded in an n-cube with edge *dilation* one and *expansion* one. Moreover, any loop of even length can be embedded with dilation one. Any odd length loop must have at least one edge of dilation two, when embedded in the cube [14]. The expansion for a loop with N_L nodes embedded in an n-cube is $\frac{N}{N_L}$, which is at most $2 - \frac{4}{N+2}$.

A multidimensional array $N_1 \times N_2 \times \ldots N_r$ can be embedded in a Boolean cube preserving adjacency by simply partitioning the address space of the cube node addresses such that $\lceil \log_2 N_i \rceil$ bits are assigned to the embedding of the nodes in dimension i of the array. The nodes in each dimension are embedded using a Gray code. With this simple embedding the expansion is 1 if $N_i = 2^{n_i}$, $\forall i \in \{1, 2, \ldots, r\}$, but can be as high as $\prod_{i=1}^{r}(2 - \frac{4}{N_i+2})$. Reduced expansion can be obtained at the expense of increased dilation [2,14,11].

4   Spanning Graphs, Broadcasting, and Personalized Communication

Matrix multiplication, as many other linear algebra algorithms, implies a broadcasting of elements from one location to all other locations, or a subset of other locations. A degenerate form of spanning tree is a Hamiltonian path. Such a tree has a maximum height. The path can be generated by a binary-reflected Gray code. The minimum time for broadcasting is clearly bounded from below by the length of the longest path. To reduce the time for broadcasting compared to that given by a Hamiltonian path, it is necessary to use a spanning tree with a shorter longest path; for instance, a tree of minimum height. A *Spanning Binomial Tree* [7,1,14] is such a tree. However, broadcasting based on such a spanning tree does not necessarily minimize the time [17] for broadcasting. We will now briefly describe the embedding of Hamiltonian paths, Spanning Binomial Trees, n Edge-Disjoint Spanning Binomial Trees, Spanning Balanced n-Trees, and n Rotated Spanning Binomial Trees. The communication complexities for routing according to these different spanning graphs are given. For details of the derivations see [17]. The different graphs are all optimal for at least one of the algorithms considered here. The data set to be communicated to a node from the source is M. Hence, in broadcasting the data set in the source is M, but in personalized communication it is $(N - 1)M$.

4.1   One-to-All Broadcasting

The matrix multiplication algorithms we will describe all require some form of broadcasting, in most cases *all-to-all broadcasting*, but since the *all-to-all broadcasting* is a composition of one-to-all broadcasting we first describe the simpler case. The communication complexities are summarized in Table 1.

4.1.1   Hamiltonian Paths

A Hamiltonian path is the simplest form of broadcasting tree. With *one-port* communication, the time for broadcasting is proportional to the time for the first packet to propagate to the furthest node, and the number of subsequent packets arriving during every other cycle. With a Hamiltonian path generated by a binary-reflected Gray code the distribution of edges over the different dimensions is $\frac{1}{2}N$, $\frac{1}{4}N$, ..., 1. We denote the Hamiltonian path routing based on a binary-reflected Gray code by GC. The estimated routing time is given in Table 1.

If *n-port* communication is possible, n different paths can be generated by rotating the dimensions used in the Gray code such that for path i dimension k of the initial path is translated into dimension $(i + k)$ mod n. For instance, let sequence 0 be the original sequence, then the three rotated sequences for a 3-cube are as follows: *sequence* $0 = (0, 1, 0, 2, 0, 1, 0)$, *sequence* $1 = (1, 2, 1, 0, 1, 2, 1)$, and *sequence* $2 = (2, 0, 2, 1, 2, 0, 2)$. For *n-port* communication the data set M is partitioned into n sets, and each set broadcasted along a separate path. However, the n paths are not edge-disjoint, and several messages along the same path cannot be pipelined with messages along all other paths. For instance, it can be shown that there does not exist 3 (directed) edge-disjoint Hamiltonian circuits in a 3-cube, but there exist 4 (directed) edge-disjoint Hamiltonian circuits in a 4-cube.

4.1.2   Spanning Binomial Trees

The most commonly used spanning tree for broadcasting in a Boolean cube, or the reverse operation, reduction, as in inner product computations, is a *Spanning Binomial Tree* (SBT). An n-level binomial tree can be constructed recursively by adding one edge between the roots of two $(n - 1)$-level binomial trees, and making either root the new root. A 0-level binomial tree has one node. It follows that:

- An n-level binomial tree has $\binom{n}{i}$ nodes at level i, i.e., the same as the number of nodes at distance i form a node in a Boolean cube.

- The n-level binomial tree is composed of n subtrees each of which is a binomial tree of $0, 1, \ldots, n - 1$ levels respectively. The k-level subtree has 2^k nodes.

Figure 2 shows a 5-level binomial tree, which is also a spanning tree of the 5-cube.

For *one-port* communication the source node first sends a packet to the largest subtree, then the broadcasting task is effectively reduced to broadcasting in two same-sized binomial trees, each having half the number of nodes of the original tree. The number of routing steps is minimal for a maximum packet size $B_m \geq M$. However, the bandwidth is not used effectively. A lower bound for the broadcasting time is $T_{l\,b}(1, 1) = \max(Mt_c, n\tau)$. The minimum time for SBT(1,1) routing is higher than the lower bound by a factor of n for the data transmission time.

With *n-port* communication, pipelining can be employed. The routing time is reduced approximately by a factor of n, Table 1.

4.1.3   Edge-Disjoint Spanning Binomial Trees

A spanning binomial tree uses $N - 1$ of a total of $\frac{N}{2} \log N$ or $N \log N$ communication channels in the cube. Increased use of the bandwidth of the cube can be accomplished by dividing the data set up into n pieces, sending each such piece to a distinct neighbor of the source, and then

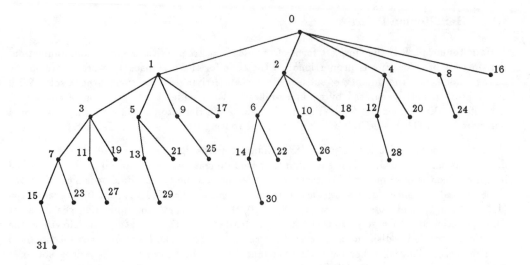

Figure 2: A 5-level binomial tree.

performing a concurrent broadcast from these n secondary sources. Each such broadcast can be done using SBT routing. If these n SBTs are distinct rotations of each other, then it can be shown that they are edge-disjoint [9]. We refer to this spanning graph as an nESBT graph for n *Edge-disjoint Spanning Binomial Trees*. It uses $(N-1)\log N$ (directed) edges, i.e., all cube edges except those directed towards the source with bidirectional internode communication. Furthermore, it is possible to devise scheduling disciplines for *one-port* communication such that no contention for communication channels occurs [9]. The speed-up of the nESBT(1,1) routing over the SBT(1,1) routing is n for $\frac{M}{B_m} \gg n$.

Note that the nESBT routing requires less temporary storage than SBT routing. The optimum packet size for SBT routing is larger by a factor of $\sqrt{nM\frac{t_c}{\tau}}$. Note that if $M \le \frac{\tau}{nt_c}$ then the optimum packet size, B_{opt}, is M. So, if $M \le \frac{\tau}{nt_c}$ and $B_m \ge M$, then the SBT is superior to the nESBT by one routing step. Note further that the routings SBT(n,1) and nESBT(1,1) are approximately equal in complexity, as are the corresponding optimal packet sizes.

The Intel iPSC effectively is restricted to communication on one port at a time. Figure 3 shows the measured times for SBT and nESBT routing as well as the relative speed-up as functions of cube dimensions.

A lower bound for *n-port one-to-all broadcasting* is $T_{lb}(n,1) = \max(\frac{M}{n}t_c, n\tau)$. The nESBT($n$, 1) routing is higher than this lower bound by at most a factor of 2 (as in the *one-port* case). The nESBT(n, 1) routing is faster than the SBT(n, 1) routing by a factor of n, if $\frac{M}{B_m} \gg n$. The optimum packet size for the SBT(n, 1) routing is larger than that of the nESBT(n, 1) routing by a factor of approximately $\sqrt{n}$.

4.1.4   Rotated Spanning Binomial Trees

A higher edge utilization than in the SBT graph is obtained by superimposing n distinctly rotated spanning binomial trees. The data set is divided into n sets, and the load on the edges

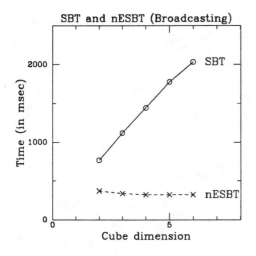
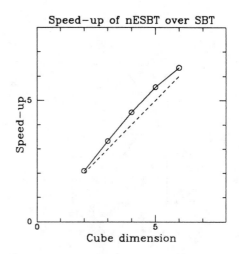

Figure 3: Measured broadcast times of the SBT and nESBT routings on the Intel iPSC for a 60k bytes message with packet size 1k bytes. On the right, the dashed line means speed-up = $\log N$.

from the source is perfectly balanced if M mod $n = 0$. We call this form of spanning graph nRSBT for n *Rotated Spanning Binomial Trees* [17]. The different instances of the SBTs are clearly not edge-disjoint. The maximum edge-load, i.e., the maximum number of elements that traverse an edge is the same as for the SBT graph, and a factor of n higher than for the nESBT graph. Concurrent communication on n ports reduces the data transfer time by a factor of n, and the number of start-ups by a factor of approximately 2 compared to *one-port* communication. Though the nRSBT($*, 1$) routing is not competitive with the nESBT($*, 1$) routing, it is an effective routing scheme for *all-to-all broadcasting* as described in the next section.

4.1.5   Spanning Balanced n-Trees

Yet another tree that can be used for lower bound routing algorithms in the case of *all-to-all broadcasting* is a *Spanning Balanced n-Tree* (SBnT) [9,17,12]. In such a tree the node set of the cube is divided into n approximately equal sets, with each such set forming a subtree of the source node.

Let $M(i, j)$ be the maximum set of consecutive indices containing all the 0-bit positions immediately to the right of bit j in the binary encoding of i, cyclically. Bit 0 is the least significant bit. We also make use of the *base* of i defined as the number of right rotation of i that minimizes the rotated value. Let $R(i) = (a_0 a_{n-1} a_{n-2} \ldots a_1)$, where $i = (a_{n-1} a_{n-2} \ldots a_0)$. Furthermore, let $J = \{j_0, j_1, \ldots, j_m\}$, $j_0 < j_1 < \ldots j_m$, where $R^j(i) < R^k(i)$, for all $j \in J$, $k \notin J$. Then $base(i) = j_0$. We use j to denote $base(i)$ in the following. For the definition of the *parent* and *children* functions we first find the position k of the first bit cyclically to the right of bit j ($j = base(i)$) that is equal to 1, i.e., $a_k = 1$, and $a_m = 0, \forall m \in M(i, j)$. $k = j$ if

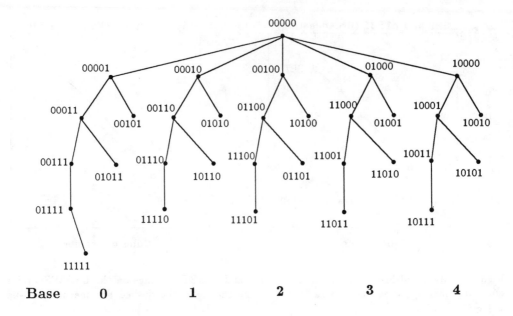

Figure 4: A *Spanning Balanced n-tree* in a 5-cube.

$i = (0...01_j0...0)$, and $k = -1$ if $i = 0$. Then

$$children_{SBnT}(i,0) = \begin{cases} \{(a_{n-1}a_{n-2}...\bar{a}_m...a_0)\}, \forall m \in \{0, 1, ..., n-1\}, & \text{if } i = 0; \\ \{q_m = (a_{n-1}a_{n-2}...\bar{a}_m...a_0)\}, \\ \qquad \forall m \in M(i,j) \text{ and } base(q_m) = base(i), & \text{if } i \neq 0. \end{cases}$$

$$parent_{SBnT}(i,0) = \begin{cases} \phi, & \text{if } i = 0; \\ (a_{n-1}a_{n-2}...\bar{a}_k...a_0), & \text{otherwise}. \end{cases}$$

Figure 4 shows a SBnT for a 5-cube. For *one-to-all* broadcasting the SBnT routing is of higher complexity than the nESBT routing, but it is superior for *all-to-all* broadcasting.

4.1.6   Summary and Discussion

A complete binary tree cannot be embedded in a Boolean cube of the same size preserving adjacency [21,3,6,23], but it can be embedded such that only one tree edge is mapped into a path of length two, and the intermediate node is the "extra" node of the cube. Such a tree is referred to as a *Two-rooted Complete Binary Tree*. (A complete binary tree of $2^n - 1$ nodes can be embedded in an $(n + 1)$-cube preserving adjacency [14,3]).

Note that routing according to a Hamiltonian path yields a lower complexity than the SBT routing if $\frac{M}{B_m} > \frac{N-3}{n-2}$ [17]. *One-to-all* broadcasting based on the two-rooted complete binary tree is inferior to the nESBT routing, but may be superior to the SBT routing and the Hamiltonian path routing. Routing based on the nRSBT graph is inferior to the SBT routing for *one-to-all* broadcasting for *one-port* communication, and is superior for *n-port* communication.

The nESBT(1,1) routing is of lowest complexity, except if $B_m \geq M$ and $M \leq \frac{\tau}{nt_c}$ in which case the SBT(1,1) requires one less cycle. Similarly, the nESBT(n, 1) routing is superior to

Algorithm	Element transfers	start-ups	B_{opt}	*min* start-ups
GC(1,1)	$M+(N-2)B$	$\lceil\frac{M}{B}\rceil + N - 2$	$\sqrt{\frac{M\tau}{(N-2)t_c}}$	$N - 2 + 2\sqrt{(N-2)M\frac{t_c}{\tau}}$
SBT-b(1,1)	Mn	$\lceil\frac{M}{B_m}\rceil n$	M	n
nESBT-b(1,1)	$M + nB_m$	$\lceil\frac{M}{B_m}\rceil + n$	$\sqrt{\frac{M\tau}{nt_c}}$	$n + 2\sqrt{nM\frac{t_c}{\tau}}$
nRSBT-b(1,1)	Mn	$2\sum_{i=0}^{n-1}\lceil\frac{Mi}{nB_m}\rceil + \lceil\frac{M}{B_m}\rceil$	M	$2n-1$
GC(n,1)	$\frac{M}{n}(N-1)$	$\lceil\frac{M}{nB_m}\rceil(N-1)$	$\frac{M}{n}$	$N-1$
SBT-b(n,1)	$M + (n-1)B$	$\lceil\frac{M}{B}\rceil + n - 1$	$\sqrt{\frac{M\tau}{(n-1)t_c}}$	$n - 1 + 2\sqrt{(n-1)M\frac{t_c}{\tau}}$
nESBT-b(n,1)	$\frac{M}{n} + nB$	$\lceil\frac{M}{nB}\rceil + n$	$\frac{1}{n}\sqrt{\frac{M\tau}{t_c}}$	$n + 2\sqrt{M\frac{t_c}{\tau}}$
nRSBT-b(n,1)	M	$\lceil\frac{M}{nB_m}\rceil n$	$\frac{M}{n}$	n

Table 1: Estimated *one-to-all broadcasting* times for various spanning graphs. The upper part is for *one-port* communication and the lower part is for *n-port* communication.

the other routings, except if $B_m \geq \frac{M}{n}$ and $M \leq \frac{\tau}{t_c}$ in which case the nRSBT$(n, 1)$ routing is superior.

The *one-to-all broadcasting* complexity estimates are summarized in Table 1.

4.2   All-to-All Broadcasting

For matrix multiplication, $A \leftarrow C \times D + E$ every element of a row of D has to interact with every element of the corresponding column of C. *All* elements of a subset of elements are broadcasted to *all* elements of another subset. In the case of matrix multiplication the elements of the subsets can be aligned such that the elements in a subset have contiguous addresses. We assume this form of alignment in all of the algorithms we present. For each source, one of the spanning graphs described previously can be used. The instances can be pure *translations* of each other, or translations combined with some other operation such as *rotation*, *reflection*, or other *permutation*.

4.2.1   N Hamiltonian Paths

One possibility is to embed a single Hamiltonian path by a binary-reflected Gray code, and use this path for broadcasting all the elements. The path is used as a conveyor belt. Another alternative is to let the path for the elements of node i be a translation of the path for elements of say node 0. In the latter case the first edge of every path is in the same dimension, so is the second, etc. Figure 5 shows the paths for nodes 0 - 3 in a 3-cube.

We refer to the first routing as a *Cyclic Rotation Algorithm* (CRA), and the latter as a *Gray Code Exchange Algorithm* (GCEA), because the sequence of exchange dimensions is exactly the sequence of dimensions encountered in traversing the cube in the binary-reflected Gray code order. For a 3-cube, the sequence of dimensions is $(0, 1, 0, 2, 0, 1, 0)$. In the *cyclic rotation algorithm*, a node always sends to and receives from the same neighbors for all routing steps, whereas in the latter all the nodes have the same exchange sequence.

The *cyclic rotation algorithm* can be expressed as follows in pseudo code. In the following,

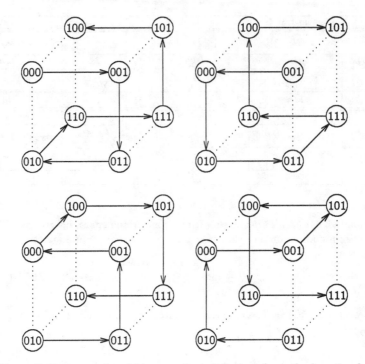

Figure 5: Four translated binary reflected Gray-code paths in a 3-cube.

G and IG represent the Gray code function and the inverse Gray code function respectively.

```
/* The Cyclic Rotation Algorithm, one-port communication: */
/* Let port [j] connect to the neighbor of dimension j. */
/* pid is the processor address in binary repr.*/

SUBROUTINE INIT_CRA
COMMON /CRA/ outport, inport
gid = IG (pid)
outport = port [j] where j is the rightmost 0-bit of gid.
inport = port [j] where j is the rightmost 0-bit of (gid+1) mod N
END

SUBROUTINE CRA (buf, length)
COMMON /CRA/ outport, inport
CALL SEND (outport, buf, length)
CALL RECV (inport, buf, length)
END
```

and the *Gray Code Exchange Algorithm* as

```
/* The Gray Code Exchange Algorithm, one-port communication: */

SUBROUTINE GCEA (i, buf, length)
j = the position of the rightmost 0-bit of i-1        /* lsb = position 0. */
CALL SEND (port [j], buf, length)
```

```
CALL RECV (port [j], buf, length)
END
```

With *one-port* communication both algorithms yield the same communication time. With *n-port* communication the generalization of the *cyclic rotation algorithm* leads to n (directed) Hamiltonian circuits. The *Gray code exchange algorithm* is generalized by using n distinctly rotated Gray code sequences. The paths of the $CRA(n, N)$ algorithm are not edge-disjoint, and the load non-uniform. However, in the $GCEA(n, N)$ algorithm, even though the paths are not edge-disjoint the load is even, and minimal.

The *Gray Code Exchange Algorithm* for *n-port* communication can be written as

```
/* The Gray Code Exchange Algorithm, n-port communication: */

SUBROUTINE GCEA_n (i, buf, length)
Split buf into n parts.
buf1 [k] = k^{th} part of buf, k = 0, 1, ..., n-1.
j = the position of the rightmost 0-bit of i-1
FOR k = 0, 1, ..., n-1 DO concurrently
        CALL SEND (port [(j+k) mod n], buf1 [k], length/n)
        CALL RECV (port [(j+k) mod n], buf1 [k], length/n)
ENDFOR
END
```

4.2.2 Spanning Binomial Trees

In the *Gray code exchange algorithm* the data volume is the same in each exchange operation. An alternative exchange algorithm is obtained by noticing that after the first exchange each of the two subcubes can contain the entire data set, with each node containing its original data and the data of its neighbor in the exchange dimension. The process can be repeated recursively. Hence, n steps are needed instead of $N - 1$ steps for the *Gray code exchange algorithm*. The penalty is a requirement for larger memory. In the final exchange half of the entire data set is involved, i.e., $\frac{1}{2}NM$. This alternate exchange algorithm [17,20] is equivalent to the embedding of N spanning binomial trees. The different trees are translations of each other. We refer to it as the SBT-b$(*, N)$ (-b for broadcasting). The maximum number of tree edges mapped to a cube edge is $\frac{1}{2}N$. In the ith step of the *one-port* version $2^{i-1}M$ data elements are exchanged.

$T^{SBT}_{min}(1, N)$ is in fact proportional to the lower bound for *one-port* communication, since each processor needs to send/receive $(N - 1)M$ elements. Note also that if $B_m \leq M$, then $T^{SBT}(1, N) = T^{GCEA}(1, N)$. In the $GCEA(1, N)$ algorithm, $\frac{M}{B_m}$ packets are exchanged along all interprocessor connections in a given dimension for each routing step. One dimension is used $\frac{1}{2}N$ times, another $\frac{1}{4}N$ times, etc. In the SBT-b$(1, N)$ algorithm each dimension is only routed once, but the number of packets are $\frac{M}{B_m}$, $2\frac{M}{B_m}$, ..., $\frac{N}{2}\frac{M}{B_m}$ for $B_m \leq M$.

For *n-port* communication the lower bound for the data transfer time is $\frac{(N-1)M}{n}t_c$. Pipelining the communications in the *SBT exchange algorithm* reduces the data transfer time only by a factor of 2. No further reduction is possible due to the fact that $\frac{1}{2}N$ tree edges are mapped onto some cube edges. However, all-to-all broadcasting in a time proportional to the lower bound is possible by using N nRSBT graphs, or N SBnT graphs for the routing [17].

4.2.3   Spanning Balanced n-Trees and n Rotated Spanning Binomial Trees

The nRSBT and SBnT routings can also be used. The time for data transmission in the case of *one-port* communication is the same as for the SBT-b$(1, N)$ routing, but $n - 1$ additional start-ups are required for the optimum case. However, the required buffer space is lower. For buffer spaces lower than the optimum for nRSBT-b$(1, N)$ and SBnT-b$(1, N)$ the communication complexities are comparable.

The nRSBT and SBnT routings offer a potential for lower bound routing in the case of *n-port* communication. $T_{min}^{nRSBT-b}(n, N) = T_{min}^{SBnT-b}(n, N) = \frac{(N-1)M}{n}t_c + n\tau \leq 2T_{lb}(n, N)$. The main difference between nRSBT-b(n, N) routing and SBnT-b(n, N) routing is that in the SBnT-b(n, N) routing the node set is divided into n parts, whereas in the nRSBT-b(n, N) the data set is divided into n parts.

The SBnT-b(n, N) and nRSBT-b(n, N) routing algorithms for *n-port* communication in pseudo codes are as follows:

```
/* The SBnT Algorithm for n-port all-to-all broadcasting: */

SUBROUTINE SBnT (init_data, length, final_data)
final_data [pid] = init_data
msg = pid || init_data
M = (length of pid) + length
DO i = 0, n-1
      outbuf [i] = msg
ENDDO
DO step = 1, n
      CALL SEND (port [i], outbuf [i]), for i = 0, 1, ..., n-1 concurrently.
      CALL RECV (port [i], inbuf [i]), for i = 0, 1, ..., n-1 concurrently.
      FOR i = 0 to n-1 DO
            FOR each msg of length M in inbuf [i] DO
                  /* Let msg = src || curr_data. */
                  {c [1], c [2], ..., c [k]} = children (pid, src)
                  /* At the last step, children will be empty. */
                  /* Let p [j] be the output port connecting to c [j]. */
                  DO j = 1, k
                        append msg of length M to outbuf [p [j]].
                  ENDDO
                  final_data [src] = curr_data
            ENDFOR
      ENDFOR
ENDDO
```

```
/* The nRSBT Algorithm for n-port all-to-all broadcasting: */

SUBROUTINE nRSBT (init_data, length, final_data)
EQUIVALENCE (A, final_data)
Split init_data into n parts.
curr_length = length / n          /* initial length of SEND and RECV */
DO i = 1, length
      A [(pid * curr_length) + (i mod curr_length), i / curr_length] = init_data [i]
ENDDO
```

Model	Algorithm	Element transfers	start-ups	B_{opt}	min start-ups
one-port	CRA$(1,N)$	$(N-1)M$	$\lceil\frac{M}{B_m}\rceil(N-1)$	M	$N-1$
	GCEA$(1,N)$	$(N-1)M$	$\lceil\frac{M}{B_m}\rceil(N-1)$	M	$N-1$
	SBT-b$(1,N)$	$(N-1)M$	$\sum_{i=0}^{n-1}\lceil\frac{2^iM}{B_m}\rceil$	$\frac{NM}{2}$	n
	SBnT-b$(1,N)$	$(N-1)M$	$\max(2n-1,\frac{(N-1)M}{B_m})$	$\frac{(N-1)M}{n}$	$2n-1$
	nRSBT-b$(1,N)$	$(N-1)M$	$\max(2n-1,\frac{(N-1)M}{B_m})$	$\frac{(N-1)M}{n}$	$2n-1$
n-port	GCEA(n,N)	$\frac{1}{n}(N-1)M$	$\lceil\frac{M}{nB_m}\rceil(N-1)$	$\frac{M}{n}$	$N-1$
	SBT-b(n,N)	$\frac{1}{2}NM$	$\sum_{i=0}^{n-1}\lceil\binom{n-1}{i}\frac{M}{B_m}\rceil$	$\frac{NM}{\sqrt{2\pi(n-1)}}$	n
	SBnT-b(n,N)	$\frac{1}{n}(N-1)M$	$\sum_{i=1}^{n}\lceil\binom{n}{i}\frac{M}{nB_m}\rceil$	$\sqrt{\frac{2}{\pi}\frac{NM}{n^{3/2}}}$	n
	nRSBT-b(n,N)	$\frac{1}{n}(N-1)M$	$\sum_{i=1}^{n}\lceil\binom{n}{i}\frac{M}{nB_m}\rceil$	$\sqrt{\frac{2}{\pi}\frac{NM}{n^{3/2}}}$	n

Table 2: The communication complexity of all-to-all broadcasting.

```
send_ptr = pid * curr_length + 1        /* initial index of row in A for send */
DO i = 0, n-1
      CALL SEND (port [(i + k) mod n], A [send_ptr, k], curr_length),
            for k = 0, 1, ..., n-1 concurrently.
      IF (i^{th} bit of pid .EQ. 0) THEN
            recv_ptr = send_ptr + curr_length
      ELSE
            recv_ptr = send_ptr - curr_length
            send_ptr = recv_ptr
      ENDIF
      CALL RECV (port [(i + k) mod n], A [recv_ptr, k], curr_length),
            for k = 0, 1, ..., n-1 concurrently.
      curr_length = curr_length * 2
ENDDO
```

4.2.4   Summary and Comparison

The times for *all-to-all* broadcasting using *one-port* and *n-port* communications are summarized in Table 2.

For *one-port* communication the SBT-b$(1,N)$ algorithm is optimal within a factor of 2 for sufficiently large maximum packet size, $B_m \geq \frac{NM}{2}$. For $B_m \leq \frac{(N-1)M}{n}$ the routing complexity of SBT-b$(1,N)$, SBnT-b$(1,N)$, and nRSBT-b$(1,N)$ are approximately equal. For $B_m \leq M$ the routing complexity of all algorithms presented here are approximately equal, i.e., no better than a Hamiltonian path based routing.

For *n-port* communication the nRSBT-b(n,N) and SBnT-b(n,N) routings are optimal within a factor of 2 for $B_m \geq \sqrt{\frac{2}{\pi}\frac{NM}{n^{3/2}}}$. For $B_m \leq \frac{M}{n}$ these two routings are no better than the GCEA(n,N) routing. The SBT-b(n,N) routing is inferior.

4.3   One-to-All Personalized Communication

In broadcasting the data set M is replicated $N-1$ times, such that every node gets a copy of the same data set. In *one-to-all personalized communication* there are $N-1$ distinct sets M to be sent from the source node. The root is the bottleneck. In personalized communication each internal node of the spanning graphs sends out data for all the nodes in the subgraph for which it is the root. In *one-to-all broadcasting* the data volume across an edge is the same for all edges of the routing graph, but in personalized communication the data volume decreases with increased distance from the source.

One-to-all personalized communication is the same as transposing a vector stored entirely in one node. The transpose of the vector is stored across all processors. *All-to-all personalized communication* is the operation performed in transposing a matrix stored by one-dimensional partitioning.

The lower bound for *one-port, one-to-all personalized communication* is $T_{lb} = \max((N-1)Mt_c, n\tau)$. The SBT-p(1,1) is optimal within a factor of 2 for sufficiently large maximum packet size, $B_m \geq \frac{1}{2}NM$.

The spanning binomial tree is very unbalanced. Half of the nodes are in one subtree, a quarter in another, etc. With *n-port* communication the transmission time can be reduced by at most a factor of 2, since $\frac{1}{2}NM$ data elements have to be passed over the same communication channel. The SBT-p(n, 1) routing is not optimal. The lower bound for *n-port* communication is $\max(\frac{(N-1)M}{n}t_c, n\tau)$.

The nRSBT-p$(n,1)$ and SBnT-p$(n,1)$ routings is optimal within a factor of 2 if $B_m \geq \sqrt{\frac{2}{\pi}}\frac{NM}{n^{3/2}}$.

4.4   All-to-All Personalized Communication

All-to-all personalized communication can be performed by N SBTs. This algorithm amounts to a sequence of exchange operations in the different dimensions with *one-port* communication. Unlike the case in all-to-all broadcasting, the data volume being exchanged remains constant through all steps, and equal to the maximum in the broadcasting case, i.e., $\frac{1}{2}NM$. The SBT-p$(1, N)$ routing is optimal within a factor of 2.

With *n-port* communication the lower bound for the transmission time is reduced by a factor of n. Hence, $T_{lb} = \max(\frac{NM}{2}t_c, n\tau)$. The SBT-p$(n, N)$ routing cannot attain the lower bound [17]. But, the nRSBT-p(n, N) and the SBnT-p(n, N) routings can route in a time proportional to the lower bound if $B_m \geq \frac{NM}{2n}$ (or $\geq \frac{(N-1)M}{n}$ for the latter) [17].

4.5   Summary and Comparison

Tables 3 and 4 summarize the communication complexities for *personalized communications*.

On the Intel iPSC the communication start-up time is significant, so it is desirable to reduce the number of start-ups by sending long messages. In the SBT-p$(*, N)$ algorithm blocks to be exchanged between processors are not necessarily contiguous, and vary throughout the algorithm. Hence, minimizing the communication time requires internal data movement. However, the copy time is also significant on the iPSC. We have not included the time for data movement internal to a node in the expressions above for reasons of clarity. There exists a block size

Model	Algorithm	Element transfers	start-ups	B_{opt}	min start-ups
one-port	SBT-p(1,1)	$(N-1)M$	$\sum_{i=0}^{n-1}\lceil\frac{2^i M}{B_m}\rceil$	$\frac{NM}{2}$	n
n-port	SBT-p(n,1)	$\frac{1}{2}NM$	$\sum_{i=0}^{n-1}\lceil\binom{n-1}{i}\frac{M}{B_m}\rceil$	$\frac{NM}{\sqrt{2\pi(n-1)}}$	n
	SBnT-p(n,1)	$\frac{1}{n}(N-1)M$	$\sum_{i=1}^{n}\lceil\binom{n}{i}\frac{M}{nB_m}\rceil$	$\sqrt{\frac{2}{\pi}}\frac{NM}{n^{3/2}}$	n
	nRSBT-p(n,1)	$\frac{1}{n}(N-1)M$	$\sum_{i=1}^{n}\lceil\binom{n}{i}\frac{M}{nB_m}\rceil$	$\sqrt{\frac{2}{\pi}}\frac{NM}{n^{3/2}}$	n

Table 3: The communication complexity of *one-to-all personalized communication*.

Model	Algorithm	Element transfers	start-ups	B_{opt}	min start-ups
one-port	SBT-p(1,N)	$\frac{1}{2}nNM$	$\lceil\frac{NM}{2B_m}\rceil n$	$\frac{NM}{2}$	n
n-port	SBnT-p(n,N)	$\frac{1}{2}NM$	$\sum_{i=1}^{n}\lceil\sum_{j=i}^{n}\binom{n}{j}\frac{M}{nB_m}\rceil$	$\frac{(N-1)M}{n}$	n
	nRSBT-p(n,N)	$\frac{1}{2}NM$	$\lceil\frac{NM}{2nB_m}\rceil n$	$\frac{NM}{2n}$	n

Table 4: The communication complexity of *all-to-all personalized communication*.

$B_{copy} < B_m$ above which it is better to minimize copy time than start-up time. For details see [10].

Ignoring copy time the SBT-p$(1, N)$ algorithm is of the same order as the lower bound performance for *one-port* communication: $T = (\frac{NM}{2}t_c + \tau)n$ if $B \geq \frac{1}{2}NM$. For *n-port* communication SBnT(n, N) and nRSBT(n, N) routings are optimum within a factor of 2, if $B_m \geq \frac{(N-1)M}{n}$ and $B_m \geq \frac{NM}{2n}$, respectively.

5   Dense Matrix Multiplication

For multiprocessors configured as one-, two- or multidimensional arrays both one- and two-dimensional partitionings of matrices are common. The partitioning can be done either by rows or columns, or both, or by diagonals. One-dimensional partitionings are natural for linear arrays and two-dimensional partitionings for meshes. In addition, the partitioning can be made either cyclically, or consecutively [15]. In the two-dimensional *cyclic* storage, matrix element (i, j) is stored in processors $PID(i)\|PID(j)$ where $PID(i) = i \bmod N_1$, $PID(j) = j \bmod N_2$, $N_1 \times N_2 = N$. In the *consecutive* storage, matrix element (i, j) is stored in processor $PID(i)\|PID(j)$, where $PID(i) = \lfloor\frac{i}{\lceil\frac{P}{N_1}\rceil}\rfloor$, and $PID(j) = \lfloor\frac{j}{\lceil\frac{Q}{N_2}\rceil}\rfloor$ for a $P \times Q$ matrix. In the *consecutive* partitioning matrix elements with the same high order bits are allocated to the same processor, i.e., the high order bits are used to assign an element to a processor, if P (or Q) is a power of 2. In the *cyclic* partitioning, elements in the same processor have the same low order bits.

A Boolean cube can simulate both one- and two-dimensional arrays without any communications overhead, and has additional communication capabilities. For the multiplication of a $P \times Q$ matrix by a $Q \times R$ matrix on N processors, one- and two-dimensional partitionings yield a linear speed-up of the arithmetic operations if at least P, or R, is a multiple of N. For $P, R < N \leq PR$, the two-dimensional partitioning yields a linear speed-up of the arithmetic operations. However, the communication complexity for the different algorithms and partitionings is not the same.

5.1   One-Dimensional Partitioning

In a one-dimensional partitioning with columns or rows divided evenly among the processors, cyclically or consecutively, a linear array algorithm is an obvious choice. Assume that the computation is $A \leftarrow C \times D + E$ and that all matrices are stored in the same manner. With the matrices partitioned columnwise *all-to-all broadcasting* can be performed on C. A is computed *in-place*, i.e., the products forming an element of A are accumulated in a fixed location (the same as the location of the corresponding element of D). Alternatively, C can be transposed and either followed by an *all-to-all broadcasting* for an *in-place* algorithm, or an *all-to-all broadcasting* performed on D, which yields A^T. A transpose of A^T yields A. A fourth alternative is to transpose D, which implies a computation of inner products throughout space, and the elements of A computed by a reduction over the number of processors for each element. The reduction is an *all-to-all reduction* on A. Several variations for each of the basic algorithms are also considered. The basic algorithms are:

- **Algorithm 1.** Compute A *in-place* by *all-to-all broadcasting* of C. Processor $k = PID(j)$ computes $CD(*, \lfloor \frac{j}{\lceil \frac{R}{N} \rceil} \rfloor)$ for all j mapped to k.

- **Algorithm 2.** Compute A by a transpose of C and an *all-to-all broadcasting* of C^T. Processor $k = PID(j)$ computes $CD(*, \lfloor \frac{j}{\lceil \frac{R}{N} \rceil} \rfloor)$ for all j mapped to k.

- **Algorithm 3.** Compute A by a transpose of C, *all-to-all broadcasting* of D, and transpose of A^T. Processor $k = PID(j)$ computes $C(\lfloor \frac{j}{\lceil \frac{P}{N} \rceil} \rfloor, *)D$.

- **Algorithm 4.** Compute A *in-space* by a transpose of D, and *all-to-all reduction* of partial inner products of A.

The second alternative is clearly inferior to the first, so we only consider the other three in the following. However, for the two-dimensional partitioning, the corresponding one of algorithm 2 may perform better than any other corresponding algorithm for certain aspect ratios.

For row partitioning the roles of C and D are interchanged. Figure 6 characterizes the basic algorithms. The two subscripts in sequence are used to denote the ordinal numbers of block rows and block columns among the N partitioned blocks rows (or columns). The superscript denotes the ordinal number of the partial inner product result. The number in the square brackets (eg. [R] in algorithm 1) is the minimum maximum number of processors to minimize the arithmetic time for each algorithm.

The total number of arithmetic operations is the same in all cases. We only consider the classical algorithm with $PR(2Q - 1)$ arithmetic operations. The parallel arithmetic complexity is $2PQ\lceil \frac{R}{N} \rceil$ for algorithm 1, $2QR\lceil \frac{P}{N} \rceil$ for algorithm 3, and $PR(2\lceil \frac{Q}{N} \rceil - 1) + P(\lceil \frac{R}{N} \rceil + \sum_{i=1}^{n} \lceil \frac{R}{2^i} \rceil)$ for algorithm 4. The second term of the last expression is bounded from below by $P(n + 1)$ and from above by $P\lceil \frac{R}{N} \rceil N$. If all dimensions are multiples of N there is no difference in the arithmetic complexity, but if for instance $P = c_1 N$, $Q = c_2 N$ and $R = 1$, then the arithmetic complexities are $2c_1 c_2 N^2$, $2c_1 c_2 N$, and $2c_1 c_2 N + c_1 n N$, respectively. Distributing D in space (algorithms 3 and 4) is clearly more effective than distributing C. Similarly, if $P = 1$ and Q and R are multiples of N, then distributing C is preferable with respect to the parallel arithmetic complexity (algorithms 1 and 4).

Column Partitioning:

$A1: \quad C_{*k}, D_{*k} \xrightarrow{\text{brd. C, } \leftrightarrow} C_{**}, D_{*k} \xrightarrow{\text{mpy., [R]}} A_{*k}$

$A3: \quad C_{*k}, D_{*k} \xrightarrow{\text{txp. C, } \diagup} C_{k*}, D_{*k} \xrightarrow{\text{brd. D, } \leftrightarrow} C_{k*}, D_{**} \xrightarrow{\text{mpy., [P]}} A_{k*} \xrightarrow{\text{txp. A, } \diagup} A_{*k}$

$A4: \quad C_{*k}, D_{*k} \xrightarrow{\text{txp. D, } \diagup} C_{*k}, D_{k*} \xrightarrow{\text{mpy., [Q]}} A_{**}^{k} \xrightarrow{\text{red. A, } \leftrightarrow} A_{*k}$

Row Partitioning:

$A1: \quad C_{k*}, D_{k*} \xrightarrow{\text{brd. D, } \updownarrow} C_{k*}, D_{**} \xrightarrow{\text{mpy., [P]}} A_{k*}$

$A3: \quad C_{k*}, D_{k*} \xrightarrow{\text{txp. D, } \diagup} C_{k*}, D_{*k} \xrightarrow{\text{brd. C, } \updownarrow} C_{**}, D_{*k} \xrightarrow{\text{mpy., [R]}} A_{*k} \xrightarrow{\text{txp. A, } \diagup} A_{k*}$

$A4: \quad C_{k*}, D_{k*} \xrightarrow{\text{txp. C, } \diagup} C_{*k}, D_{k*} \xrightarrow{\text{mpy., [Q]}} A_{**}^{k} \xrightarrow{\text{red. A, } \updownarrow} A_{*k}$

Figure 6: Notation summary of algorithms for one-dimensional partitioning.

Figure 7: Computing $A \leftarrow C \times D + E$ by rotation of C.

The matrix transpose operation implies *all-to-all personalized communication*. Hence, the three types of algorithms considered consist of different combinations of *all-to-all broadcasting/reduction* and *all-to-all personalized communication* on matrices of different shapes, in addition to the arithmetic operations. The communication complexity of the different operations are given in the previous sections. Tables 5, 6, and 7 give the communication complexity for the different multiplication algorithms (assuming column partitioning).

For *one-port* communication the CRA$(1, N)$, GCEA$(1, N)$, and SBT$(1, N)$ algorithms are of interest. The first two are included only because they yield the same complexity as the SBT$(1, N)$ algorithm if $B_m \leq M$.

With the CRA$(1, N)$ algorithm and either cyclic or consecutive storage, the number of communication steps is $N - 1$ and the number of arithmetic steps is N. In the *in-place* algorithm C is rotated $N - 1$ times to the right (or left), and in the *in-space* algorithm D and the partial accumulation of A are rotated left (or right). In the *in-place* algorithm products are formed on the shaded parts of D during step i, $i = \{0, 1, \ldots, N - 1\}$, Figure 7. Sample codes for column partitioning, consecutive storage, and an *in-place* algorithm based on the CRA$(1, N)$ and GCEA$(1, N)$ *all-to-all broadcasting* algorithms are given below.

/* Matrix multiplication using the Cyclic Rotation Algorithm: */

```
/* Gray code encoding. */

gid = IG (pid)
/* Let C and D and A be the gid^{th} (or pid^{th} for binary code encoding) */
/* block columns of matrices C, D and A respectively. */
CALL INIT_CRA
A = C * gid^{th} block rows of D          /* block matrix multiplication */
/* For binary code encoding: A = C * pid^{th} block rows of D. */
DO i = 1, N-1
        CALL CRA (C, P⌈Q/N⌉)
        A = A + C * ((gid + i) mod N)^{th} block rows of D
        /* For binary code encoding:
                A = A + C * G((pid + i) mod N)^{th} block rows of D. */
ENDDO


/* Matrix multiplication using the Gray Code Exchange Algorithm: */
/* Binary code encoding. */

gid = IG (pid)
/* Let C and D and A be the pid^{th} block columns. */
/* of matrices C, D and A respectively. */
A = C * pid^{th} block rows of D
/* For Gray code encoding: A = C * (gid)^{th} block rows of D. */
DO i = 1, N-1
        CALL GCEA (i, C, P⌈Q/N⌉)
        A = A + C * (pid ⊕ G(i))^{th} block rows of D
        /* For Gray code encoding: A = A + C * (gid ⊕ i)^{th} block rows of D. */
ENDDO
```

The $SBT(1, N)$ algorithm takes advantage of the topology of the Boolean cube, in that the spanning tree is of minimum height. The $SBT\text{-}b(1, N)$ and $SBT\text{-}p(1, N)$ algorithms are optimal for *one-port* communication and unlimited buffer size, i.e., $B_m \geq \frac{1}{2}PQ$ for *all-to-all broadcasting* or *all-to-all personalized communication* of a $P \times Q$ matrix partitioned evenly by rows or columns. Figure 8 displays the steps during which a $\frac{Q}{N} \times \frac{R}{N}$ block of D is multiplied by a $P \times \frac{2^{i-1}Q}{N}$ block column of C for partitioning by columns and the *in-place* algorithm.

Figure 9 (left) shows the measured times of the GCEA and the SBT algorithms on the iPSC with fixed matrices, $P = Q = R = 32$, and varying cube dimensions. The communication times of the SBT algorithm are less than 10% for cubes with 4 or fewer dimensions. For the GCEA, the communication times are greater than the arithmetic times for cubes with 4 or more dimensions. For the GCEA communication routine the total time for a matrix multiplication has a minimum for a 4-cube. The arithmetic times of an algorithm based on the GCEA communication are higher than that of the SBT communication due to the larger loop overhead. With the GCEA communication N multiplication steps are required, whereas in the SBT communication one or two steps are sufficient. The measured multiplication time for the GCEA based multiplication routine is 10% - 100% higher than that of the SBT based routine as shown on the right of Figure 9.

While the number of start-ups of the SBT algorithm grows linearly with the number of cube dimensions, the maximum required temporary storage and the optimum buffer size grow exponentially, if the size of the partitioned matrices is fixed. If the maximum buffer size is

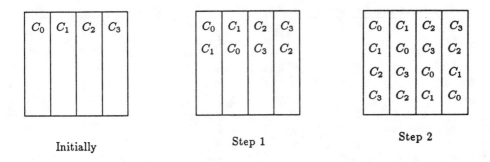

Figure 8: Computing $A \leftarrow C \times D + E$ by an *in-place* SBT-b$(1, N)$ algorithm applied to C.

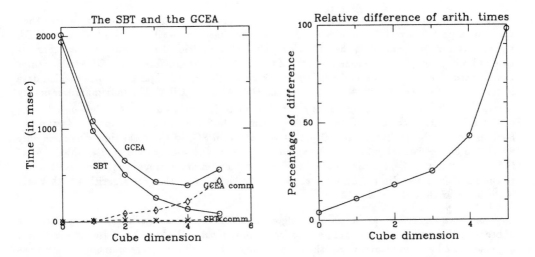

Figure 9: Measured times for matrix multiplication using the GCEA and the SBT algorithms on the iPSC. $P = Q = R = 32$. On the left, the solid lines are total times and the dashed lines are communication times. On the right, the relative difference of the arithmetic time is shown as a function of cube dimensions.

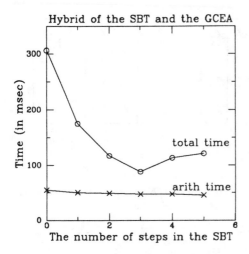
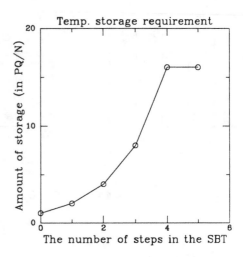

Figure 10: Measured times for matrix multiplication using the hybrid method of the GCEA and the SBT algorithms on a 5-dimensional cube of the iPSC. $P = Q = R = 32$.

less than half the matrix size, additional start-ups are needed. If the buffer size is less than the matrix partition residing in a processor, then the time complexities of the SBT and GCEA algorithms are the same. But, the SBT algorithm needs additional temporary storage. For the case of limited temporary storage a hybrid of the SBT and the GCEA (or the CRA) algorithms can be used. The hybrid method will perform k steps of the SBT algorithm during which data is cumulated, followed by $2^{n-k} - 1$ steps of the GCEA or the CRA. The maximum temporary storage and the optimum buffer size is $\frac{2^k PQ}{N}$. Figure 10 (left) shows the total time on a 5-cube of the iPSC with $P = Q = R = 32$. The optimum buffer sizes required for the 4- and the 5-cubes exceed the $1k$ bytes internal packet size of the iPSC, so the total time decreases only up to the 3-dimensional cube. The total times of the 4- and 5-cubes are greater than that of the 3-cube due to different overheads involved. The temporary storages required with respect to the number of steps in the SBT are shown on the right. Note that the algorithm with $k = n$ is the same as that of $k = n - 1$.

The above algorithms are all *in-place* algorithms. The *in-space* algorithms use one instance of broadcasting and one instance of personalized communication. Algorithm 3 uses two instances of personalized communication. For the *in-space* algorithm and *one-port* communication we use the SBT-p$(1, N)$ algorithm for the transpose operation and the SBT-b$(1, N)$ algorithm for the gathering of inner products. The following is a sample code.

```
/* Matrix multiplication in-space by matrix transposition: */

CALL TRANSPOSE (D)
DO i = 1, P
     DO j = 1, R
          A (i, j) = C (i, 1) * D (j, 1)
     ENDDO
ENDDO
DO k = 2, ⌈Q/N⌉
```

```
        DO i = 1, P
            DO j = 1, R
                A (i, j) = A (i, j) + C (i, k) * D (j, k)
            ENDDO
        ENDDO
    ENDDO
    curr_A = A          /* A is a P × R matrix */
    DO i = 0, n-1
        IF (the iᵗʰ bit of pid .EQ. 0) THEN
                outbuf = right half block columns of curr_A
                curr_A = left half block columns of curr_A
        ELSE
                outbuf = left half block columns of curr_A
                curr_A = right half block columns of curr_A
        ENDIF
        CALL SEND (port [i], outbuf, P⌈R/2^{i+1}⌉)
        CALL RECV (port [i], inbuf, P⌈R/2^{i+1}⌉)
        curr_A = curr_A + inbuf          /* Matrix addition */
    ENDDO
```

For the transposition of D each block column is divided into $\frac{Q}{N} \times \frac{R}{N}$ blocks, and each such block sent to a distinct processor. After this communication and the associated arithmetic operations there are N partial inner products, one per processor, for each element of A. The accumulation of the partial sums amounts to sending a $P \times \lceil \frac{R}{N} \rceil$ block from every processor to the processor storing the corresponding block column of A. The total temporary storage required per processor is $P \times R$.

With *n-port* communication the GCEA(n, N) algorithm can be employed instead of the GCEA$(1, N)$ algorithm. The data transfer time is thereby reduced by a factor of n, and the total start-up time too, if $B_m \leq \lceil \frac{M}{n} \rceil$. It is also possible to use the SBT(n, N) algorithm. The latter algorithm does not fully utilize the bandwidth of the cube. While the former algorithm does fully utilize the bandwidth of the cube, it requires many more start-ups, in general. The SBnT(n, N) and nRSBT(n, N) algorithms yield a lower time for data transfer regardless of the maximum packet size, and offers the potential for lower bound *all-to-all broadcasting* and *all-to-all personalized communication*.

An *in-place* matrix multiplication algorithm for column partitioning and consecutive storage using *all-to-all broadcasting* based on SBnT-b(n, N) (or nRSBT-b(n, N)) routing can be expressed as follows:

```
/* Matrix multiplication using the SBnT (or nRSBT) Algorithm: */

CALL SBnT (C, P⌈Q/N⌉, C2)
/* or CALL nRSBT (C, P⌈Q/N⌉, C2) */
A = C2 [0] * 0ᵗʰ block rows of D
DO i = 1, N-1
        A = A + C2 [i] * iᵗʰ block rows of D
ENDDO
```

For an *in-space* algorithm and *n-port* communication we choose the SBnT-p(n, N) and SBnT-b(n, N) (or nRSBT-p(n, N) and nRSBT-b(n, N)) algorithms.

Communication model	Algorithm	Communication operations
one-port	$A1'(1)$	$\text{CRA}(1,N)[C]$ or $\text{GCEA}(1,N)[C]$
	$A1(1)$	$\text{SBT-b}(1,N)[C]$
	$A3(1)$	$\text{SBT-p}(1,N)[C]+\text{SBT-b}(1,N)[D]+\text{SBT-p}(1,N)[A]$
	$A4(1)$	$\text{SBT-p}(1,N)[D]+\text{SBT-b}(1,N)[A]$
n-port	$A1'(n)$	$\text{GCEA}(n,N)[C]$
	$A1(n)$	$\text{SBnT-b}(n,N)[C]$ or $n\text{RSBT-b}(n,N)[C]$
	$A3(n)$	$\text{SBnT-p}(n,N)[C]+\text{SBnT-b}(n,N)[D]+\text{SBnT-p}(n,N)[A]$
	$A4(n)$	$\text{SBnT-p}(n,N)[D]+\text{SBnT-b}(n,N)[A]$

Table 5: Algorithm classification.

Algorithm	Element transfers	start-ups
$A1'(1)$	$(N-1)P\lceil\frac{Q}{N}\rceil$	$\lceil\frac{PQ}{NB_m}\rceil(N-1)$
$A1(1)$	$(N-1)P\lceil\frac{Q}{N}\rceil$	$\sum_{i=0}^{n-1}\lceil\frac{2^i PQ}{NB_m}\rceil$
$A3(1)$	$((N-1)Q+\frac{n}{2}P)\lceil\frac{R}{N}\rceil+\frac{n}{2}P\lceil\frac{Q}{N}\rceil$	$(\lceil\frac{PQ}{2NB_m}\rceil+\lceil\frac{PR}{2NB_m}\rceil)n+\sum_{i=0}^{n-1}\lceil\frac{2^i PR}{NB_m}\rceil$
$A4(1)$	$((N-1)P+\frac{n}{2}Q)\lceil\frac{R}{N}\rceil$	$\lceil\frac{RQ}{2NB_m}\rceil n+\sum_{i=0}^{n-1}\lceil\frac{2^i PR}{NB_m}\rceil$
$A1'(n)$	$\frac{1}{n}(N-1)P\lceil\frac{Q}{N}\rceil$	$\lceil\frac{PQ}{nNB_m}\rceil(N-1)$
$A1(n)$	$\frac{1}{n}(N-1)P\lceil\frac{Q}{N}\rceil$	$\sum_{i=1}^{n}\lceil\binom{n}{i}\frac{PQ}{nNB_m}\rceil$
$A3(n)$	$\frac{1}{n}\{((N-1)Q+\frac{n}{2}P)\lceil\frac{R}{N}\rceil+\frac{n}{2}P\lceil\frac{Q}{N}\rceil\}$	$\approx(\lceil\frac{PQ}{2nNB_m}\rceil+\lceil\frac{PR}{2nNB_m}\rceil)n+\sum_{i=1}^{n}\lceil\binom{n}{i}\frac{QR}{nNB_m}\rceil$
$A4(n)$	$\frac{1}{n}((N-1)P+\frac{n}{2}Q)\lceil\frac{R}{N}\rceil$	$\approx\lceil\frac{QR}{2nNB_m}\rceil n+\sum_{i=1}^{n}\lceil\binom{n}{i}\frac{PR}{nNB_m}\rceil$

Table 6: The communication complexity of matrix multiplication using one-dimensional column partitioning.

5.1.1 Summary and Comparison

We summarize the communication complexities of the multiplication algorithms in Tables 5, 6, and 7. Table 5 defines the algorithms in terms of communication operations. All the algorithms use the Boolean cube topology unless superscripted by l, which denotes a linear array algorithm. The argument denotes the number of ports for concurrent communication. Note that in $A3(n)$, the $\text{SBnT-p}(n,N)[C]$ and the $\text{SBnT-b}(n,N)[D]$ can in fact be combined into one complicated routing so that n start-ups results if $B_m\geq\frac{P}{2n}\lceil\frac{Q}{N}\rceil+\sqrt{\frac{2}{\pi}\frac{QR}{n^{3/2}}}$.

For row partitioning a corresponding set of algorithms can be devised. The roles of C and D are interchanged. If it is possible to choose the partitioning form, column partitioning should be used for $P\leq R$ for a given type of algorithm.

For the column partitioning scheme and *one-port* communication, the $A4$ algorithm yields lower complexity than the $A1$ algorithm if $(N-1)P\lceil\frac{Q}{N}\rceil>((N-1)P+\frac{n}{2}Q)\lceil\frac{R}{N}\rceil$, or with $\alpha=\lceil\frac{R}{N}\rceil$ and $\beta=\lceil\frac{Q}{N}\rceil$, if $P\geq\frac{n}{2}\frac{\alpha\beta}{\beta-\alpha}$ approximately. Hence, if D is a vector, then in many instances $Q\gg R$, and the above condition yields $P>\frac{n}{2}\alpha$.

The matrix shapes for which the different algorithms yield the lowest total estimated running times for a few combinations of machine parameters are given in Figures 11 to 14. All these Figures consist of four plots. Plot (a), the upper left plot, shows the two boundary planes which

Algorithm	B_{opt}	min start-ups	Arithmetic
$A1'(1)$	$P\lceil\frac{Q}{N}\rceil$	$N-1$	$2PQ\lceil\frac{R}{N}\rceil$
$A1(1)$	$\frac{PQ}{2}$	n	$2PQ\lceil\frac{R}{N}\rceil$
$A3(1)$	$\frac{PQ}{2N}, \frac{1}{2}QR, \frac{PR}{2N}$	$3n$	$2QR\lceil\frac{P}{N}\rceil$
$A4(1)$	$\frac{1}{2}Q\lceil\frac{R}{N}\rceil, \frac{1}{2}PR$	$2n$	$PR(2\lceil\frac{Q}{N}\rceil-1)+P(\lceil\frac{R}{N}\rceil+\sum_{i=1}^{n}\lceil\frac{R}{2^i}\rceil)$
$A1'(n)$	$\frac{1}{n}P\lceil\frac{Q}{N}\rceil$	$N-1$	$2PQ\lceil\frac{R}{N}\rceil$
$A1(n)$	$\sqrt{\frac{2}{\pi}\frac{PQ}{n^{3/2}}}$	n	$2PQ\lceil\frac{R}{N}\rceil$
$A3(n)$	$\frac{P}{2n}\lceil\frac{Q}{N}\rceil, \sqrt{\frac{2}{\pi}\frac{QR}{n^{3/2}}}, \frac{P}{2n}\lceil\frac{R}{N}\rceil$	$3n$	$2QR\lceil\frac{P}{N}\rceil$
$A4(n)$	$\frac{Q}{2n}\lceil\frac{R}{N}\rceil, \sqrt{\frac{2}{\pi}\frac{PR}{n^{3/2}}}$	$2n$	$PR(2\lceil\frac{Q}{N}\rceil-1)+P(\lceil\frac{R}{N}\rceil+\sum_{i=1}^{n}\lceil\frac{R}{2^i}\rceil)$

Table 7:   The *optimum* communication complexity of matrix multiplication using one-dimensional column partitioning. For the amount of element transfers, see Table 6.

partition the $16 \times 16 \times 16$ parameter cube into 3 disjoint regions. The region for the A1 is below the lower plane (and above the $\frac{P}{N} = 0$ plane). The region for the A4 is between these two planes. The region for the A3 is above the upper plane (and below the $\frac{P}{N} = 16$ plane). Plot (b), the upper right plot, shows the lower plane. Plot (c), the lower left plot, shows the upper plane. Plot (d), the lower right plot, shows the contour of the upper plane. As the aspect ratio of $\frac{\tau}{t_c}$ increases as from Figure 11 to Figure 12, the regions of the A3 and the A4 are gradually taken over by the A1. As the number of processors increase, part of the A1 region is taken over by the A3 and the A4. For sufficiently large number of processors (such as $N = 1024$) the cube is partitioned into three symmetric regions of approximately equal size according to the three axes, Figure 13. Note that for $\frac{P}{N} = \frac{Q}{N} = \frac{R}{N}$, the communication complexity of the A1 is less than that of the A4, which in turn is less than the A3 as shown in Table 7, and Figures 11 to 13. The special case where $1 \leq P, Q, R \leq N$ is shown in Figure 14.

With *n-port* communication the $SBnT(n, N)$ or $nRSBT(n, N)$ based algorithms offer a reduction in the data transfer time by a factor of n. The reduction in the number of start-ups is a factor of n for $B_m \leq \frac{PQ}{nN}$ for the algorithm A1. The $SBnT(n, N)$-based (or the $nRSBT(n, N)$-based) algorithm has the same communication complexity as the $GCEA(n, N)$ algorithm if $B_m \leq \frac{PQ}{nN}$. The reduction in the number of start-ups for the $SBnT(n, N)$ and $nRSBT(n, N)$ algorithms is $\frac{N-1}{n}$ for $B_m \geq \left(\frac{n}{2}\right)\frac{PQ}{nN}$ (and larger temporary storage).

The criterion for choosing between the A1 or A4 algorithms is the same in the *n-port* and *one-port* cases. The plot which shows the region of the lowest complexity algorithm with $\frac{\tau}{t_c} = \gamma$ and *one-port* communication is the same as that of $\frac{\tau}{t_c} = \frac{\gamma}{n}$ and *n-port* communication.

If $Q < N$ and $R < N$ and the linear array is embedded in a Boolean cube, then the number of steps can be reduced to k, where $2^{k-1} < \max(Q, R) \leq 2^k$.

All the algorithms described work for both binary code and Gray code encodings due to the fact that summing the inner product can be done in an arbitrary order. While the local data are accessed differently, the communication patterns are the same.

5.2   Two-Dimensional Partitioning

For the two-dimensional partitioning we assume a binary-reflected Gray code embedding of the $N_1 \times N_2$ grid in the Boolean cube. However, it can be shown that with a binary code embedding

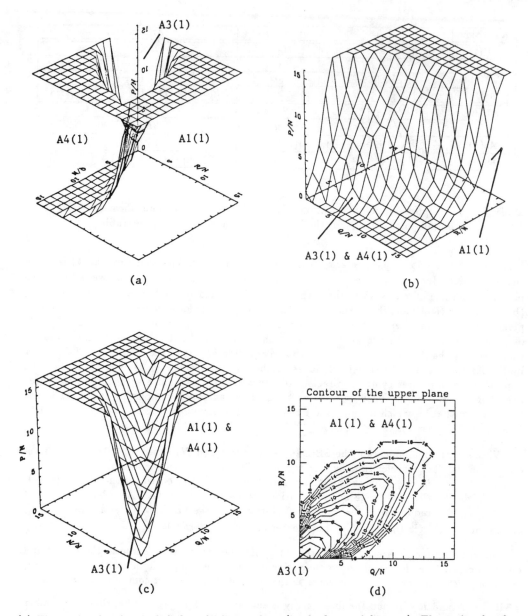

(a) The region for the $A1$ is below the lower plane (in the lower right part). The region for the $A4$ is between the two planes (in the lower left part). The region for the $A3$ is above the upper plane (in the upper central part). Note that these two boundary planes coalesce on the right side. (b) The lower plane. (c) The upper plane. Note that (a), (b) and (c) are shown from different views. (d) The contour of the upper plane.

Figure 11: Lowest complexity algorithm as a function of matrix shape; $N = 16$, $\tau = t_c$, $B_m = \infty$, column partitioning, *one-port* communication.

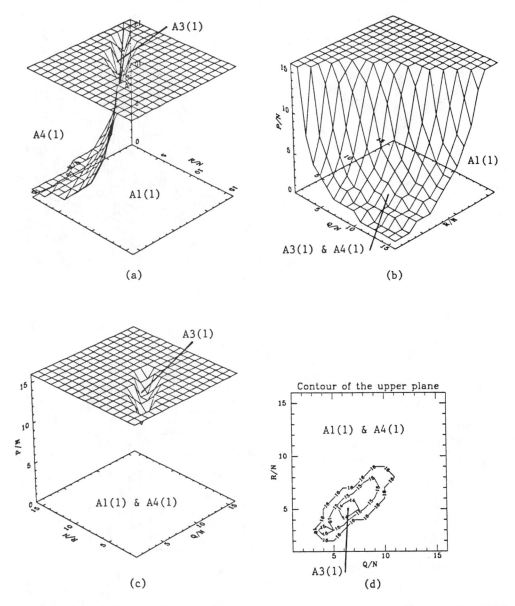

(a) The region for the $A1$ is below the lower plane (in the lower right part). **The region for the $A4$** is between the two planes (in the lower left part). The region for the $A3$ **is above the upper** plane (in the upper central part). (b) The lower plane. (c) The upper plane. **(d) The contour** of the upper plane.

Figure 12: Lowest complexity algorithm as a function of matrix shape; $N = 16$, $\tau = 1000t_c$, $B_m = \infty$, column partitioning, *one-port* communication.

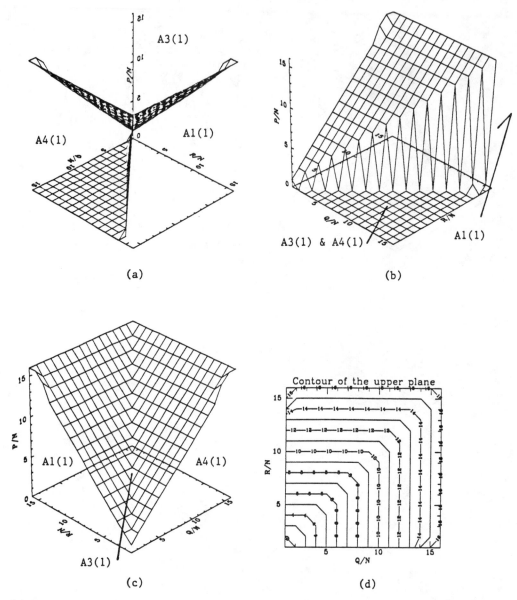

(a) The region for the $A1$ is below the lower plane (in the lower right part). The region for the $A4$ is between the two planes (in the lower left part). The region for the $A3$ is above the upper plane (in the upper central part). (b) The lower plane. (c) The upper plane. (d) The contour of the upper plane.

Figure 13: Lowest complexity algorithm as a function of matrix shape; $N = 1024$, $\tau = t_c$, $B_m = \infty$, column partitioning, *one-port* communication.

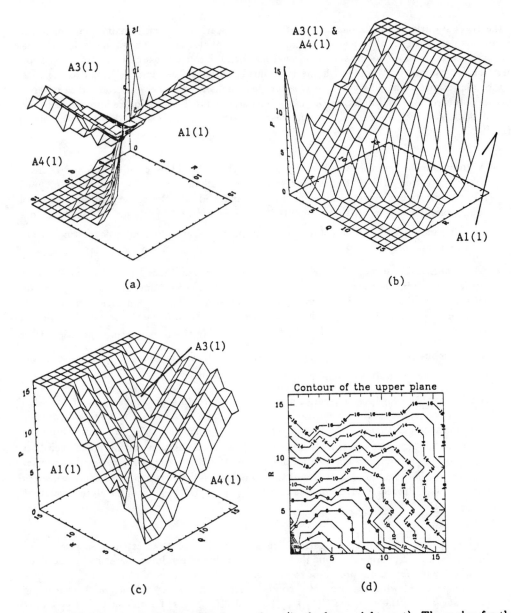

(a) The region for the $A1$ is below the lower plane (in the lower right part). The region for the $A4$ is between the two planes (in the lower left part). The region for the $A3$ is above the upper plane (in the upper central part). (b) The lower plane. (c) The upper plane. (d) The contour of the upper plane.

Figure 14: Lowest complexity algorithm as a function of matrix shape; $N = 16$, $\tau = t_c$, $B_m = \infty$, column partitioning, *one-port* communication. Note that $1 \leq P, Q, R \leq N$.

of the $N_1 \times N_2$ grid in the Boolean cube, the communication pattern remains the same. The algorithms described for the one-dimensional case have analogues in the two-dimensional case. The *in-place* algorithm that in the one-dimensional case implies broadcasting of C in the row direction for column partitioning, in the two-dimensional case also implies broadcasting of D in the column direction. The two broadcasting operations need to be synchronized in order to conserve storage. We will describe the initialization and synchronization requirements below. The algorithms corresponding to the four one-dimensional algorithms ($A4$ has two variations) are

- **Algorithm 1.** Compute A *in-place* by broadcasting of C in the row direction and D in the column direction such that each processor receives all elements of the rows of C mapped into that processor row and all elements of D mapped into the corresponding column of processors. Processor k, l then computes $C(\lfloor \frac{i}{\lceil \frac{P}{N_1} \rceil} \rfloor, *) D(*, \lfloor \frac{j}{\lceil \frac{R}{N_2} \rceil} \rfloor)$ for all i mapped to k and all j mapped to l. The communication operations are *all-to-all broadcasting* within rows and columns.

- **Algorithm 2.** Transpose C, perform an *all-to-all broadcast* along processor rows for the elements of C^T in that processor row, and accumulate inner products for A through *all-to-all reduction* in the column direction (of the processors). The accumulation can be made such that $\frac{P}{N_1}$ elements for each column of D are accumulated in each processor by *all-to-all reduction*. A processor k, l receives $C(*, \lfloor \frac{i}{\lceil \frac{P}{N_1} \rceil} \rfloor)$ during the broadcasting operation, then computes the product $C(*, \lfloor \frac{i}{\lceil \frac{Q}{N_1} \rceil} \rfloor) D(\lfloor \frac{i}{\lceil \frac{Q}{N_1} \rceil} \rfloor, \lfloor \frac{j}{\lceil \frac{R}{N_2} \rceil} \rfloor)$. The summation over index i is the reduction operation along columns.

- **Algorithm 3.** Transpose C, perform *all-to-all broadcasting* of the elements of D within processor rows, accumulate inner products in the column direction. The *all-to-all reduction* is performed such that each processor receives all $\frac{P}{N_2}$ elements of $\frac{R}{N_1}$ distinct columns of D, such that A^T is computed. (Alternatively, the accumulation can be made such that $\frac{P}{\max(N_1, N_2)}$ elements for each column are accumulated in a processor selected such that the proper allocation of A is obtained through a *some-to-all personalized communication* within rows.) Processor k, l computes $C(\lfloor \frac{i}{\lceil \frac{P}{N_2} \rceil} \rfloor, \lfloor \frac{j}{\lceil \frac{Q}{N_1} \rceil} \rfloor) D(\lfloor \frac{j}{\lceil \frac{Q}{N_1} \rceil} \rfloor, *)$ for all i, j such that $\lfloor \frac{i}{\lceil \frac{P}{N_2} \rceil} \rfloor = l$ and $\lfloor \frac{j}{\lceil \frac{Q}{N_1} \rceil} \rfloor = k$.

- **Algorithm 4.** Transpose D, perform an *all-to-all broadcasting* of the elements of D^T within processor columns, accumulate the partial inner products for elements of A by *all-to-all reduction* along processor rows such that the elements of at most $\lceil \frac{R}{N_2} \rceil$ columns are accumulated within a processor column. After the transposition and broadcasting processor k, l has the elements $C(\lfloor \frac{i}{\lceil \frac{P}{N_1} \rceil} \rfloor, \lfloor \frac{j}{\lceil \frac{Q}{N_2} \rceil} \rfloor) D(\lfloor \frac{j}{\lceil \frac{Q}{N_2} \rceil} \rfloor, *)$ for all i such that $\lfloor \frac{i}{\lceil \frac{P}{N_1} \rceil} \rfloor = k$ and j such that $\lfloor \frac{j}{\lceil \frac{Q}{N_2} \rceil} \rfloor = l$.

- **Algorithm 5.** Transpose D, perform an *all-to-all broadcasting* of the elements of C within processor columns, accumulate inner products for elements of A by *all-to-all reduction* along processor rows, such that each processor receives $\frac{P}{N_2}$ elements of A^T for each of $\frac{R}{N_1}$ columns of D. Processor k, l computes $C(*, \lfloor \frac{j}{\lceil \frac{Q}{N_2} \rceil} \rfloor) D(\lfloor \frac{j}{\lceil \frac{Q}{N_2} \rceil} \rfloor, \lfloor \frac{i}{\lceil \frac{R}{N_1} \rceil} \rfloor)$ for all i such that $\lfloor \frac{i}{\lceil \frac{R}{N_1} \rceil} \rfloor = k$ and j such that $\lfloor \frac{j}{\lceil \frac{Q}{N_2} \rceil} \rfloor = l$.

Figure 15 characterizes the 5 algorithms. The two subscripts in sequence are used to denote the ordinal numbers of block rows and block columns among the $N_1 \times N_2$ partitioned blocks.

$$A1: \quad C_{kl}, D_{kl} \xrightarrow{\text{brd. C,} \leftrightarrow} C_{k*}, D_{kl} \xrightarrow{\text{brd. D,} \updownarrow} C_{k*}, D_{*l} \xrightarrow{\text{mpy., [PR]}} A_{kl}$$

$$A2: \quad C_{kl}, D_{kl} \xrightarrow{\text{txp. C,} \diagup} C_{lk}, D_{kl} \xrightarrow{\text{brd. C,} \leftrightarrow} C_{*k}, D_{kl} \xrightarrow{\text{mpy., [QR]}} A_{*l}^{k} \xrightarrow{\text{red. A,} \updownarrow} A_{kl}$$

$$A3: \quad C_{kl}, D_{kl} \xrightarrow{\text{txp. C,} \diagup} C_{lk}, D_{kl} \xrightarrow{\text{brd. D,} \leftrightarrow} C_{lk}, D_{k*} \xrightarrow{\text{mpy., [PQ]}} A_{l*}^{k} \xrightarrow{\text{red. A,} \updownarrow} A_{lk} \xrightarrow{\text{txp. A,} \diagup} A_{kl}$$

$$A4: \quad C_{kl}, D_{kl} \xrightarrow{\text{txp. D,} \diagup} C_{kl}, D_{lk} \xrightarrow{\text{brd. D,} \updownarrow} C_{kl}, D_{l*} \xrightarrow{\text{mpy., [PQ]}} A_{k*}^{l} \xrightarrow{\text{red. A,} \leftrightarrow} A_{kl}$$

$$A5: \quad C_{kl}, D_{kl} \xrightarrow{\text{txp. D,} \diagup} C_{kl}, D_{lk} \xrightarrow{\text{brd. C,} \updownarrow} C_{*l}, D_{lk} \xrightarrow{\text{mpy., [QR]}} A_{*k}^{l} \xrightarrow{\text{red. A,} \leftrightarrow} A_{lk} \xrightarrow{\text{txp. A,} \diagup} A_{kl}$$

Figure 15: Notation summary of the algorithms for two-dimensional partitioning.

The "∗" sign means union of all the block rows (or columns). The superscript denotes the ordinal number of the partial inner product result. The number in the square brackets (eg. [PR] in $A1$) is the minimum maximum number of processors to minimize the arithmetic time for each algorithm. Algorithm $A2$ has a matrix transpose in addition to the communication of C as in algorithm $A1$. But, unlike in the one-dimensional case algorithm $A2$ may have a higher processor utilization than algorithm $A1$.

5.2.1 Algorithm 1

Algorithm 1 if carried out as a sequence of *one-to-all broadcasts* with a multiplication phase between each such operation constitutes an *outer-product* algorithm, but becomes an *inner-product* algorithm, if it is implemented by *all-to-all broadcasting* followed by the multiplication operations. If storage is to be conserved, then a linear array type algorithm, such as the CRA or GCEA algorithms, needs to be used. In order to avoid $O(N_1^2, N_2^2)$ start-ups, and correspondingly high data transfer times, it is of interest to pipeline the computations for successive outer products. This effectively leads to *all-to-all broadcasting* with constant storage. Alignment of the two matrices C and D may be explicit or implicit. We describe one algorithm of the latter type suitable for MIMD architectures, and two algorithms of the first type. For a few variations see [14].

With the mapping of the matrices defined previously, only the diagonal blocks have the proper index sets for the multiplication operation assuming $N_1 = N_2 = \sqrt{N}$. The outer products can all be initiated at the same time. The computations proceeds as triangle shaped wave fronts emanating from the main diagonal towards the bottom and right for each outer product. It can be shown that for $\sqrt{N}$ being odd, $2\sqrt{N} - 1$ steps suffice to complete the algorithm with constant size buffer. Each step consists of communications of two block matrices, one block matrix multiplication and one block matrix addition. For $\sqrt{N}$ being even, we can put one more buffer at the boundary processors and delay sending the message to the opposite side of the boundary processors. $2\sqrt{N} + 1$ steps are sufficient to complete the algorithm.

Figure 16 illustrates some of the steps. A total of $2\sqrt{N} + 1$ steps are needed. Each step requires only nearest neighbor communication. For a MIMD mode of operation the coding of the algorithm is straightforward. In a SIMD mode masking is required to define the set of active processors in each step. Notice that if more than one matrix multiplication are performed, the subsequent matrix multiplications can be initiated every $\sqrt{N}$ cycles from the main diagonal without any communication and computation conflict. Hence, a total of K matrix multiplications only require $(K + 1)\sqrt{N} + 1$ steps compared to approximately $\frac{3K}{2}\sqrt{N}$ steps by Cannon's algorithm as described next.

Cannon [4,5] describes a matrix multiplication algorithm suitable for SIMD architectures

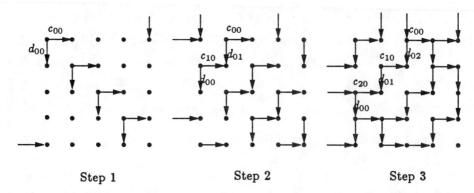

Step 1   Step 2   Step 3

Figure 16: Computing $A \leftarrow C \times D + E$ by a pipelined outer product algorithm.

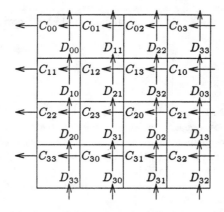

Figure 17: Matrix multiplication on a mesh according to [4,5].

configured as two-dimensional arrays. The algorithm consists of two phases; an alignment phase and a multiplication phase including $2Q$ (or $\max(N_1, N_2)$ for both N_1, N_2 being powers of 2) communication steps for *one-port communication*. During the alignment phase the matrix C is rotated left and the matrix D rotated up. The alignment of the matrices allows all processors to participate in each step of the multiplication phase. After the alignment phase the matrix C is stored such that diagonals are aligned with columns of the array, and diagonals of D aligned with rows of the array. During the multiplication phase the matrix C is rotated left one step at a time, and the matrix D rotated up one step at a time. Figure 17 shows the data structures after the alignment phase. The alignment defines a particular permutation and any suitable routing algorithm for the Boolean cube can be used. If the permutation is carried out as a sequence of shifts, and the CRA algorithm is used, then for *one-port* communication the row shifts use $\text{CRA}(1, N_2)$ and require $\lfloor \frac{N_2}{2} \rfloor$ steps, and the column shifts require $\lfloor \frac{N_1}{2} \rfloor$ steps by $\text{CRA}(1, N_1)$.

The total data volume communicated across an edge for the alignment of C is $\lceil \frac{P}{N_1} \rceil \lceil \frac{Q}{N_2} \rceil \lfloor \frac{N_2}{2} \rfloor$. For the alignment of D, replace P, N_1 and N_2 by R, N_2 and N_1 respectively. There are $\max(N_1, N_2) - 1$ steps of the algorithm, and each such step requires communication of $\lceil \frac{P}{N_1} \rceil \lceil \frac{Q}{N_2} \rceil$ elements for the rotation of C and $\lceil \frac{Q}{N_1} \rceil \lceil \frac{R}{N_2} \rceil$ elements for the rotation of D.

/* Matrix multiplication according to Cannon's Algorithm: */

/* Gray code encoding. Assume $N_1 \geq N_2$ and $\frac{N_1}{N_2} = k$. */

rid = IG ($\lfloor \frac{pid}{N_2} \rfloor$)
cid = IG (pid mod N_2)
gid = rid || cid
/* Let C, D and A be the (rid, cid) block of the matrices C, D and A, respectively. */
/* Partition the local matrix C into k column blocks denoted C[i], i = {1, ..., k}. */
/* Similarly for the local matrices D and A. */
/* Alignment phase: */
DO i = 1, rid
        /* C is rotated left. */
        CALL CRA_row (C, $\lceil \frac{P}{N_1} \rceil \lceil \frac{Q}{N_2} \rceil$)
                /* CRA within the subcube of the least n_2 dimensions */
ENDDO
DO i = 1, cid
        /* D is rotated up. */
        CALL CRA_column (D, $\lceil \frac{Q}{N_1} \rceil \lceil \frac{R}{N_2} \rceil$)
ENDDO
/* Multiplication phase: */
DO i = 1, k
        A [i] = C [i] * D [i]
ENDDO
Do j = 1, $N_1 - 1$
        CALL CRA_row (C[1], $\lceil \frac{P}{N_1} \rceil \lceil \frac{Q}{N_1} \rceil$)
        Left rotate C[i] locally.
        CALL CRA_column (D, $\lceil \frac{Q}{N_1} \rceil \lceil \frac{R}{N_2} \rceil$)
        DO i = 1, k
                A [i] = A [i] + C [i] * D [i]
        ENDDO
ENDDO
ENDDO

In a Boolean cube the number of communication steps for the alignment of C and D can be reduced to at most $2 \log N_1$ and $2 \log N_2$ steps, respectively [14].

It is also possible to base a matrix multiplication algorithm on the GCEA algorithm. As was the case with the CRA algorithm an alignment is required between C and D, and the movement synchronized. The use of the GCEA$(1, N)$ algorithm is equivalent to the following recursive procedure. Let C be partitioned into 4 blocks: C_{00}, C_{01}, C_{10}, and C_{11}. Similarly, let D be partitioned into D_{00}, D_{01}, D_{10} and D_{11} of appropriate sizes. Then, an exchange of blocks C_{10} and C_{11} and of blocks D_{01} and D_{11} respectively brings block matrices into positions such that four independent matrix multiplications can be performed on matrices of half the number of rows and columns of the original problem. To complete the matrix multiplication an exchange of blocks in the same row is made for C and in the same column for D followed by a new multiplication of half sized matrices. For the multiplication phase there are $N_2 - 1$ communication steps for C in the x-direction, each step communicating $\lceil \frac{P}{N_1} \rceil \lceil \frac{Q}{N_2} \rceil$ elements. For D there are N_1-1 steps of $\lceil \frac{Q}{N_1} \rceil \lceil \frac{R}{N_2} \rceil$ each. The communications are between adjacent processors, if the matrices are embedded in the Boolean cube by a binary encoding of partitions.

Dekel [5] describes the above algorithm in detail for $P = Q = R = \sqrt{N}$. For $P = 2^{\alpha_1} N_1$, $Q = 2^{\alpha_2} N_1 = 2^{\alpha_3} N_2$ and $R = 2^{\alpha_4} N_2$ the algorithm is directly portable. A certain number of the low order bits are mapped to the same processor for consecutive partitioning, and communications corresponding to those bits are internal to a processor. The set-up phase requires $\log N_2$ and

$\log N_1$ communications respectively.

```
/* Matrix multiplication according to Dekel's Algorithm: */
/* Binary code encoding. One-port communication, N₁ ≥ N₂ and N₁/N₂ = k. */
```

$rid = \lfloor \frac{pid}{N_2} \rfloor$

$cid = pid \bmod N_2$

```
/* Alignment phase: */
SWAP C[j] with C[j ⊕ rid] locally for j ∈ {1, 2, ..., k}.
DO i = 1, n₂
        IF ((iᵗʰ bit of rid) .EQ. 1) THEN
                CALL SEND (port[i], C, PQ/N)
                CALL RECV (port[i], C, PQ/N)
        ENDIF
ENDDO
DO i = 1, n₁
        IF ((iᵗʰ bit of cid) .EQ. 1) THEN
                CALL SEND (port[n₂ + i], D, QR/N)
                CALL RECV (port[n₂ + i], D, QR/N)
        ENDIF
ENDDO
/* Multiplication phase: */
DO i = 1, k
        A [i] = C [i] * D [i]
ENDDO
DO i = 1, N₁ − 1
        IF (i mod k .EQ. 0) THEN
                CALL GCEA (i/k, C, PQ/N)
        ELSE
                u = the position of the rightmost 0-bit of i-1
                SWAP C[j] with C[j ⊕ 2ᵘ] locally for j ∈ {1, 2, ..., k}.
        ENDIF
        CALL GCEA (i, D, QR/N)
        DO i = 1, k
                A [i] = A [i] + C [i] * D [i]
        ENDDO
ENDDO
```

It is also possible to design a matrix multiplication algorithm based on the SBT-b$(1, N)$ algorithm. With this algorithm the number of communication steps for the multiplication phase is reduced to $\log N_2$ and $\log N_1$ respectively. The need for temporary storage is equal to $\frac{1}{2} Q(\lceil \frac{P}{N_1} \rceil + \lceil \frac{R}{N_2} \rceil)$. The alignment described for Dekel's algorithm is applicable. With a temporary storage of $Q(\lceil \frac{P}{N_1} \rceil + \lceil \frac{R}{N_2} \rceil)$, the alignment step can be eliminated. In this case, the computation is performed only after all necessary communications are done.

```
/* Matrix multiplication using the SBT-b(1, N) Algorithm: */
CC [cid] = C
DD [rid] = D
CALL sub_SBT (0, n₂ − 1, CC, PQ/N) /* within subcube of dimensions 0 to n₂ − 1 */
CALL sub_SBT (n₂, n − 1, DD, QR/N)
A = CC [0] * DD [0]
```

```
DO i = 1, N₁ − 1
    A = A + CC [i] * DD [i]
ENDDO
```

For *n-port* communication we only consider *all-to-all broadcasting* and the SBnT-b(n, N) and nRSBT-b(n, N) algorithms. The maximum edge load is reduced compared to the *one-port* case. The communication time is

$$\min \left(\frac{(N_2 - 1)}{n_2} \left\lceil \frac{P}{N_1} \right\rceil \left\lceil \frac{Q}{N_2} \right\rceil t_c + \sum_{i=1}^{n_2} \left[\binom{n_2}{i} \left\lceil \frac{P}{N_1} \right\rceil \left\lceil \frac{Q}{N_2} \right\rceil \frac{1}{n_2 B_m} \right] \tau, \right.$$

$$\left. \frac{(N_1 - 1)}{n_1} \left\lceil \frac{Q}{N_1} \right\rceil \left\lceil \frac{R}{N_2} \right\rceil t_c + \sum_{i=1}^{n_1} \left[\binom{n_1}{i} \left\lceil \frac{Q}{N_1} \right\rceil \left\lceil \frac{R}{N_2} \right\rceil \frac{1}{n_1 B_m} \right] \tau \right).$$

The reduction in the element transfer time is by a factor of $\frac{n}{2}$. The number of start-ups is also reduced by the same factor if $B < \frac{2}{n} \lceil \frac{PQ}{N} \rceil$.

5.2.2   Algorithm 2

For the transposition of C we use a transpose algorithm as described in [10,8]. The *all-to-all broadcasting* of C^T can be made with algorithm CRA$(1, N_2)$, GCEA$(1, N_2)$, or SBT-b$(1, N_2)$ for *one-port* communication. The reduction can be carried out by the same algorithms, but in the other direction.

Let N_{max} and N_{min} be $\max(N_1, N_2)$ and $\min(N_1, N_2)$, respectively. The transposition of the $P \times Q$ matrix partitioned by a $N_1 \times N_2$ processor hypercube can be viewed as $2 \log_2 N_{min}$ steps of matrix transposition exchanging $\lceil \frac{P}{N_1} \rceil \lceil \frac{Q}{N_2} \rceil$ elements between processors, $\log_2 \frac{N_{max}}{N_{min}}$ steps in which $\frac{1}{2} \lceil \frac{P}{N_1} \rceil \lceil \frac{Q}{N_2} \rceil$ elements are exchanged between processors, and the transposition of $\frac{N_{max}}{N_{min}}$ local matrices of size $\frac{P}{N_{max}} \frac{Q}{N_{max}}$.

$$T_{txp,1-port}(N_1, N_2; P, Q) = 2 \log N_{min} \left(\left\lceil \frac{P}{N_1} \right\rceil \left\lceil \frac{Q}{N_2} \right\rceil t_c + \left[\left\lceil \frac{P}{N_1} \right\rceil \left\lceil \frac{Q}{N_2} \right\rceil \frac{1}{B_m} \right] \tau \right)$$

$$+ \log \frac{N_{max}}{N_{min}} \left(\frac{1}{2} \left\lceil \frac{P}{N_1} \right\rceil \left\lceil \frac{Q}{N_2} \right\rceil t_c + \left[\left\lceil \frac{P}{N_1} \right\rceil \left\lceil \frac{Q}{N_2} \right\rceil \frac{1}{2B_m} \right] \tau \right)$$

$$= \left(\frac{n}{2} + \min(n_1, n_2) \right) \left(\left\lceil \frac{P}{N_1} \right\rceil \left\lceil \frac{Q}{N_2} \right\rceil t_c + \tau \right), \quad B_m \geq \left\lceil \frac{P}{N_1} \right\rceil \left\lceil \frac{Q}{N_2} \right\rceil$$

$$\leq n \left(\left\lceil \frac{P}{N_1} \right\rceil \left\lceil \frac{Q}{N_2} \right\rceil t_c + \tau \right), \quad B_m \geq \left\lceil \frac{P}{N_1} \right\rceil \left\lceil \frac{Q}{N_2} \right\rceil.$$

With *n-port* communication, pipelining can be used. The communication time becomes

$$T_{txp,n-port}(N_1, N_2; P, Q) = \left(\left\lceil \left\lceil \frac{P}{N_1} \right\rceil \left\lceil \frac{Q}{N_2} \right\rceil \frac{1}{B} \right\rceil + n - 1 \right) (Bt_c + \tau)$$

$$= \left(\sqrt{\left\lceil \frac{P}{N_1} \right\rceil \left\lceil \frac{Q}{N_2} \right\rceil} t_c + \sqrt{(n-1)\tau} \right)^2, \quad B_{opt} = \sqrt{\frac{\lceil \frac{P}{N_1} \rceil \lceil \frac{Q}{N_2} \rceil \tau}{(n-1)t_c}}.$$

5.2.3   Algorithm 3

For version 1 of algorithm 3 two matrix transpose operations are needed, one on the matrix C, and one on the matrix A. For these operations we use the transpose algorithms in [10]. For

Model	Algorithm	Communication operations
one-port	$A1(1)$	$\text{SBT-b}(1,N_2)[C] + \text{SBT-b}(1,N_1)[D]$
	$A2(1)$	$\text{TXP}(1,N)[C] + \text{SBT-b}(1,N_2)[C] + \text{SBT-b}(1,N_1)[A]$
	$A3(1)$	$\text{TXP}(1,N)[C] + \text{SBT-b}(1,N_2)[D] + \text{SBT-b}(1,N_1)[A] + \text{TXP}(1,N)[A]$
	$A4(1)$	$\text{TXP}(1,N)[D] + \text{SBT-b}(1,N_1)[D] + \text{SBT-b}(1,N_2)[A]$
	$A5(1)$	$\text{TXP}(1,N)[D] + \text{SBT-b}(1,N_1)[C] + \text{SBT-b}(1,N_2)[A] + \text{TXP}(1,N)[A]$
n-port	$A1(n)$	$\text{SBnT-b}(n_2,N_2)[C] + \text{SBnT-b}(n_1,N_1)[D]$
	$A2(n)$	$\text{TXP}(n,N)[C] + \text{SBnT-b}(n_2,N_2)[C] + \text{SBnT-b}(n_1,N_1)[A]$
	$A3(n)$	$\text{TXP}(n,N)[C] + \text{SBnT-b}(n_2,N_2)[D] + \text{SBnT-b}(n_1,N_1)[A] + \text{TXP}(n,N)[A]$
	$A4(n)$	$\text{TXP}(n,N)[D] + \text{SBnT-b}(n_1,N_1)[D] + \text{SBnT-b}(n_2,N_2)[A]$
	$A5(n)$	$\text{TXP}(n,N)[D] + \text{SBnT-b}(n_1,N_1)[C] + \text{SBnT-b}(n_2,N_2)[A] + \text{TXP}(n,N)[A]$

Table 8: Algorithm classification of two-dimensional partitioning.

the *all-to-all broadcasting* of D within rows algorithm $\text{SBT-b}(1,N_2)$ can be used. For the *all-to-all reduction* $\text{SBT-b}(1,N_1)$ is a possible choice. Recall that the complexity of the $\text{SBT-b}(1,*)$ is the same as that of the $\text{CRA}(1,*)$ or $\text{GCEA}(1,*)$ if the buffer size $B_m \leq \lceil \frac{Q}{N_1} \rceil \lceil \frac{R}{N_2} \rceil$, and $B_m \leq \lceil \frac{P}{N_1} \rceil \lceil \frac{R}{N_2} \rceil$, respectively. With *n-port* communication the $\text{SBnT-b}(n,*)$ or the $\text{nRSBT-b}(n,*)$ routings are used instead.

For version 2 of algorithm 3 the *all-to-all reduction* is carried out such that the inner products for the set of $\frac{P}{N_2}$ rows of A allocated to a column of processors are accumulated with contiguous sets of $\frac{P}{N_1}$ inner products per processor in the same column, and in the processor row in which the inner product shall finally reside. The divide and conquer strategy is applied to $\frac{P}{N_2}$ (if $N_1 > N_2$), and repeated R times, since every processor column contains every column of D. After this reduction operation the elements of A are in the proper processor row, but all elements of a row are confined to one or a few processors in that row. The desired distribution is obtained by *one-to-all personalized communication*, or *some-to-all personalized communication* if $N_1 < N_2$. For *one-port* communication we choose the $\text{SBT-p}(1,*)$ algorithm, and for *n-port* communication either the $\text{SBnT-p}(n,*)$ or $\text{nRSBT-p}(n,*)$ algorithm.

5.2.4 Summary and Comparison

Tables 8 to 11 summarize the communication and arithmetic complexities. The optimum values of N_1 and N_2 depend on the algorithm we choose and the values of P, Q and R. In deriving the optimum values of N_1 and N_2, we assume that P is a multiple of N_1, Q a multiple of N_1 and N_2 and R a multiple of N_2. Table 12 lists the optimum values of N_1 and N_2 for the five algorithms we consider. Figure 18 shows the optimum values of N_1 for the $A1$ algorithm as a function of $\frac{P}{N_1}$, $\frac{R}{N_2}$ and N. The choice of N_1 does not depend on Q. The circle symbol denotes the boundary location, which has two minimum values of N_1. Note that the ratio of the slopes of the successive boundary lines is 4. The same Figure also applies to other algorithms by the appropriate relabeling of the axis. Figure 19 shows the measured and communication times of the $A1(1)$ algorithm on the iPSC as a function of $\frac{N_1}{N_2}$ for different values of $\frac{P}{R} = \{2, 8, 32\}$. The measured minima are the same as the predicted.

Figures 20 to 23 show the best algorithm of the above five algorithms with respected to $\frac{\tau}{t_c}$, $\frac{P}{N}$, $\frac{Q}{N}$, $\frac{R}{N}$ and N. The comparison is made based on the times of each algorithm with its own optimum N_1 and N_2. The plot does not depend on the arithmetic rate by assuming that P, Q, R are all multiples of N. All Figures contains four plots. Plot (a), the upper left plot, shows the

Algorithm	Element transfers	start-ups
$A1(1)$	$(N_2-1)\lceil\frac{P}{N_1}\rceil\lceil\frac{Q}{N_2}\rceil + (N_1-1)\lceil\frac{Q}{N_1}\rceil\lceil\frac{R}{N_2}\rceil$	$\sum_{i=0}^{n_2-1}\lceil\lceil\frac{P}{N_1}\rceil\lceil\frac{Q}{N_2}\rceil\frac{2^i}{B_m}\rceil + \sum_{i=0}^{n_1-1}\lceil\lceil\frac{Q}{N_1}\rceil\lceil\frac{R}{N_2}\rceil\frac{2^i}{B_m}\rceil$
$A2(1)$	$\lceil\frac{P}{N_1}\rceil\lceil\frac{Q}{N_2}\rceil n + \lceil\frac{Q}{N_1}\rceil\lceil\frac{P}{N_2}\rceil(N_2-1) + \lceil\frac{P}{N_1}\rceil\lceil\frac{R}{N_2}\rceil(N_1-1)$	$\lceil\lceil\frac{P}{N_1}\rceil\lceil\frac{Q}{N_2}\rceil\frac{1}{B_m}\rceil n + \sum_{i=0}^{n_2-1}\lceil\lceil\frac{Q}{N_1}\rceil\lceil\frac{P}{N_2}\rceil\frac{2^i}{B_m}\rceil + \sum_{i=0}^{n_1-1}\lceil\lceil\frac{P}{N_1}\rceil\lceil\frac{R}{N_2}\rceil\frac{2^i}{B_m}\rceil$
$A3(1)$	$\lceil\frac{P}{N_1}\rceil\lceil\frac{Q}{N_2}\rceil n + \lceil\frac{P}{N_1}\rceil\lceil\frac{R}{N_2}\rceil(N_2-1) + \lceil\frac{R}{N_1}\rceil\lceil\frac{P}{N_2}\rceil(N_1-1) + \lceil\frac{R}{N_1}\rceil\lceil\frac{P}{N_2}\rceil n$	$\lceil\lceil\frac{P}{N_1}\rceil\lceil\frac{Q}{N_2}\rceil\frac{1}{B_m}\rceil n + \sum_{i=0}^{n_2-1}\lceil\lceil\frac{P}{N_1}\rceil\lceil\frac{R}{N_2}\rceil\frac{2^i}{B_m}\rceil + \sum_{i=0}^{n_1-1}\lceil\lceil\frac{R}{N_1}\rceil\lceil\frac{P}{N_2}\rceil\frac{2^i}{B_m}\rceil + \lceil\lceil\frac{R}{N_1}\rceil\lceil\frac{P}{N_2}\rceil\frac{1}{B_m}\rceil n$
$A4(1)$	$\lceil\frac{Q}{N_1}\rceil\lceil\frac{R}{N_2}\rceil n + \lceil\frac{R}{N_1}\rceil\lceil\frac{Q}{N_2}\rceil(N_1-1) + \lceil\frac{P}{N_1}\rceil\lceil\frac{R}{N_2}\rceil(N_2-1)$	$\lceil\lceil\frac{Q}{N_1}\rceil\lceil\frac{R}{N_2}\rceil\frac{1}{B_m}\rceil n + \sum_{i=0}^{n_1-1}\lceil\lceil\frac{R}{N_1}\rceil\lceil\frac{Q}{N_2}\rceil\frac{2^i}{B_m}\rceil + \sum_{i=0}^{n_2-1}\lceil\lceil\frac{P}{N_1}\rceil\lceil\frac{R}{N_2}\rceil\frac{2^i}{B_m}\rceil$
$A5(1)$	$\lceil\frac{Q}{N_1}\rceil\lceil\frac{R}{N_2}\rceil n + \lceil\frac{P}{N_1}\rceil\lceil\frac{Q}{N_2}\rceil(N_1-1) + \lceil\frac{R}{N_1}\rceil\lceil\frac{P}{N_2}\rceil(N_2-1) + \lceil\frac{R}{N_1}\rceil\lceil\frac{P}{N_2}\rceil n$	$\lceil\lceil\frac{Q}{N_1}\rceil\lceil\frac{R}{N_2}\rceil\frac{1}{B_m}\rceil n + \sum_{i=0}^{n_1-1}\lceil\lceil\frac{P}{N_1}\rceil\lceil\frac{Q}{N_2}\rceil\frac{2^i}{B_m}\rceil + \sum_{i=0}^{n_2-1}\lceil\lceil\frac{R}{N_1}\rceil\lceil\frac{P}{N_2}\rceil\frac{2^i}{B_m}\rceil + \lceil\lceil\frac{R}{N_1}\rceil\lceil\frac{P}{N_2}\rceil\frac{1}{B_m}\rceil n$

Table 9: The communication complexity of matrix multiplication using two-dimensional partitioning.

Algorithm	B_{opt}	min start-ups	Arithmetic
$A1(1)$	$\frac{N_2}{2}\lceil\frac{P}{N_1}\rceil\lceil\frac{Q}{N_2}\rceil, \frac{N_1}{2}\lceil\frac{Q}{N_1}\rceil\lceil\frac{R}{N_2}\rceil$	n	$2Q\lceil\frac{P}{N_1}\rceil\lceil\frac{R}{N_2}\rceil$
$A2(1)$	$\lceil\frac{P}{N_1}\rceil\lceil\frac{Q}{N_2}\rceil, \frac{N_2}{2}\lceil\frac{Q}{N_1}\rceil\lceil\frac{P}{N_2}\rceil, \frac{N_1}{2}\lceil\frac{P}{N_1}\rceil\lceil\frac{R}{N_2}\rceil$	$2n$	$(2\lceil\frac{Q}{N_2}\rceil-1)\lceil\frac{R}{N_2}\rceil P + \sum_{i=1}^{n_1}\lceil\frac{R}{N_2}\rceil\lceil\frac{P}{2^i}\rceil + \lceil\frac{R}{N_2}\rceil\lceil\frac{P}{N_1}\rceil$
$A3(1)$	$\lceil\frac{P}{N_1}\rceil\lceil\frac{Q}{N_2}\rceil, \frac{N_2}{2}\lceil\frac{Q}{N_1}\rceil\lceil\frac{R}{N_2}\rceil, \frac{N_1}{2}\lceil\frac{R}{N_1}\rceil\lceil\frac{P}{N_2}\rceil, \lceil\frac{R}{N_1}\rceil\lceil\frac{P}{N_2}\rceil$	$3n$	$(2\lceil\frac{Q}{N_1}\rceil-1)\lceil\frac{P}{N_2}\rceil R + \sum_{i=1}^{n_1}\lceil\frac{P}{N_2}\rceil\lceil\frac{R}{2^i}\rceil + \lceil\frac{P}{N_2}\rceil\lceil\frac{R}{N_1}\rceil)$
$A4(1)$	$\lceil\frac{Q}{N_1}\rceil\lceil\frac{R}{N_2}\rceil, \frac{N_1}{2}\lceil\frac{R}{N_1}\rceil\lceil\frac{Q}{N_2}\rceil, \frac{N_2}{2}\lceil\frac{P}{N_1}\rceil\lceil\frac{R}{N_2}\rceil$	$2n$	$(2\lceil\frac{Q}{N_1}\rceil-1)\lceil\frac{P}{N_1}\rceil R + \sum_{i=1}^{n_2}\lceil\frac{P}{N_1}\rceil\lceil\frac{R}{2^i}\rceil + \lceil\frac{P}{N_1}\rceil\lceil\frac{R}{N_2}\rceil$
$A5(1)$	$\lceil\frac{Q}{N_1}\rceil\lceil\frac{R}{N_2}\rceil, \frac{N_1}{2}\lceil\frac{P}{N_1}\rceil\lceil\frac{Q}{N_2}\rceil, \frac{N_2}{2}\lceil\frac{R}{N_1}\rceil\lceil\frac{P}{N_2}\rceil, \lceil\frac{R}{N_1}\rceil\lceil\frac{P}{N_2}\rceil$	$3n$	$(2\lceil\frac{Q}{N_2}\rceil-1)\lceil\frac{R}{N_1}\rceil P + \sum_{i=1}^{n_2}\lceil\frac{R}{N_1}\rceil\lceil\frac{P}{2^i}\rceil + \lceil\frac{R}{N_1}\rceil\lceil\frac{P}{N_2}\rceil)$

Table 10: The *optimum* communication complexity of matrix multiplication using two-dimensional partitioning with *one-port* communication. For the amount of element transfers, see Table 9.

Algorithm	B_{opt}	T_{min} − arith. time
$A1(n)$	$\sqrt{\frac{2}{\pi}\frac{N_2}{n_2^{3/2}}\lceil\frac{P}{N_1}\rceil\lceil\frac{Q}{N_2}\rceil}$, $\sqrt{\frac{2}{\pi}\frac{N_1}{n_1^{3/2}}\lceil\frac{Q}{N_1}\rceil\lceil\frac{R}{N_2}\rceil}$	$\max(\frac{N_2-1}{n_2}\lceil\frac{P}{N_1}\rceil\lceil\frac{Q}{N_2}\rceil t_c + n_2\tau,$ $\frac{N_1-1}{n_1}\lceil\frac{Q}{N_1}\rceil\lceil\frac{R}{N_2}\rceil t_c + n_1\tau)$
$A2(n)$	$\sqrt{\lceil\frac{P}{N_1}\rceil\lceil\frac{Q}{N_2}\rceil}\frac{\tau}{(n-1)t_c}$, $\sqrt{\frac{2}{\pi}\frac{N_2}{n_2^{3/2}}\lceil\frac{Q}{N_1}\rceil\lceil\frac{P}{N_2}\rceil}$, $\sqrt{\frac{2}{\pi}\frac{N_1}{n_1^{3/2}}\lceil\frac{P}{N_1}\rceil\lceil\frac{R}{N_2}\rceil}$	$n\tau + (\sqrt{\lceil\frac{P}{N_1}\rceil\lceil\frac{Q}{N_2}\rceil t_c} + \sqrt{(n-1)\tau})^2$ $+(\lceil\frac{Q}{N_1}\rceil\lceil\frac{P}{N_2}\rceil\frac{N_2-1}{n_2} + \lceil\frac{P}{N_1}\rceil\lceil\frac{R}{N_2}\rceil\frac{N_1-1}{n_1})t_c$
$A3(n)$	$\sqrt{\lceil\frac{P}{N_1}\rceil\lceil\frac{Q}{N_2}\rceil}\frac{\tau}{(n-1)t_c}$, $\sqrt{\lceil\frac{R}{N_1}\rceil\lceil\frac{P}{N_2}\rceil}\frac{\tau}{(n-1)t_c}$, $\sqrt{\frac{2}{\pi}\frac{N_2}{n_2^{3/2}}\lceil\frac{Q}{N_1}\rceil\lceil\frac{R}{N_2}\rceil}$, $\sqrt{\frac{2}{\pi}\frac{N_1}{n_1^{3/2}}\lceil\frac{R}{N_1}\rceil\lceil\frac{P}{N_2}\rceil}$	$n\tau + (\sqrt{\lceil\frac{P}{N_1}\rceil\lceil\frac{Q}{N_2}\rceil t_c} + \sqrt{(n-1)\tau})^2$ $+(\sqrt{\lceil\frac{R}{N_1}\rceil\lceil\frac{P}{N_2}\rceil t_c} + \sqrt{(n-1)\tau})^2$ $+(\lceil\frac{Q}{N_1}\rceil\lceil\frac{R}{N_2}\rceil\frac{N_2-1}{n_2} + \lceil\frac{R}{N_1}\rceil\lceil\frac{P}{N_2}\rceil\frac{N_1-1}{n_1})t_c$
$A4(n)$	$\sqrt{\lceil\frac{Q}{N_1}\rceil\lceil\frac{R}{N_2}\rceil}\frac{\tau}{(n-1)t_c}$, $\sqrt{\frac{2}{\pi}\frac{N_1}{n_1^{3/2}}\lceil\frac{R}{N_1}\rceil\lceil\frac{Q}{N_2}\rceil}$, $\sqrt{\frac{2}{\pi}\frac{N_2}{n_2^{3/2}}\lceil\frac{P}{N_1}\rceil\lceil\frac{R}{N_2}\rceil}$	$n\tau + (\sqrt{\lceil\frac{Q}{N_1}\rceil\lceil\frac{R}{N_2}\rceil t_c} + \sqrt{(n-1)\tau})^2$ $+(\lceil\frac{R}{N_1}\rceil\lceil\frac{Q}{N_2}\rceil\frac{N_1-1}{n_1} + \lceil\frac{P}{N_1}\rceil\lceil\frac{R}{N_2}\rceil\frac{N_2-1}{n_2})t_c$
$A5(n)$	$\sqrt{\lceil\frac{Q}{N_1}\rceil\lceil\frac{R}{N_2}\rceil}\frac{\tau}{(n-1)t_c}$, $\sqrt{\lceil\frac{R}{N_1}\rceil\lceil\frac{P}{N_2}\rceil}\frac{\tau}{(n-1)t_c}$, $\sqrt{\frac{2}{\pi}\frac{N_1}{n_1^{3/2}}\lceil\frac{P}{N_1}\rceil\lceil\frac{Q}{N_2}\rceil}$, $\sqrt{\frac{2}{\pi}\frac{N_2}{n_2^{3/2}}\lceil\frac{R}{N_1}\rceil\lceil\frac{P}{N_2}\rceil}$	$n\tau + (\sqrt{\lceil\frac{Q}{N_1}\rceil\lceil\frac{R}{N_2}\rceil t_c} + \sqrt{(n-1)\tau})^2$ $+(\sqrt{\lceil\frac{R}{N_1}\rceil\lceil\frac{P}{N_2}\rceil t_c} + \sqrt{(n-1)\tau})^2$ $+(\lceil\frac{P}{N_1}\rceil\lceil\frac{Q}{N_2}\rceil\frac{N_1-1}{n_1} + \lceil\frac{R}{N_1}\rceil\lceil\frac{P}{N_2}\rceil\frac{N_2-1}{n_2})t_c$

Table 11: The *optimum* communication complexity of matrix multiplication using two-dimensional partitioning with *n-port* communication. The arithmetic time is the same as in the *one-port* case and is omitted from the last column.

Algorithm	N_1	N_2	T_{min}, $\qquad B_m \geq B_{opt}$
$A1(1)$	$\sqrt{\frac{PN}{R}}$	$\sqrt{\frac{RN}{P}}$	$\frac{2PQR}{N}t_a + \frac{Q}{\sqrt{N}}(2\sqrt{PR} - \frac{P+R}{\sqrt{N}})t_c + n\tau$
$A2(1)$	$\sqrt{\frac{QN}{R}}$	$\sqrt{\frac{RN}{Q}}$	$\frac{2PQR}{N}t_a + \frac{P}{\sqrt{N}}(2\sqrt{QR} + \frac{nQ-(Q+R)}{\sqrt{N}})t_c + 2n\tau$
$A3(1)$	$\sqrt{\frac{QN}{P}}$	$\sqrt{\frac{PN}{Q}}$	$\frac{2PQR}{N}t_a + \frac{R}{\sqrt{N}}(2\sqrt{PQ} + \frac{nP(1+\frac{Q}{R})-(P+Q)}{\sqrt{N}})t_c + 3n\tau$
$A4(1)$	$\sqrt{\frac{PN}{Q}}$	$\sqrt{\frac{QN}{P}}$	$\frac{2PQR}{N}t_a + \frac{R}{\sqrt{N}}(2\sqrt{PQ} + \frac{nQ-(P+Q)}{\sqrt{N}})t_c + 2n\tau$
$A5(1)$	$\sqrt{\frac{RN}{Q}}$	$\sqrt{\frac{QN}{R}}$	$\frac{2PQR}{N}t_a + \frac{P}{\sqrt{N}}(2\sqrt{QR} + \frac{nR(1+\frac{Q}{R})-(Q+R)}{\sqrt{N}})t_c + 3n\tau$

Table 12: The *optimum* values of N_1 and N_2 for P, Q and R being multiples of N and *one-port* communication.

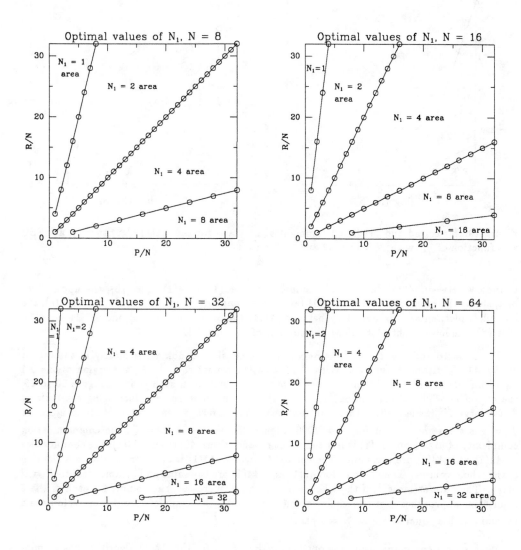

Figure 18: Optimal values of N_1 for the $A1$ algorithm with *one-port* communication.

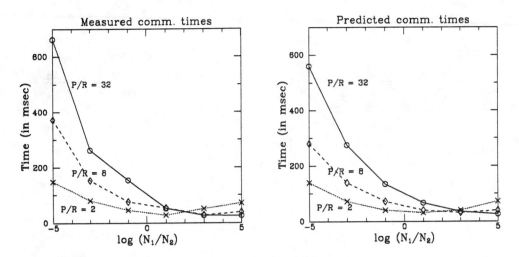

Figure 19: Measured and predicted communication times for the $A1(1)$ algorithm on an iPSC as a function of $\frac{N_1}{N_2}$ with $N = Q = 32$ and $PR = 1024N$.

boundary between $A2(1)$ (above the boundary) and $A1(1) + A4(1)$. Plot (b), the upper right plot, shows the boundary between $A4(1)$ (above the boundary) and $A1(1) + A2(1)$. Plot (c), the lower left plot, shows the boundary between $A1(1)$ (below the boundary) and $A2(1) + A4(1)$. Plot (d), the lower right plot, shows the contour of the plot (c).

For $N = 16$ and $\tau = t_c$, the volume within the considered domain is mostly in the region of the $A1$ algorithm, Figure 20. With the increasing aspect ratio of $\frac{\tau}{t_c}$, the region of the $A1$ algorithm also increases. As the number of processors increases, such as from Figure 20 to 23, the region in which algorithms $A2(1)$ or $A4(1)$ is optimum increases. Increasing the ratio of $\frac{\tau}{t_c}$ for large N has less effect than that for small N. In fact, when $N = 1024$, the Figure for $\frac{\tau}{t_c} = 1$ is the same as that for $\frac{\tau}{t_c} = 1000$, Figure 23. For $\frac{P}{N} = \frac{Q}{N} = \frac{R}{N}$, the communication complexity of algorithm $A1(1)$ is less than that of algorithms $A2(1)$ and $A4(1)$; the complexities of $A2(1)$ and $A4(1)$ are the same. The volume for which $A1(1)$ is optimum is always at least $\frac{1}{3}$ of the whole volume. The volumes for $A2(1)$ and $A4(1)$ are the same and symmetrical to $P = R$ plane. They are at most $\frac{1}{3}$ of the whole volume. As N increases, the volume for each of the 3 algorithms approaches $\frac{1}{3}$ of the whole volume. For $A1(1)$, the shape of its optimum volume is a pyramid with a square base at $\frac{Q}{N} = 0$ plane.

With n-port communication, the optimum value of N_1 for the $A2(n)$ algorithm has to minimize $R\frac{(N_1-1)}{n_1} + Q\frac{(N_2-1)}{n_2}$ if P, Q, R are multiples of N. Figure 24 shows the optimum values of N_1 for the $A2(n)$ algorithm. For algorithms $A3(n)$, $A4(n)$ and $A5(n)$, (Q, R) are replaced by (Q, P), (P, Q) and (R, Q) respectively. For algorithm $A1(n)$, Q is replaced by P, approximately.

Figures 25 and 26 show the partitioning of the P, Q, R space according to the algorithm of minimum complexity with n-port communication. The four plots of each Figure are organized the same way as in the *one-port* case. For P, Q, and R multiples of N, algorithm $A1(n)$ is preferable with respect to execution time for most values of P, Q, and R. Algorithm $A1(n)$ shall be chosen if P, $R \geq Q$. Algorithm $A2(n)$ shall be chosen only if Q, $R > P$, and $A4(n)$ only if Q, $P > R$. The volume for $A2(n)$ ($A4(n)$) is significantly smaller than that for $A2(1)$

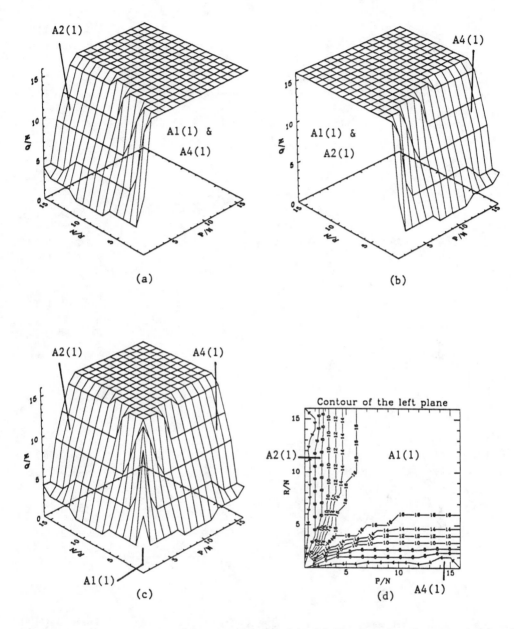

(a) The boundary between $A2(1)$ and $A1(1) + A4(1)$. (b) The boundary between $A4(1)$ and $A1(1) + A2(1)$. (c) The boundary between $A1(1)$ and $A2(1) + A4(1)$. (d) Contour plot of (c).

Figure 20: Lowest complexity algorithm as a function of matrix shape; $N = 16$, $\tau = t_c$, $B_m = \infty$, two-dimensional partitioning, *one-port* communication.

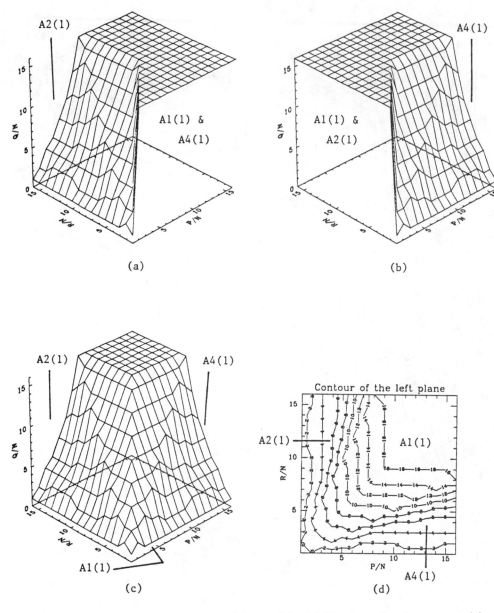

(a) The boundary between $A2(1)$ and $A1(1) + A4(1)$. (b) The boundary between $A4(1)$ and $A1(1) + A2(1)$. (c) The boundary between $A1(1)$ and $A2(1) + A4(1)$. (d) Contour plot of (c).

Figure 21: Lowest complexity algorithm as a function of matrix shape; $N = 128$, $\tau = t_c$, $B_m = \infty$, two-dimensional partitioning, one-port communication.

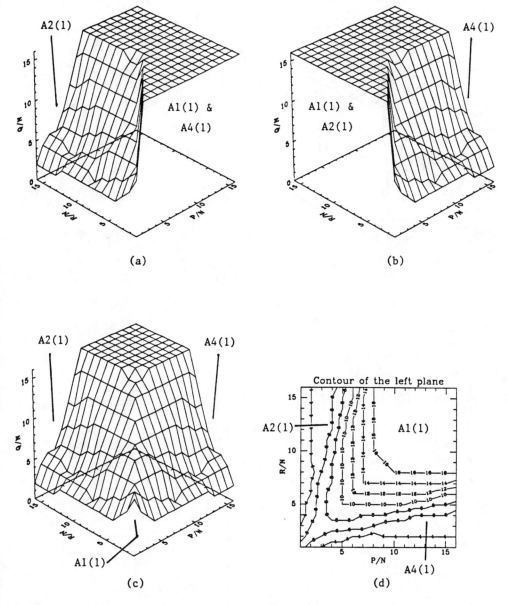

(a) The boundary between $A2(1)$ and $A1(1) + A4(1)$. (b) The boundary between $A4(1)$ and $A1(1) + A2(1)$. (c) The boundary between $A1(1)$ and $A2(1) + A4(1)$. (d) Contour plot of (c).

Figure 22: Lowest complexity algorithm as a function of matrix shape; $N = 128$, $\tau = 1000t_c$, $B_m = \infty$, two-dimensional partitioning, *one-port* communication.

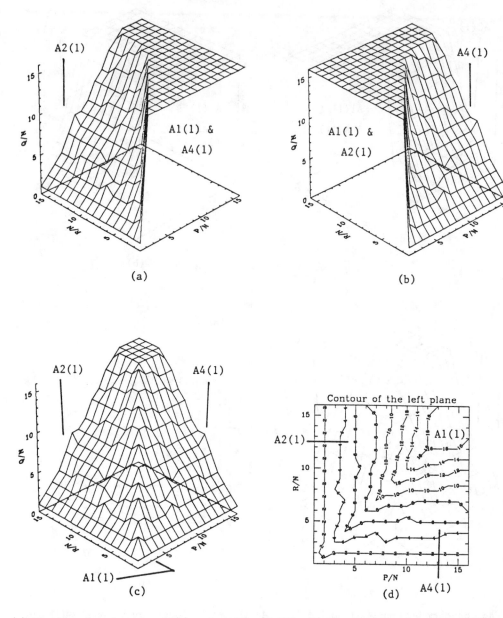

(a) The boundary between $A2(1)$ and $A1(1) + A4(1)$. (b) The boundary between $A4(1)$ and $A1(1) + A2(1)$. (c) The boundary between $A1(1)$ and $A2(1) + A4(1)$. (d) Contour plot of (c).

Figure 23: Lowest complexity algorithm as a function of matrix shape; $N = 1024$, $\frac{\tau}{t_c} = 1$ to 1000, two-dimensional partitioning, *one-port* communication.

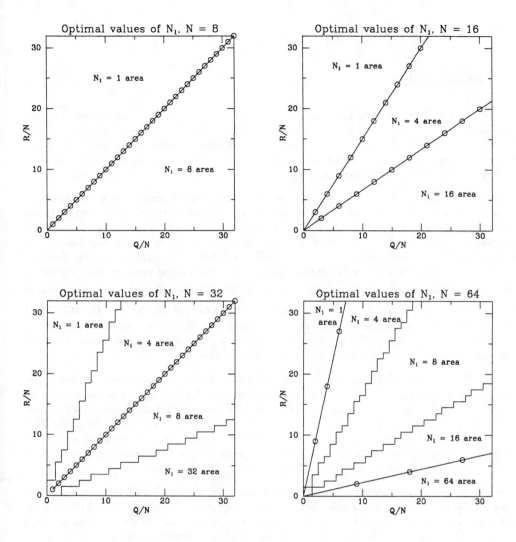

Figure 24: Optimal values of N_1 for algorithm $A2(n)$ with *n-port* communication.

$(A4(1))$ of the corresponding *one-port* case.

6   Conclusions

A two-dimensional partitioning yields a complexity that is at most the same as that of a one-dimensional partitioning. In the one-dimensional partitioning the processors shall be aligned with the axis with the largest number of elements. In the two dimensional partitioning the processing plane shall be aligned with the matrix plane with the maximum number of elements. The aspect ratio of the processing array shall be the same as that of the matrix plane.

For the Boolean cube a reduction in the number of start-ups is possible in exchange for an increase in buffer sizes, and temporary storage. With a temporary storage that is equal to the size of the partitioned matrices, $O(N)$ communication steps are required for the one-dimensional partitioning while only $O(N_1, N_2)$ communication steps are required for the two-dimensional partitioning. The two-dimensional partitioning offers a reduction in element transfer time and number of start-ups by a factor of approximately $\frac{2}{\sqrt{N}}$ in the case of *one-port* communication and optimum aspect ratio for the partitioning $\left(\frac{N_1}{N_2}\right)$. The number of start-ups is also reduced by a factor of approximately $\frac{2}{\sqrt{N}}$ for the optimum aspect ratio if $B_m < \frac{PQ}{N}$. For sufficiently large values of B_m the number of start-ups is the same in both the one- and two-dimensional partitioning, but the value of B_m at which the minimum number of start-ups is achieved is lower by a factor of approximately $\sqrt{N}$ in the two-dimensional case.

The CRA and the GCEA algorithms in one and two dimensions preserves storage requirements. The Spanning Binomial Tree algorithm only requires $\log N$ communication steps at the expense of larger temporary storage and optimum buffer size. With limited temporary storage (and maximum buffer size), a hybrid method can be used by performing k steps of the SBT algorithm and $2^{n-k} - 1$ steps of a linear time algorithm. The number of communication steps can be halved, approximately, by doubling the temporary storage and the optimum buffer size. With *n-port* communication, the edge load is reduced by a factor of n.

We have also devised algorithms with three-dimensional partitioning of the matrices as described in [16]. It shows that if the initial matrices are properly located, or if the maximum packet size is small relative to the matrix size, or if the communication start-up times are small relative to the data transmission times, three-dimensional partitioning is always preferable.

Throughout the paper it is implicitly assumed that the matrices are stored in the processors local storage by a consecutive strategy [14]. The complexity results also hold for cyclic storage. All the algorithms described work for binary code and Gray code encodings. The communication patterns are the same; only the local data accessing schemes differ.

Acknowledgement

This work has been supported in part by the Office of Naval Research under Contracts N00014-84-K-0043 and N00014-86-K-0564.

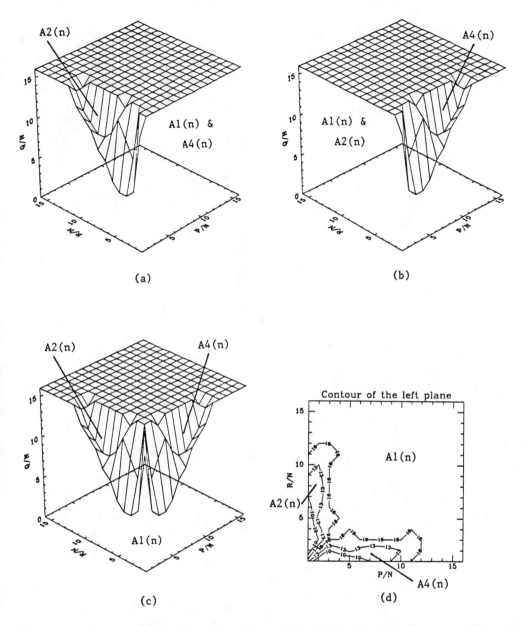

(a) The boundary between $A2(1)$ and $A1(1) + A4(1)$. (b) The boundary between $A4(1)$ and $A1(1) + A2(1)$. (c) The boundary between $A1(1)$ and $A2(1) + A4(1)$. (d) Contour plot of (c).

Figure 25: Lowest complexity algorithm as a function of matrix shape; $N = 16$, $\tau = t_c$, $B_m = \infty$, two-dimensional partitioning, n-port communication.

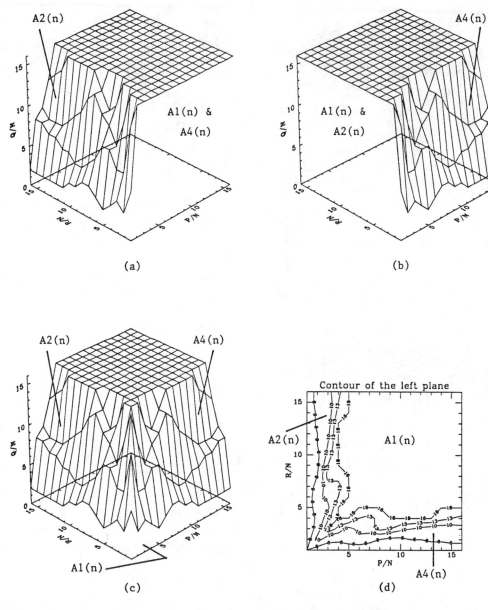

(a) The boundary between $A2(1)$ and $A1(1) + A4(1)$. (b) The boundary between $A4(1)$ and $A1(1) + A2(1)$. (c) The boundary between $A1(1)$ and $A2(1) + A4(1)$. (d) Contour plot of (c).

Figure 26: Lowest complexity algorithm as a function of matrix shape; $N = 1024$, $\tau = t_c$, $B_m = \infty$, two-dimensional partitioning, n-port communication.

References

[1] Alfred V. Aho, John E. Hopcroft, and Jeffrey D. Ullman. *The Design and Analysis of Computer Algorithms*. Addison-Wesley, 1974.

[2] Romas Aleliunas and Arnold L. Rosenberg. On embedding rectangular grids in square grids. *IEEE Trans. Computers*, C-31(9):907–913, September 1982.

[3] Sandeep N. Bhatt and Ilse I.F. Ipsen. *How to Embed Trees in Hypercubes*. Technical Report YALEU/CSD/RR-443, Yale University, Dept. of Computer Science, December 1985.

[4] L.E. Cannon. *A Cellular Computer to Implement the Kalman Filter Algorithm*. PhD thesis, Montana State University, 1969.

[5] Eliezer Dekel, David Nassimi, and Sartaj Sahni. Parallel matrix and graph algorithms. *SIAM J. Computing*, 10:657–673, 1981.

[6] Sanjay R. Deshpande and Roy M. Jenevin. Scaleability of a binary tree on a hypercube. In *International Conference on Parallel Processing*, pages 661–668, IEEE Computer Society, 1986. TR-86-01, Univ. Texas at Austin.

[7] Michael J. Fischer. *Efficiency of Equivalence Algorithms*, pages 153–167. Plenum Press, 1972.

[8] Ching-Tien Ho and S. Lennart Johnsson. Algorithms for matrix transposition on Boolean n-cube configured ensemble architectures. In *Int. Conf. on Parallel Processing*, pages 621–629, IEEE Computer Society, 1987.

[9] Ching-Tien Ho and S. Lennart Johnsson. Distributed routing algorithms for broadcasting and personalized communication in hypercubes. In *1986 Int. Conf. Parallel Processing*, pages 640–648, IEEE Computer Society, 1986. Tech. report YALEU/CSD/RR-483.

[10] Ching-Tien Ho and S. Lennart Johnsson. *Matrix Transposition on Boolean n-cube Configured Ensemble Architectures*. Technical Report YALEU/CSD/RR-494, Yale University, Dept. of Computer Science, September 1986.

[11] Ching-Tien Ho and S. Lennart Johnsson. On the embedding of arbitrary meshes in Boolean cubes with expansion two dilation two. In *Int. Conf. on Parallel Processing*, pages 188–191, IEEE Computer Society, 1987.

[12] Ching-Tien Ho and S. Lennart Johnsson. *Spanning Balanced Trees in Boolean cubes*. Technical Report YALEU/CSD/RR-508, Yale University, Dept. of Computer Science, January 1987.

[13] *Intel iPSC System Overview*. Intel Corp., January 1986.

[14] S. Lennart Johnsson. Communication efficient basic linear algebra computations on hypercube architectures. *Journal of Parallel and Distributed Computing*, 4(2):133–172, April 1987. (Report YALEU/CSD/RR-361, January 1985).

[15] S. Lennart Johnsson. *Data Permutations and Basic Linear Algebra Computations on Ensemble Architectures*. Technical Report YALEU/CSD/RR-367, Yale University, Dept. of Computer Science, February 1985.

[16] S. Lennart Johnsson and Ching-Tien Ho. *Algorithms for Multiplying Matrices of Arbitrary Shapes Using Shared Memory Primitives on a Boolean Cube*. Technical Report YALEU/CSD/RR-569, Department of Computer Science, Yale University, October 1987.

[17] S. Lennart Johnsson and Ching-Tien Ho. *Spanning Graphs for Optimum Broadcasting and Personalized Communication in Hypercubes*. Technical Report Report YALEU/CSD/RR-500, Yale University, Dept. of Computer Science, November 1986. To appear in IEEE Trans. Computers.

[18] Flynn M.J. Very high-speed computing systems. *Proc. of the IEEE*, 12:1901–1909, 1966.

[19] E M. Reingold, J Nievergelt, and N Deo. *Combinatorial Algorithms*. Prentice Hall, 1977.

[20] Yousef Saad and Martin H. Schultz. *Data Communication in Hypercubes*. Technical Report YALEU/DCS/RR-428, Dept. of Computer Science, Yale University, October 1985.

[21] Yousef Saad and Martin H. Schultz. *Topological properties of Hypercubes*. Technical Report YALEU/DCS/RR-389, Dept. of Computer Science, Yale University, June 1985.

[22] Charles L. Seitz. Ensemble architectures for VLSI – a survey and taxonomy. In P. Penfield Jr., editor, *1982 Conf on Advanced Research in VLSI*, pages 130 – 135, Artech House, January 1982.

[23] Angela Y. Wu. Embedding of tree networks in hypercubes. *Journal of Parallel and Distributed Computing*, 2(3):238–249, 1985.

CHAPTER 9

The Force on the Flex: Global Parallelism and Portability*

Harry F. Jordan†

ABSTRACT

A parallel programming methodology, called the force, supports the construction of programs to be executed in parallel by an unspecified, but potentially large, number of processes. The methodology was originally developed on a pipelined, shared memory multiprocessor, the Denelcor HEP, and embodies the primitive operations of the force in a set of macros which expand into multiprocessor Fortran code. A small set of primitives is sufficient to write large parallel programs, and the system has been used to produce 10,000 line programs in computational fluid dynamics. The level of complexity of the force primitives is intermediate. It is high enough to mask detailed architectural differences between multiprocessors but low enough to give the user control over performance.

The system is being ported to a medium scale multiprocessor, the Flex/32, which is a 20 processor system with a mixture of shared and local memory. Memory organization and the type of processor synchronization supported by the hardware on the two machines lead to some differences in efficient implementations of the force primitives, but the user interface remains the same. An initial implementation was done by retargeting the macros to Flexible Computer Corporation's ConCurrent C language. Subsequently, the macros were caused to directly produce the system calls which form the basis for ConCurrent C. The implementation of the Fortran based system is in step with Flexible Computer Corporations's implementation of a Fortran system in the parallel environment.

* Research was supported in part by NASA Contracts No. NAS1-17070 and No. NAS1-18107 and by the Air Force Office of Scientific Research under Grant No. AFOSR 85-1089 while the author was in residence at ICASE, NASA Langley Research Center, Hampton, VA 23665.

† University of Colorado, Boulder, CO 80309-0425.

The Global Parallelism Concept

The unifying idea behind the programming environment discussed in this paper is that of "global" parallelism. In contrast to the dataflow point of view we retain the idea of multiple instruction streams but insulate the user from the detailed management of the streams on an individual basis. One view of this unifying idea is as a way of incorporating parallelism into the structural hierarchy of a program. It is in contrast to the encapsulation of parallelism into one or more program modules and can be viewed as parallelism with the largest possible "grain" size.

The view of a computation as an hierarchically structured set of functions is well established and maps into the subroutine calling hierarchy in most programming languages. The level of the (usually tree structured) functional hierarchy at which parallelism enters into the description of an algorithm is an important issue. The leaf level, where SIMD parallelism is appropriate can be denoted as fine grained parallelism. As MIMD parallelism is applied at higher levels, we can speak of algorithms with coarser grained parallelism. With fine grained parallelism, the major issue in expressing the computation is to specify exactly what is to be done in parallel in each of the small grains. Very tight synchronization must be the rule (as in SIMD) for fine grained parallelism to make sense. In a program with coarse grained parallelism the amount of code devoted to expressing the parallelism may be very small and localized in a high level module. In exchange, the specification of synchronization becomes the major issue and may appear explicitly at any level of structure, all the way down to the leaf.

One possible way to fit MIMD parallelism into the calling hierarchy is to try to encapsulate parallelism below a certain level, or grain size. This has the advantage that the upper levels of the program can be written without knowing anything about parallel computation. Using the Fork/Join mechanism [1] to manage parallel processes, a single instruction stream would fork within some subroutine into multiple streams which would perform a parallel computation and then join into a single stream before returning from the subroutine. The drawbacks in this scheme lie in the area of performance. It is well known that even a small amount of sequential code in an otherwise parallel program can decrease efficiency significantly on a system with a large degree of parallelism. The encapsulation idea forces all code above a certain level of structure to be sequential. Furthermore, there is overhead associated with managing processes and execution environments in fork and join which is invoked whenever the program passes into or out of the parallel level of structure.

Since encapsulation overheads tend to make larger grained parallelism more efficient regardless of the grain size, there is a good reason to locate parallelism at the highest level of program structure in the MIMD environment. Experience shows that it is quite feasible to write applications programs with "global" parallelism. In this environment one begins a program under the assumption that it may be executed by an arbitrary number P of processes. There is no explicit code for process management. The processes are managed by entry level, system dependent code which chooses the number of processes on the basis of hardware structure and available knowledge of algorithm needs. The explicitly appearing code to deal with parallelism is all related to process synchronization and data sharing. The idea of global parallelism applies to the decomposition of algorithms on the basis of data rather than function. With a high degree of parallelism some data decomposition of an algorithm is surely necessary since the number of independent functions is limited. Thus this idea is probably most appropriate to systems supporting many processes.

The above concept of global parallelism has been incorporated into a programming methodology called the "force". The force [2] methodology for parallel programming arose in trying to produce high performance parallel programs in a shared-memory multiprocessor running up to 200 processes on the same user program [3]. Multiprogramming was not an issue, and all emphasis was on single problem solution speed. Partly for performance measurement purposes and partly for program manageability, a programming style emerged in which a single piece of code was written which could be executed by a force of processes in parallel. The number of processes constituting the force is constant during execution but is bound as late as the beginning of execution, and may be one. Similar techniques have been developed for programming some more recent multiprocessors, notably the Bolt Beranek and Newman Butterfly [4] and the IBM research processor RP3[5].

Several advantages arise out of independence from the number of processes. It is not necessary to design algorithms with a detailed dependence on the, potentially very large, number of processes executing them. The choice of the optimal number of processes can be made at run time on the basis of system hardware configuration and load. Since complete independence from the number of processes implies correct execution with only one process, the issues of arithmetic correctness and multi-process synchronization can be separated in the testing of a program.

Statements written in a force program are implicitly executed by all processes in parallel. Variables appearing in statements are divided into local variables, having separate instances for each process, and global variables, shared among all processes of the force. An assignment statement, for example, may combine the values of global and local variables to produce a local or global result. If the result is local, no assignment conflict is possible. If it is global, then assignment conflict must be prevented, either by allocation of disjoint sections of a global data structure to multiple processes or by synchronizing the assignment across processes, say by enclosing it in a critical section or by using producer/consumer synchronization on the variable assigned. Library or user subroutines which are either free of side effects or carefully synchronized can be invoked in parallel, one copy for each process.

Realization of the Concept

The programming language associated with the force consists of some simple extensions to the Fortran language, which are currently implemented as macros expanded by a language independent preprocessor. The target

Fortran system must, of course, include ways of creating multiple processes and of supporting synchronized access to global variables. The macros interact through the variables of a parallel environment, which contains some general information such as the number of processes and some machine dependent items.

The macros currently constituting the force can be divided into several classes, as shown in Fig. 1. The first class deals with parallel program structure. The macros *Force* and *Forcesub* respectively begin parallel main programs and parallel subroutines. They make the parallel environment variables available to the macros within that program module as well as making the number of processes and a unique identifier for the current process available to the user at run time. An *End Declarations* macro marks the beginning of executable code and provides target locations for declarations and start up code which may be generated by the macros. A *Join* macro terminates the parallel main program. It is the last statement executed by all processes of the force.

Macros of the second class deal with variable declaration. This class currently includes only *Global* and *Local* macros. Global variables are associated with Fortran common while local variables are ordinary Fortran variables local to a separately compiled program module. Sharing of local variables among several program modules, but local to one process, can only be accomplished by parameter passing. The static allocation flavor of Fortran makes it difficult to build a structure of common variables with one instance for each process when the number of processes is not known until execution time.

Macros of another class distribute work across processes. The most familiar construct is the DOALL, which is employed when instances of a loop body for different index values are independent and can thus be executed in any order. Two versions are provided. The *Presched DO* divides index values among processes in a fixed manner which depends only on the index range and the number of processes. The *Selfsched DO* allows processes to schedule themselves over index values by obtaining the next available value of a shared index as they become free to do work. For situations in which it is desirable to parallelize over both indices of a doubly nested loop, both prescheduled, *Pre2DO*, and self scheduled, *Self2DO*, macros are available. Independence of the loop body instances over both indices is, of course, required for correct operation. A similar construct is the parallel case, *Pcase*, which distributes different single stream code blocks over the processes of the force. Execution conditions can be associated with each block, and any number of these conditions may be true simultaneously. No order of evaluation of the conditions is specified, and each will be evaluated by one arbitrarily selected process. Thus conditions depending only on global variables are most meaningful.

At the heart of the force methodology are the synchronization macros. They characterize the approach to parallel programming and provide the means for controlling the force so that coherent and deterministic computation can be performed. Two subclasses of synchronization are control flow

Macros associated with program structure:
```
    Force <name> of <# procs> ident <proc #>
        <declarations>
    End declarations
        <force program>
    Join

    Forcesub <name> of <#procs> ident <proc #>
        <declarations>
    End header
        <subroutine body>
    RETURN

    Forcecall <name>(<parameters>)
```

Declaration macros:
```
    Global <variable names>
    Local <Fortran declaration>
```

Macros specifying parallel execution:
```
    Pcase on <variable>
        <code block>
    Usect
        <code block>
    ...
    End pcase

    [Pre|Self]sched DO <n> <var> = <i1>, <i2>, <i3>
        <loop body>
<n>   End [pre|self]sched DO
```

Synchronizing macros:
```
    Barrier
        <code block>
    End barrier

    Critical $<variable>
        <code block>
    End critical

    Produce <variable> = <expression>          (producer)
    ... = ... Use(<variable>) ...          (consumer)
```

Figure 1: Specific Macros for a Force Program

oriented synchronizations and data oriented synchronizations. The key control oriented synchronization is the barrier since it provides control of the entire force. Its semantics are that all processes must execute a *Barrier* macro before one arbitrarily chosen process executes the code block between *Barrier* and *End Barrier*. When the code block is complete, the entire force begins execution at the statement following the *End Barrier*. Although all but one process are temporarily suspended by a barrier, no process termination or creation takes place and all local process states are preserved across the barrier. Operations which depend on the past computation, or determine the future progress, of the entire force are typically enclosed in a barrier.

Another control based synchronization is the critical section, familiar from the operating systems literature. Statements between *Critical* <*variable*> and *End Critical* may only be executed by one process of the force at a time. This mutual exclusion extends to any other critical section with the same associated variable. Data oriented synchronization is provided by the elementary producer-consumer mechanism, in which global variables have a binary state, full or empty, as well as a value. Execution by some process of the macro, *Produce* <*variable*> = <*expression*>, waits for the variable to be in the empty state, sets its value to that of the expression and makes it full, all in a manner which is atomic with respect to the progress of any other process. Similarly, the macro, *Use(*<*variable*>*)*, appearing in an expression returns the value of the variable when it becomes full and sets it empty. Variables in the wrong state may cause these macros to block the progress of a process. Auxiliary macros for full/empty variables are *Purge* <*variable*>, which sets a variable empty regardless of its previous state, and *Copy(*<*variable*>*)*, which waits for the variable to be full and returns its value but does not empty it.

A major weakness in the current set of force macros is that it does not smoothly support decomposition of a program into parallel components on the basis of functionality. The *Pcase* macro offers the rudiments of this, but only allows one process to execute each of the parallel functions. What is desired is a macro, *Resolve,* which will resolve the force into components executing different parallel code sections. The section of code for each component would start with *Component* <*name*> *strength* <*number*>, which would name the component and specify the fraction of the force to be devoted to this component. The component strengths would be estimated by the programmer on the basis of any knowledge available about the computational complexity of each component. A macro, *Unify,* would reunite the components into a single force. The implementation of *Resolve* is complicated by the conflicting demands of generality and efficiency. If the number of components is larger than the number of processes in the force, then inter-component synchronization may deadlock unless the components are co-scheduled over the available processes. An implementation which produces process rescheduling at every possible deadlock point and is still efficient when the number of processes exceeds the number of components is under development.

Incorporation of a *Resolve* macro will make it useful to extend the barrier idea. A barrier should be able to specify whether only the processes in the current component are to be blocked or whether all processes in the parent force are to participate. In the case of recursively nested *Resolve* constructs, the barrier might specify a nesting level relative to the one in which it appears.

The *Resolve* idea promises a mechanism for functional decomposition of programs into parallel components, but there is one more capability of parallel programming environments with explicit process management which is not addressed by the force. This is the ability to give away work to "available" processes in a dynamic manner during execution. This ability is most called for by tree algorithms and dynamic divide-and-conquer methods. It would be desirable for the force to contain a mechanism for efficiently handling such algorithms without making the user responsible for explicit process management or losing the benefits of independence of the number of processes. A mechanism related to resolve might be applied at each tree node but could lead to much process management overhead in cases where the correct thing to do is merely to traverse a subtree with the one remaining process.

Status and Applications

The force macros described above represent a parallel programming environment in which process management is suppressed, and programs are independent of the number of processes executing them, except for performance. The system makes parallel execution the normal mode; sequential operation must be explicitly invoked. Two features combine to ensure that there is no topological structure to the parallel environment. First, processes are identical in capability, and, second, all variables are either strictly local to one process or uniformly shared among all of them. This eliminates much of the complexity of the "mapping problem" encountered in constructing parallel versions of algorithms for machines with visible processor topology.

Primitive operations of the force are available to support both fine-grained and coarse-grained parallelism. Many of the primitives, especially those supporting fine grained interaction, require only local analysis to determine correctness of the synchronization. This locality strengthens the case for being able to automate this analysis. The ability to recursively subdivide the force, coupled with the support for parallelization on the basis of data partitioning, orients the system towards "massive" parallelism in that the activity of large numbers of processes can be compactly specified.

The system is currently tied fairly tightly to shared memory with undifferentiated processes and, for that reason, does not support message passing. One could view the *Produce* and *Consume* primitives as a weak form of send and receive operations with the associated variable playing the role of an unbuffered, one word, message channel.

The force system has been used to produce a parallel Gaussian elimination subroutine[2] identical in interface and operation to the SGEFA routine of LINPACK[6]. As well as being effective in this library subroutine type of application, it has been used to write large parallel fluid dynamics programs, including SOR algorithms for incompressible flow[7], [8] and MacCormack's method for a shock tube model[9]. It has also been used to implement a new parallel pivoting algorithm for solving sparse systems of linear equations[10].

The Machines

The issues which arise in implementing the force on a shared memory multiprocessor will be addressed by considering implementations on two, fairly different, such machines: the Denelcor HEP[3] and the Flexible Computer Systems Flex/32[11]. Not only are the two systems fairly different in architecture, the HEP being a pipelined multiprocessor while the Flex/32 is built from multiple microprocessors, but the primitive operations for establishing and controlling parallel processes which are supported by the systems are quite different. These parallel primitive operations are a combined result of hardware, compiler support, operating system and run-time libraries. A summary of the hardware, parallelism model and primitive operations for each of the machines follows.

The HEP

The HEP computer is a multiple instruction stream computer categorized as MIMD by Flynn[12]. Several processing units, called Process Execution Modules (PEMs), may be connected to a shared memory consisting of one or more memory modules as shown in Fig. 2. Even within a single PEM, however, HEP is still an MIMD computer. Only the number of instructions actually executing simultaneously, about 12 per PEM, changes when more PEMs are added to a system. Separate memories store program and data with smaller memories devoted to registers and frequently used constants. Only data memory is shared between PEMs. We will concentrate on the

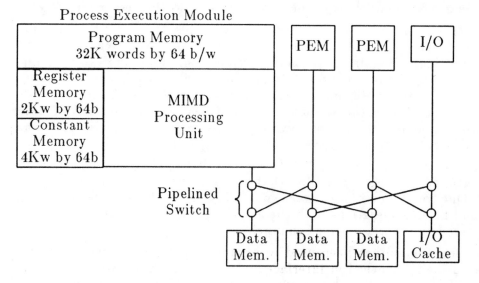

Figure 2: Architecture of the HEP Computer

architecture of a single PEM which implements multiprocessing by using the technique of pipelining.

There are several separate, interacting pipelines in a PEM but the major flavor of the architecture can be given by considering only one of them, the main execution pipeline. Heavy use has been made of pipelines in vector processors (SIMD computers). In such machines the operating units are broken into small stages with data storage in each stage. Complete processing of a pair of operands involves the data passing sequentially through all stages of the "pipeline." Parallelism is achieved by having different pairs of operands occupying different stages of the pipeline simultaneously. The main execution pipeline of HEP can be viewed as a unified structure which processes most instructions using a pipeline with eight steps. Independent instructions (along with their operands) flow through the pipeline with an instruction being completely executed in eight steps. Independence of the activities in successive stages of the pipeline is achieved not by processing independent components of vectors but by alternately issuing instructions from independent instruction streams. Multiple copies of process state, including program counter, are kept for a variable number of processes. A PEM is an MIMD processor in exactly the same sense in which a pipelined vector processor is an SIMD machine. In both, independent data items are processed simultaneously in different stages of the pipeline while in the HEP, independent instructions occupy pipeline stages along with their data.

The previous paragraph describes the register to register instructions. Those dealing with main memory (data memory) behave differently. Data memory is shared between PEMs and words are moved between register and data memories by means of a class of Storage Function Unit (SFU) instructions. The relationship between the main execution pipeline and the SFU is shown in Fig. 3. A process is characterized by a Process Status Word (PSW) containing a program counter and index offsets into both register memory and constant memory to support the writing of reentrant code. Under the assumption that multiple processes will cooperate on a given job or task and thus share memory, memory is allocated and protected on the basis of a structure called a task. There are a maximum of 16 tasks, eight supervisor tasks and eight user tasks. The 128 possible processes are divided into a maximum of 64 users and 64 supervisor processes which must belong to tasks of corresponding types. Aside from this restriction a task may have any number of processes, from zero to 64.

An active process is represented in the hardware by a Process Tag (PT) which points to one of the 128 possible PSWs. The instruction issuing operation maintains a fair allocation of resources between tasks first and between processes within a task second by means of 16 task queues, each containing up to 64 PTs and a secondary queue called the snapshot queue. PTs coming one at a time from the snapshot queue cause the issuing of an instruction from the corresponding process into the execution pipeline.

When an SFU instruction (data memory access) is issued, the PT leaves the queues of the main scheduler and enters a second set of identical queues in the SFU. When a PT comes to the head of the SFU snapshot queue a

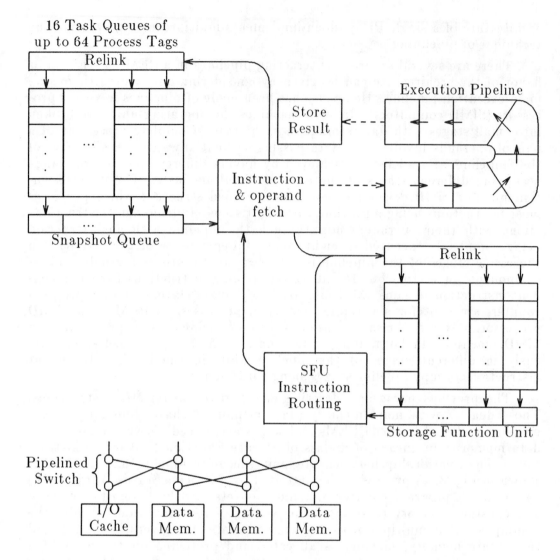

Figure 3: HEP Pipeline Architecture

memory transaction is built and sent, along with the PT, into the attached node of a pipelined, message-switched switching network. The transaction propagates through the switch to the appropriate memory bank and returns to the SFU with status and perhaps data. An SFU instruction behaves as if it were issued into a pipeline longer than the eight step execution pipeline but with the same step rate.

Hardware support for process synchronization is based on producer/consumer synchronization. Each cell in register and data memories has a full/empty state and synchronization is performed by having an instruction wait for its operands to be full and its result empty before proceeding. The synchronizing conditions are optionally checked by the instruction issuing mechanism and, if not fulfilled, cause the PT to be immediately relinked into its task queue with the program counter of the PSW unaltered.

Compiler level support consists of minimal language extensions to give the user access to the parallelism of the hardware. The extensions can be represented as subroutine calls or incorporated into the language definition. Since the force is based on Fortran, the extensions to that language are described. To allow for the fact that an independent process usually requires some local variables, the process concept is tied to the Fortran subroutine. The Fortran extension is merely a second version of the CALL statment, CREATE. Control returns immediately from a CREATE statement, but the created subroutine, with a unique copy of its local variables, is also executing simultaneously. The RETURN in a created subroutine has the effect of terminating the process executing the subroutine. Parameters are passed by address in both CALL and CREATE.

The only other major conceptual modification to Fortran allows access to the synchronizing properties of the full/empty state of memory cells. Any Fortran variable may be declared to be an "asynchronous" variable. Asynchronous variables are distinguished by names beginning with a $ symbol and may have any Fortran type. They may appear in Fortran declarative statements and adhere to implicit typing rules based on the initial letter. If such a variable appears on the right side of an assignment, wait for full, read and set empty semantics apply. When one appears on the left of an assignment, the semantics are wait for empty, write and set full. To initialize the state (not the value) of asynchronous variables, a new statement, PURGE, sets the states of asynchronous variables to empty regardless of their previous states.

The HEP Fortran extensions of CREATE and asynchronous variables are the simplest way to incorporate the parallel features of the hardware into the Fortran language. Since process creation is directly supported by the HEP instruction set and any memory reference may test and set the full/empty state that is associated with each memory cell, the Fortran extensions are direct representations of hardware mechanisms. The parallel computation model supported by the Fortran compiler and run time system can thus be viewed as shown in Fig. 4. A process with its own program counter and registers may spawn others like it using CREATE, and the processes interact by way of full/empty shared memory cells.

The parallel programming primitive operations can be characterized as in Table 1. Note that all the parallel primitives are user level operations requiring no operating system intervention. Interrupts are not present in the HEP. Conditions which would normally lead to an interrupt, including supervisor calls, result in the creation of a supervisor process to handle the condition and may or may not suspend the process giving rise to the condition.

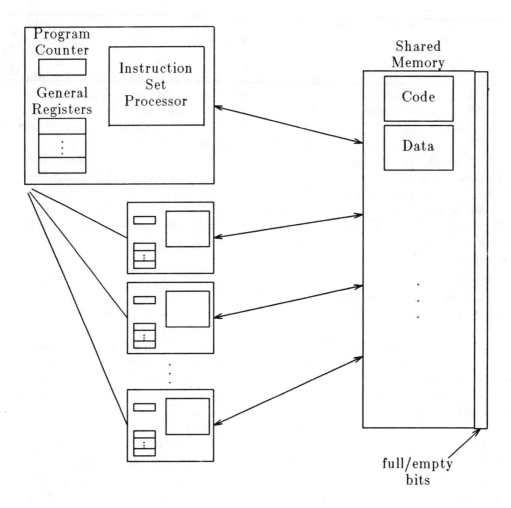

Figure 4: HEP Run Time System Model

Create
Quit and save state

Set location empty
Produce   - Wait for empty, write and fill
Consume   - Wait for full, read and empty

Table 1: HEP Parallel Primitives

The Flex/32®

The architecture of the Flex/32 is conceptually simpler than that of the HEP, but the system support for parallelism is more complex. The machine consists of a set of single board microcomputers connected by several buses to each other and to some common memory and synchronization hardware. As shown in Fig. 5, there are a set of local buses, ten of them, each of which can connect two boards, which are either single board computers consisting of processor and memory or mass memory boards. Two common buses connect the local buses together and to the common memory and synchronization hardware. The memory on the common bus is faster for a processor to access than that on the mass memory boards, but both are shared by all processors. The memory on a processor board is accessible only to that processor.

Hardware support for synchronization is supplied by an 8192 bit lock memory. This structure is meant to remove the requirement for repeated tests by a processor trying to obtain a lock. There is an interrupt system connected with each processor, which provides underlying hardware support for an event signaling mechanism between processors as well as for exception handling within a single processor.

The processor/memory boards are based on the National Semiconductor 32032 microprocessor chip. There may be one or four megabytes of memory on a board and a VME bus interface is provided to connect an individual processor to I/O devices. A self-test system, connected to all processors, provides a mechanism for testing, bootstrapping and initializing the multiprocessor.

The process model in the Flex/32 is somewhat different from that of the HEP and is shown pictorially in Fig. 6. Since not all of the address space is

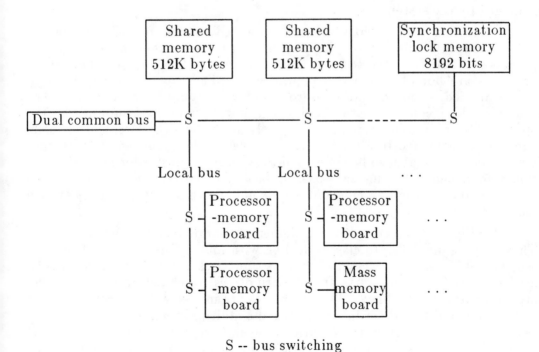

S -- bus switching

Figure 5: Flex/32 Architecture

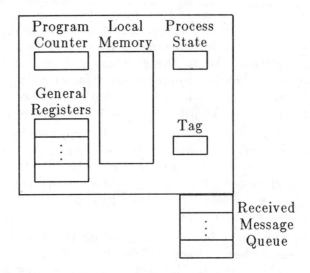

Figure 6: Flex/32 Run Time System - Process Model

shared, a process has a certain amount of strictly local memory. The system also manages a unique identifying tag for each process and maintains a process state which may be one of: running, non-existent, dormant, ready or suspended. There is also a received message queue for each process which is managed by the system.

In addition to a slightly more complicated process model, the Flex/32 system supports a more complex model of synchronization facilities linking processes. The total systems model is shown in Fig. 7. At the outset, processes are bound to individual processors. The processors may be multiprogrammed, so more than one process may be bound to a processor. The processes share communication and synchronization support supplied by the operating system. The Signaling Channels implement the Event mechanism and may be attached to a process as a receiver of the event, an originator, or both. Lock bits may also be connected to several processors for mutual exclusion enforcement. The message passing facility is represented by the received message queue in each process and is thus not shown separately in the system model.

The Flex/32 system provides numerous parallel processing primitives. They may be divided into classes dealing with four different parts of the system model: Processes, Messages, Events and Locks. The structures associated with each of these parts and the primitives which act on the structures are summarized in Table 2. The primitives are implemented through system calls. Since most of them interact with the multiprogramming of single processors, operating system intervention is usually required. Only a small part of this fairly extensive parallel programming model is needed to support the implementation of the force constructs.

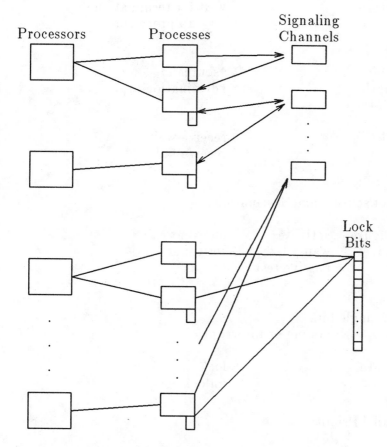

Figure 7: Flex/32 Run Time System - Overall Structure

Process
  Structure   State: •running   Tag: unique,
                         •suspended   system-wide
                         •ready   identifier
                         •dormant
                         •nonexistent

  Primitives: get tag   create
               start up   wait for termination
               kill   give up processor

Messages
  Structure: •type   •source id
               •length   •destination id
               •pointer

  Primitives: send   receive-wait
                                        receive-fail

Events
  Structure: list of sources and destinations

  Primitives: configure   activate   on event call
               remove   wait   set timer
                           passive test

Locks
  Structure: 8192 single bits
  Operating mode: polling or interrupt

  Primitives: allocate   lock
                                        unlock

Table 2: Flex/32 Parallel Primitives

Implementation of Force Primitives

Basic hardware support for synchronization on the HEP is through the produce and consume operations on full/empty memory cells. The basic hardware support for synchronization on the Flex/32 is supplied by the common lock memory and the interrupt hardware. Table 3 compares the implementation of critical sections on the two machines. The implementations are very similar, but a detailed look at the differences will introduce the issues to arise in more disjoint implementations of other primitives to follow.

The basic HEP synchronization is somewhat more powerful than is needed for critical sections. A single full/empty variable suffices to control entry to the section, but only its state is significant; the value of the variable

HEP

Ststem state and initialization:
       Single full/empty variable   -   full

Critical section code:
       Consume critical section variable
       Execute code body
       Produce critical section variable

Performance:
       Consume and produce are single user-mode instructions,
       but may result in some resource usage by waiting processes.

Flex/32

System state and initialization:
       Single bit lock   -   clear

Critical section code:
       Set critical section lock
       Execute code body
       Clear critical section lock

Performance:
       Set and clear locks are done by system calls.
       Processor rescheduling is possible, and wakeup of
       a delayed process may be by interrupt or polling.

Table 3: Implementation of Critical Sections

is unused. The Flex/32 locks are well suited in complexity to what is needed for critical section control. The process delay which may be required on critical section entry is supported by the hardware of the HEP, making critical section entry a user level operation with no operating system intervention. On the other hand, a small amount of system resources is consumed by waiting processes, which may cause congestion if many processes wait simultaneously. The Flex/32 implements locking and unlocking through system calls. This is costly in terms of performance but allows processor rescheduling. Wakeup of blocked processes may either be by polling or by interrupt.

There is considerably more structure to the implementation of the *Barrier* macro on both machines. Table 4 summarizes the implementations, including two implementations for the HEP having quite different performance characteristics. The two HEP implementations emphasize the difference between suspended and partially active waiting, which was mentioned in connection with the critical section code. This issue was not important in connection with critical sections because the control is very simple

HEP - Active Waiting

System State		Initialization
Entry lock	-	clear
Exit lock	-	set
Counter	-	zero

Barrier Code
   Wait for entry lock clear
   Count arriving process
   If last process then
     execute code body
     set entry lock
     clear exit lock
   Wait for exit lock clear
   Count exiting process
   If last process then
     set exit lock
     clear entry lock

HEP - Process Suspending

System state		Initialization
Process state save area	-	empty
Counter	-	zero

Barrier Code
   Count arriving process
   If not last one then
     save state and quit
   else
     recreate other processes
     clear counter

Flex/32

System State		Initialization
Barrier event	-	connected to all processes as source/destination
Counter	-	zero

Barrier Code
   Lock counter
     Count arriving process
     Clear counter if last
   Unlock counter
   If last process then
     Execute code body
     Activate barrier event
   else
     Wait for barrier event

Table 4: Implementation of Barriers

and because the probability that many processes will simultaneously wait on entry to critical sections with the same lock is low. In the *Barrier*, it is guaranteed that all processes simultaneously access the same blocking condition. There is only one implementation for the Flex/32 since all synchronization support is through operating system calls and involves process suspension rather than active waiting.

The critical section and the Barrier implementations serve to give an idea of the range of differences in the implementation of Force primitives on the two architectures. Many of the primitives, such as prescheduled DOALL, did not change at all between the machines, while others, such as self-scheduled DOALL, build on the same techniques used in the critical section and Barrier. One other implementation issue which deserves mention is the implementation of a data oriented synchronization on a machine which has hardware support only for control oriented synchronization.

The Force includes primitive operations for the simplest data oriented synchronization, produce and consume. The HEP hardware supports these operations directly, using the full/empty state bit for each memory cell. In the Flex/32, locks are separate items, not associated with data. To implement producer/consumer synchronization, a boolean data item must be allocated to the full/empty state and a lock must be allocated to bind the data transfer to the state change as an atomic unit. The lock itself cannot be used to model the full/empty state because there is no way to bind it to the data transmission. Furthermore, since the full/empty state is a data item, the system supported process waiting mechanism cannot be used to wait for its change. Critical section code must be repeatedly executed to monitor a change in the state variable. In contrast, it is very easy to model the lock/unlock synchronization using produce/consume. The full/empty state of a memory cell is used for the lock and the value of the cell is simply ignored.

Conclusions

The implementation of a parallel programming environment on two shared memory multiprocessors with quite different architectures has been described. The primitive operations of the system make fairly efficient implementations possible on both machines. One major difference has to do with whether parallelism is supported directly by hardware accessible to the user or is supported only through the operating system. In the latter case, the implementer must work in terms of the software run-time model presented by the system rather than in terms of a model related more directly to the hardware, which makes the prediction and optimization of performance somewhat more difficult. The mechanism by which processes wait at a synchronization is a key issue. If the waiting mechanism is tied to multiprogramming through the operating system call, throughput will be optimized, but a large overhead will be incurred for potentially short synchronization delays.

The use of interrupts in the system architecture leads to natural support for the Event concept. The implementation of Barrier type synchronizations can be tied to the event concept fairly naturally. On machines which do not support events, attention must be paid to minimizing the utilization of resources by waiting processes. The Barrier differs from the critical section in this regard because it is guaranteed that many processes will simultaneously wait at the Barrier while critical section conflict is probabilistic, and the liklihood of many processes waiting at the entry to a critical section is low in a normally constructed program.

REFERENCES

[1] J. B. Dennis and E. C. Van Horn, "Programming semantics for multiprogrammed computations," *Comm. ACM* Vol. 9, No. 3, pp. 143-155 (1966).

[2] H. F. Jordan, "Structuring parallel algorithms in an MIMD, shared memory environment," *Proc. 18th Hawaii Int'nl Conf. on Systems Sciences*, Vol. II, pp. 30-38 (1985); to appear in *Parallel Computing*, 1985.

[3] H. F. Jordan, "HEP architecture, programming and performance," in *Parallel MIMD Computation: The HEP Supercomputer and its Applications*, J. S. Kowalik, Ed., MIT Press (1985).

[4] "The Uniform System Approach to Programming the Butterfly Parallel Processor," Draft of Oct. 23, 1985, Copyright BBN Laboratories Inc. (R. H. Thomas, private communication).

[5] F. Darema-Rogers, D. A. George, V. A. Norton and G. F. Pfister, "A VM Parallel Environment," *Rept. RC11225 (#49161)*, IBM T. J. Watson Res. Ctr. (Jan. 1985).

[6] J. J. Dongarra, J. R. Bunch, C. B. Moler and G. W. Stewart, *LINPACK Users Guide*, SIAM Publications, Phil., PA (1979).

[7] N. R. Patel and H. F. Jordan, "A parallelized point rowwise successive over-relaxation method on a multiprocessor," *Parallel Computing*, Vol. 1, No. 3&4, December 1984.

[8] N. Patel, W. B. Sturek and H. F. Jordan, "A Parallelized Solution for Incompressible Flow on a Multiprocessor," *Proc. AIAA 7th Computational Fluid Dynamics Conf.*, Cincinnati, Ohio, pp. 203-213, July 1985.

[9] N. Patel, private communication.

[10] G. Alaghband and H. F. Jordan, "Multiprocessor Sparse L/U Decomposition with Controlled Fill-in," *ICASE Rept. No. 85-48*, NASA Langley Res. Ctr., Hampton, VA, 1985.

[11] *The Flex/32® System Overview*, Flexible Computer Corp., Dallas, Texas, 1986.

[12] Flynn, M. J., "Some Computer Organizations and Their Effectiveness," *IEEE Trans. on Computers*, pp. 948-960 (1972).

CHAPTER 10

SCHEDULE: An Aid to Programming Explicitly Parallel Algorithms in Fortran*

J. J. Dongarra[†]
D. C. Sorensen[‡]

1. Introduction

Many new parallel computers are now emerging as commercial products[7]. Exploitation of the parallel capabilities requires either extensions to an existing language such as Fortran or development of an entirely new language. A number of activities[11, 12] are under way to develop new languages that promise to provide the ability to exploit parallelism without the considerable effort that may be required in using an inherently serial language that has been extended for parallelism. We applaud such activities and expect they will offer a true solution to the software dilemma in the future. However, in the short term we feel there is a need to confront some of the software issues, with particular emphasis placed on transportability and use of existing software.

Our interests lie mainly with mathematical software typically associated with scientific computations. Therefore, we concentrate here on using the Fortran language. Each vendor of a parallel machine designed primarily for numerical calculations has provided its own parallel extensions to Fortran. These extensions have taken many forms already and are usually dictated by the underlying hardware and by the capabilities that the vendor feels appropriate for the user. This has led to widely different extensions ranging from the ability to synchronize on every assignment of a variable with a full empty property[9] to attempts at automatically detecting loop-based parallelism with a preprocessing compiler aided by user directives[2]. The act

* Work supported in part by the Applied Mathematical Sciences subprogram of the Office of Energy Research, U.S. Department of Energy, under Contracts W-31-109-Eng-38, DE-AC05-840R21400, and DE-FG02-85ER25001.

† Mathematics and Computer Science Division, Argonne National Laboratory, 9700 Cass Avenue, Argonne, Illinois, 60439-4844.

‡ Center for Supercomputing Research and Development, University of Illinois-Champaign, 305 Talbot Laboratory, 104 South Wright Street, Urbana, Illinois, 61801-2932.

of getting a parallel process executing on a physical processor ranges from a simple "create" statement[9] which imposes the overhead of a subroutine call, to "tskstart" [1] which imposes an overhead on the order of 10^6 machine cycles, to no formal mechanism whatsoever[2]. All of these different approaches reflect characteristics of underlying hardware and operating systems. It is too early to impose a standard on these vendors, yet it is disconcerting that there is no agreement among any of them on which extensions should be included. There is not even an agreed-upon naming convention for extensions that have identical functionality. Program developers interested in producing implementations of parallel algorithms that will run on a number of different parallel machines are therefore faced with an overwhelming task. The process of developing portable parallel packages is complicated by additional factors that lie beyond each computer manufacturer supplying its own, very different mechanism for parallel processing. A given implementation may require several different communicating parallel processes, perhaps with different levels of granularity. An efficient implementation may require the ability to dynamically start processes, perhaps many more than the number of physical processors in the system. This feature is either lacking or prohibitively expensive on most commercially available parallel computers. Instead, many of the manufacturers have limited themselves to providing one-level loop-based parallelism.

This paper describes an environment for the transportable implementation of parallel algorithms in a Fortran setting. By this we mean that a user's code is virtually identical for each machine. The package, called SCHEDULE, can help a programmer familiar with a Fortran programming environment to implement a parallel algorithm in a manner that will lend itself to transporting the resulting program across a wide variety of parallel machines. The package is designed to allow existing Fortran subroutines to be called through SCHEDULE, without modification, thereby permitting users access to a wide body of existing library software in a parallel setting. Machine intrinsics are invoked within the SCHEDULE package, and considerable effort may be required on our part to move SCHEDULE from one machine to another. On the other hand, the user of SCHEDULE is relieved of the burden of modifying each code he disires to transport from one machine to another.

Our work has primarily been influenced by the work of Babb [3], Browne [4], and Lusk and Overbeek [10]. We present here our approach, which aids in the programming of explicitly parallel algorithms in Fortran and which allows one to make use of existing Fortran libraries in the parallel setting. The approach taken here should be regarded as minimalist: it has a very limited scope. There are two reasons for this. First, the goal of portability of user code will be less difficult to achieve. Second, the real hope for a solution to the software problems associated with parallel programming lies with new programming languages or perhaps with the "right" extension to Fortran. Our approach is expected to have a limited lifetime. Its purpose is to allow us to exploit existing hardware immediately.

2. Terminology

Within the science of parallel computation there seems to be no standard definition of terms. A certain terminology will be adopted here for the sake of dialogue. It will not be "standard" and is intended only to apply within the scope of this document.

Process - A unit of computation, an independently executable Fortran
   subroutine together with calling sequence parameters, common
   data, and externals.

Task   - A main program, processes, and a virtual processor.

Virtual Processor - A process designed to assume the identity of every
   process within a given task (through an appropriate subroutine call).

Processor - A physical device capable of executing a main program or a
   virtual processor.

Shared Data - Variables that are read and/or written by
   more than one process (including copies of processes).

Data Dependency - A situation wherein one process (A) reads any shared
   data that another process (B) writes. This data dependency
   is satisfied when B has written the shared data.

Schedulable Process - A process whose data dependencies have all
   been satisfied.

3. Parallel Programming Ideas

When designing a parallel algorithm one is required to describe the data dependencies, parallel structures, and shared variables involved in the solution. Typically, such algorithms are first designed at a conceptual level and later implemented in Fortran and its extensions. Each manufacturer provides a different set of extensions and targets these extensions at different implementation levels. For example, some manufacturers allow only test-and-set along with spawn-a-process, while others allow concurrent execution of different loop iterations.

Our attempt here is to allow the user to define the data dependencies, parallel structures, and shared variables in his application and then to implement these ideas in a Fortran program written in terms of subroutine calls to our environment. Each set of subroutine calls to the environment specifies the subroutine, or process (unit of computation), along with the calling parameters and the data dependencies necessary to coordinate the parallel execution.

The basic philosophy here is that Fortran programs are naturally broken into subroutines that identify units of computation that are self-contained and that operate on shared data structures. This allows one to call on existing library subroutines in a parallel setting without modification, and without having to write an envelope around the library subroutine call in order to conform to some unusual data-passing conventions imposed by a given parallel programming environment.

A parallel(izable) program is written in terms of calls to subroutines which, in principle, may be performed either independently or according to data dependency requirements that the user is responsible for defining. The result is a serial program that can run in parallel given a way to schedule the units of computation on a system of parallel processors while obeying the data dependencies.

4. Parallel Programming Using SCHEDULE

The package SCHEDULE requires a user to specify the subroutine calls along with the execution dependencies in order to carry out a parallel computation. Each of these calls represents a process, and the user must take the responsibility of ensuring that the data dependencies represented by the graph are valid. This concept is perhaps difficult to grasp without some experience with writing parallel programs. We shall try to explain it in this section by example; in the following section we shall describe the underlying concepts and the SCHEDULE mechanism.

To use SCHEDULE, one must be able to express (i.e., program) an algorithm in terms of processes and execution dependencies among the processes. A convenient way to view this is through a computational graph. For example, the following graph

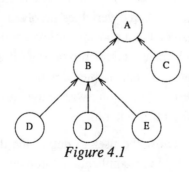

Figure 4.1

denotes five subroutines A, B, C, D, and E (here with two "copies" of subroutine D operating on different data). We intend the execution to start simultaneously on subroutines C,D,D, and E since they appear as leaves in the data dependency graph (D will be started twice with different data). Once D,D,and E have completed then B may execute. When B and C have completed execution then A may start and the entire computation is finished when A has completed. To use SCHEDULE, one is required to specify the subroutine calling sequence of each of the six schedulable units of computation, along with a representation of this dependency graph.

For each node in the graph, SCHEDULE requires two subroutine calls. One contains information about the user's routine to be called, such as the name of the routine, calling sequence parameters, and a simple tag to identify the process. The second subroutine call defines the dependency in the graph to nodes above and below the one being specified, and specifies the tag to identify the process. In this example, after an initial call to set up the environment for SCHEDULE, six pairs of calls would be made to define the relationships and data in the computational graph.

These concepts are perhaps more easily grasped through an actual Fortran example. A very simple example is a parallel algorithm for computing the inner product of two vectors. The intention here is to illustrate the mechanics of using SCHEDULE. This algorithm and the use of SCHEDULE on a problem of such small granularity are not necessarily recommended.

Problem: Given real vectors a and b, each of length n, compute $\sigma = a^T b$.

Parallel Algorithm:
$$\text{Let } a^T = (a_1^T, a_2^T, ..., a_k^T) \text{ and } b^T = (b_1^T, b_2^T, ..., b_k^T)$$
be a partitioning of the vectors a and b into smaller vectors a_i and b_i.

Compute (in parallel)

$$\sigma_j = a_j^T b_j \, , j = 1, k \, .$$

When all done

$$\sigma = \sigma_1 + \sigma_2 + \cdots + \sigma_k \, .$$

Each of the parallel processes will execute code of the following form:

```
      subroutine inprod(m,a,b,sig)
      integer m
      real a(*),b(*),sig
      sig = 0.0
      do 100 j = 1,m
          sig = sig + a(j)*b(j)
100   continue
      return
      end
```

The following routine is used to accumulate the result:

```
      subroutine addup(k,sigma,temp)
      integer k
      real sigma,temp(*)
      sigma = 0.0
      do 100 j = 1,k
          sigma = sigma + temp(j)
100   continue
      return
      end
```

The first step in constructing a code is to understand the parallel algorithm in terms of schedulable processes and a data dependency graph. Then the algorithm is expressed in a standard (serial) Fortran code. This code consists of a main program which initializes the shared data and a "parallel" subroutine **parprd** to compute the inner product by invoking the parallel processes **inprd** and **addup**. The program and associated data dependency graph are shown below.

Serial Code:

```
      program main
      integer n,k
      real a(1000),b(1000),temp(50),sigma
      read (5,*) n,k
      do 100 j = 1,n
          a(j) = j
          b(j) = 1
100   continue
c
      call parprd(n,k,a,b,temp,sigma)
c
      write(6,*) ' sigma = ',sigma
      stop
      end


      subroutine parprd(n,k,a,b,temp,sigma)
c
c     declare shared variables
c
      integer n,k
      real a(*),b(*),temp(*),sigma
c
c     declare local variables
```

```
c
      integer m,indx,j
c
      m = n/k
      indx = 1
      do 200 j = 1,k
c
         call inprod(m,a(indx),b(indx),temp(j))
c
         indx = indx + m
         if (j .eq. k-1) m = n - indx + 1
  200 continue
c
      call addup(k,sigma,temp)
c
      return
      end
```

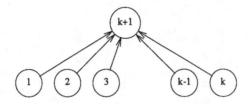

Figure 4.2

In this data dependency graph we have identified k processes

$$inprod(m, a(indx), b(indx), temp(j)), \quad j = 1, 2,..., k \quad, \quad indx = 1 + (j-1)*m$$

which are not data dependent. Each of them reads a segment of the shared data a, b and writes on its own entry of the array *temp*, but none of them needs to read data that some other process will write. This fact is evident in the graphical representation where they are *leaves*. One process,

$$addup(k, sigma, temp),$$

labeled $k+1$ is data dependent on each of the processes $1,2,...,k$. This is because **addup** needs to read each entry of the array *temp* in order to compute the sum and place it into σ.

From this data dependency graph we may proceed to write the parallel program. Once we have understood the computation well enough to have carried out these two steps, the invocation of SCHEDULE to provide for the parallel execution of schedulable processes is straightforward. Calls to **parprd**, **inprod**, and **addup** are replaced by calls to SCHEDULE to identify the routines to be executed as well as the information relating to the dependency graph. The modified code follows.

Parallel Main:

```
      program main
      integer n,k
c
      EXTERNAL PARPRD
c
      real  a(1000),b(1000),temp(50),sigma
      read (5,*) n,k,NPROCS
      do 100 j = 1,n
         a(j) = j
         b(j) = 1
  100 continue
c
      CALL  SCHED(nprocs,PARPRD,n,k,a,b,temp,sigma)
c
      write(6,*) ' sigma = ',sigma
      stop
      end


      subroutine parprd(n,k,a,b,temp,sigma)
c
c     declare shared variables
c
      integer n,k
      real  a(*),b(*),temp(*),sigma
c
c     declare local variables
c
      integer m1,m2,indx,j,jobtag,icango,ncheks,mychkn(2)
c
      EXTERNAL INPROD,ADDUP
      save m1,m2
c
      m1   = n/k
      indx = 1
      do 200 j = 1,k-1
c
c         express data dependencies
c
          JOBTAG = j
          ICANGO = 0
          NCHEKS = 1
          MYCHKN(1) = k+1
c
          CALL  DEP(jobtag,icango,ncheks,mychkn)
          CALL  PUTQ(jobtag,INPROD,m1,a(indx),b(indx),temp(j))
c
          indx = indx + m1
  200 continue
      m2 = n - indx + 1
c
c     express data dependencies for clean up step
c
          JOBTAG = k
          ICANGO = 0
          NCHEKS = 1
          MYCHKN(1) = k+1
c
```

```
        CALL   DEP(jobtag,icango,ncheks,mychkn)
        CALL   PUTQ(jobtag,INPROD,m2,a(indx),b(indx),temp(k))
c
        indx = indx + m1
c
        JOBTAG = k+1
        ICANGO = k
        NCHEKS = 0
c
        CALL   DEP(jobtag,icango,ncheks,mychkn)
        CALL   PUTQ(jobtag,ADDUP,k,sigma,temp)
c
        return
        end
```

The code that will execute in parallel has been derived from the serial code by replacing calls to **parprd, inprd, addup** with calls to SCHEDULE routines that invoke these routines. The modifications are signified by putting calls to SCHEDULE routines in capital letters. Let us now describe the purpose of each of these calls.

```
        CALL  SCHED(nprocs,PARPRD,n,k,a,b,temp,sigma)
```

This replaces the call to **parprd** in the serial code. The effect is to devote *nprocs* virtual processors to the parallel subroutine **parprd**. The parameter list following the subroutine name consist of the calling sequence one would use to make a normal call to **parprd**. Each of these parameters must be called by reference and not by value. No constants or arithmetic expressions should be passed as parameters through a call to **sched**. This call to **sched** will activate *nprocs* copies of a virtual processor **work**. This virtual processor is a SCHEDULE procedure (written in C) that is internal to the package and not explicitly available to the user.

```
        JOBTAG = j
        ICANGO = 0
        NCHEKS = 1
        MYCHKN(1) = k+1
c
        CALL   DEP(jogtag,icango,ncheks,mychkn)
        CALL   PUTQ(jobtag,INPROD,m,a(indx),b(indx),temp(j))
```

This code fragment shows the $j-th$ instance of the process **inprod** being placed on a queue. The information needed to schedule this process is contained in the data dependency graph. In this case, the $j-th$ instance of a call to **inprod** is being placed on the queue, so *jobtag* is set to j. The value zero is placed in *icango*, indicating that this process does not depend on any others. If this process were dependent on p, other processes then *icango* would be set to p.

The mechanism just described allows static scheduling of parallel processes. In this program the partitioning and data dependencies are known in advance even though they are parameterized. It is possible to dynamically allocate processes; this procedure will be explained later. It might be worthwhile at this point to discuss the mechanism that this package relies on.

5. The SCHEDULE Mechanism

The call to the SCHEDULE routines **dep** and **putq**, respectively, places process dependencies and process descriptors on a queue. A unique user supplied identifier *jobtag* is associated with each node of the dependency graph. This identifier is a positive integer. Internally it represents a pointer to a process. The items needed to specify a data dependency are non-negative integers *icango* and *ncheks* and an integer array *mychkn*. The *icango* specifies the number of processes that process *jobtag* depends on. The *ncheks* specifies the number of processes that depend on process *jobtag*. The *mychkn* is an integer array whose first *ncheks* entries contain the identifiers (i.e., *jobtag* s) of the processes that depend on process *jobtag*.

icango = 2

ncheks = 3

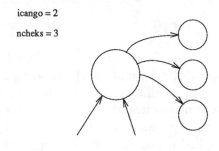

Figure 5.1. A Node in a Dependency Graph

In Figure 5.1 a typical node of a data dependency graph is shown. This node has two incoming arcs and three outgoing arcs. As shown to the right of the node one would set *icango* = 2, *ncheks* = 3, and the first three entries of *mychkn* to the identifiers of the processes pointed to by the outgoing arcs.

The initial call to *sched* (nprocs,subname,<parms>) results in *nprocs* virtual processors called **work** to begin executing on *nprocs* separate physical processors. Typically *nprocs* should be set to a value that is less than or equal to the number of physical processors available on the given system. These **work** routines access a ready queue of *jobtag* s for schedulable processes. Recall that a schedulable process is one whose data dependencies have been satisfied. After a **work** routine has been successful in obtaining the *jobtag* of a schedulable process, it makes the subroutine call associated with that *jobtag* during the call to **putq**. When this subroutine executes a *return*, control is returned to **work**, and a SCHEDULE routine **chekin** is called which decrements the *icango* counter of each of the *ncheks* processes that depend on process *jobtag*. If any of these *icango* values has been decremented to zero, the identifier of that process is placed on the ready queue immediately.

We depict this situation in Figure 5.2 . The array labeled **parmq** holds a process descriptor for each *jobtag*. A process descriptor consists of data dependency information and a subroutine name together with a calling sequence for that subroutine. This information is placed on **parmq** through the two calls

```
CALL DEP(jobtag,icango,ncheks,mychkn)
CALL PUTQ(jobtag,<subname>,<parms>).
```

When making these two calls the user has assured that a call to *subname* with the argument list *parms* is valid in a data dependency sense whenever the counter *icango* has been decremented to the value zero. When a **work** routine has finished a call to **chekin** , it gets the *jobtag* of the next available schedulable process off the *readyq* and then assumes the identity of the appropriate subroutine by making a call to *subname* with the argument list *parms* .

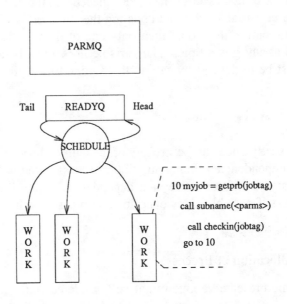

Figure 5.2. The SCHEDULE Mechanism

6. Low-Level Synchronization

Ideally, the mechanism we have just described will relieve the user of explicitly invoking any synchronization primitives. Unfortunately, some powerful parallel constructs are not so easily described by this mechanism. It may be desirable to have two processes executing simultaneously that are not truly data independent of each other. A typical example is in pipelining a computation, that is, when several parallel processes are writing on the same data in a specified order which is coordinated through explicit synchronization. To provide this capability, two low-level synchronization primitives have been made available within SCHEDULE. They are **lockon** and **lockoff**. Each takes an integer argument. An example of usage is

```
call lockon(ilock)
     ilocal = indx
     indx = indx + 5
call lockoff(ilock)
```

In this example a critical section has been placed around the act of getting a local copy of the shared variable *indx* and updating the value of *indx*. If several concurrent processes are executing this code, then only one of them will be able to occupy this critical section at any given time. The variable *ilock* must be a globally shared variable and it must be initialized by calling the routine **lockasgn**. In the above example the statement

```
call lockasgn(ilock,0)
```

must execute exactly once and before any of the calls to **lockon** are made. If there are low-level data dependencies among any of the processes that will be scheduled, then it will be necessary to enforce those data dependencies using locks. It is preferable to avoid using locks if possible. However, in certain cases such as pipelining, locks will be required.

7. Dynamic Allocation of Processes

The scheme presented above might be considered static allocation of processes. By this we mean that the number of processes and their data dependencies were known in advance. Therefore the entire data structure (internal to SCHEDULE) representing the computational graph could be recorded in advance of the computation and is fixed throughout the computation. In many situations, however, we will not know the computational graph in advance, and we will need the ability for one process to start or spawn another depending on a computation that has taken place up to a given point in the spawning process. This dynamic allocation of processes is accomplished through the use of the SCHEDULE subroutine **spawn**. The method of specifying a process is similar to the use of **putq** described above.

We shall use the same example to illustrate this mechanism.

Processes:

subroutine inprod .... same as above

```
      subroutine addup(myid,n,k,a,b,sigma,temp)
      integer myid,n,k
      real a(*),b(*),sigma,temp(*)
c
c     declare local variables
c
      integer j,jdummy,m1,m2
c
      LOGICAL WAIT
      EXTERNAL INPROD
      save m1,m2
c
      go to (1111,2222), IENTRY(myid)
 1111 continue
c
      m1 = n/k
      indx = 1
      do 200 j = 1,k-1
c
c         replace the call to inprod  with a call to spawn
c
          CALL SPAWN(myid,jdummy,INPROD,m1,a(indx),b(indx),temp(j))
          indx = indx + m1
  200 continue
      m2 = n - indx + 1
c
c     clean up step
c     replace the call to inprod  with a call to spawn
c
      CALL SPAWN(myid,jdummy,INPROD,m2,a(indx),b(indx),temp(k))
c
      nprocs = k
      L2222 = 2
c
c     If any of the spawned process have not completed, RETURN
c     to the scheduler and help out.  This avoids busy waiting
c     and allows this code to be executed by one processor.
c
          if (WAIT(myid,nprocs,L2222)) return
 2222     continue
c
c     All have checked in, now addup the results.
c
      sigma = 0.0
      do 100 j = 1,k
         sigma = sigma + temp(j)
  100 continue
```

```
        return
        end
```

The subroutine **parprd** must change somewhat.

```
        subroutine parprd(n,k,a,b,temp,sigma)
c
c       declare shared variables
c
        integer n,k
        real a(*),b(*),temp(*),sigma
c
c       declare local variables
c
        integer mychkn(1),icango,ncheks,jobtag
        EXTERNAL ADDUP
        save jobtag
c
        JOBTAG = 1
        ICANGO = 0
        NCHEKS = 0
c
        CALL DEP(jobtag,icango,ncheks,mychkn)
        CALL PUTQ(jobtag,ADDUP,jobtag,n,k,a,b,sigma,temp)
c
        return
        end
```

8. Experience with SCHEDULE

At present the experience with using SCHEDULE is limited but encouraging. Versions are running successfully on the VAX 11/780, Alliant FX/8, and CRAY-2 computers. That is, the same user code executes without modification on all three machines. Only the SCHEDULE internals are modified, and these modifications are usually minor, but can be difficult in some cases. They involve such things as naming and parameter-passing conventions for the C - Fortran interface. They also involve coding the low-level synchronization primitives and managing to "create" the **work** processes.

On the CRAY-2 process creation is accomplished using **taskstart,** and the low-level synchronization already matches the low-level synchronization routines provided by the CRAY multitasking library[1]. For the Alliant FX/8 we coded the low-level synchronization primitives using their test-and-set instruction. To "create" the work routines, we used the CVD$L CNCALL directive before a loop that performed *nprocs* calls to the subroutine **work.**

In addition to some toy programs used for debugging SCHEDULE, several codes have been written and executed using SCHEDULE. These codes include the algorithm TREEQL for the symmetric tridiagonal eigenvalue problem [8], a domain decomposition code for singularly perturbed convection-diffusion PDE [5], and a block preconditioned conjugate gradient code for systems arising in reservoir simulation [6].

References

1.   *CRAY 2 Multitasking Users Guide,* Cray Research Inc, Minn, MN (1986).

2.   *Alliant FX/Fortran Programmer's Handbook, Alliant Computer Systems Corp,* Acton Mass., 1985.

3.   R.G. Babb , "Parallel Processing with Large Grain Data Flow Techniques," *IEEE Computer* **17, 7** , pp. 55-61 (July 1984).

4.   J.C. Browne, "Framework for Formulation and Analysis of Parallel Computation Structures," *Parallel Computing* **3**, pp. 1-9 (1986).

5.   R. Chin, G. Hedstrom, F. Howes, and J. McGraw, "Parallel Computation of Multiple-Scale Problems," pp. 134-151 in *New Computing Environments: Parallel, Vector, and Systolic*, ed. Ed. A. Wouk, Siam Pub., Philadelphia (1986).

6.   J.C. Diaz, "Calculating the Block Preconditioner on Parallel Multivector Processors," *Proceedings of the Workshop on Applied Computing in The Energy Field*, Stillwater, Oklahoma, (October 10, 1986).

7.   J.J. Dongarra and I.S. Duff, "Advanced Architecture Computers," Argonne National Laboratory Report, ANL-MCS-TM-57 (October, 1985).

8.   J.J. Dongarra and D.C. Sorensen, "A Fully Parallel Algorithm for the Symmetric Eigenvalue Problem," *To appear SIAM SSISC*.

9.   H. Jordan, "HEP Architecture, Programming and Performance," in *Parallel MIMD Compuation: HEP Supercomputer and Its Applications*, ed. Ed. J. Kowalik, MIT Press (1985).

10.   E. Lusk and R. Overbeek, "Implementation of Monitors with Macros: A Programming Aid for the HEP and Other Parallel Processors," Argonne National Laboratory Report, ANL-83-97 (1983).

11.   John VanRosendale and Piyush Mehrotra, "The BLAZE Language: A Parallel Language for Scientific Programming," ICASE Report # 85-29 (1985).

12.   J.R. McGraw, et al., "SISAL: Streams and Iteration in a Single Assignment Language," Language Reference Manual, Ver. 1.2, Lawerence Livermore National Laboratory

Dynamic Grid Manipulation for Partial Differential Equations on Hypercube Parallel Processors*

William D. Gropp†

Abstract. Adaptive methods for PDEs can be considered as a problem in managing a dynamic graph on a parallel processor. The properties we want for this graph are that edges in the graph, as much as possible, map to nearest neighbor links in the parallel processor, and that changes to the graph not require a major re-arrangement of the mapping of the nodes of the graph onto the processor. We will discuss a simple restricted set of transformations which are easy to implement on a message passing parallel processor, and discuss in detail the design choices made. These transformations are based on maintaining a graph of bounded node degree at the cost of a small amount of global communication.

In designing adaptive algorithms for parallel processors, the communication speeds of the processors can have a major effect on the design. Different hypercubes can be characterized by three parameters: the floating point speed, the I/O startup time, and the I/O transfer rate. One aspect of algorithm design which is influenced by interprocessor communication is data structure granularity. We will discuss how this affects the choice of algorithm as a function of the three parameters for our algorithm and relate this to our experiments.

1. Introduction. Parallel computing offers the possibility of greatly increased computing power. However, some problems are so large that even enormous parallel computers will not be able to handle them. Such problems include time dependent partial differential equations (PDEs) which have both a fine scale and a coarse scale structure. Such problems, solved on a uniform grid, may require a mesh of over 1000 points in each direction, for 10^9 mesh points. Further, each point may require many operations, and thousands of time steps may be needed. A conservative estimate for this kind of

*This work was supported in part by Office of Naval Research Contract #N00014-82-K-0184 and Air Force Office of Scientific Research Contract AFOSR-84-0360.

†Yale University, New Haven, Connecticut, 06520.

problem would be 10^{13} floating point operations. However, the solution being computed at this resolution is in areas of coarse scale structure unusably accurate. We can save a tremendous amount of work by adapting our computation to the structure of the problem. However, adaptive algorithms on parallel processors have received little attention. In this paper, we describe work on a major part of the problem of using adaptive methods on a parallel computer—managing the adaptive data structure. The graph management problem in general is hard and does not parallelize very well, so we consider a restricted set of graph transformations or kinds of refinement/derefinement. We performed some simple experiments to show the "correctness" of the algorithm, the difficulty in implementation, and the bottlenecks in the algorithm. Experiments on an Intel Hypercube are presented.

There are many kinds of parallel processors and ways to program them In this paper we will be concerned with loosely-coupled computers using message passing. A loosely-coupled computer is a collection of processors, each of which is connected to some subset of other processors by communication lines. There is no shared memory. All interaction between the processors takes place though the exchange of messages along these communication lines. Message passing is a programming paradigm suitable to both loosely and tightly coupled computers. A algorithm designed using message passing is data synchronized; each processor is responsible for receiving messages and acting on them. In contrast to the shared memory paradigm, no processor can act directly on the memory or data of another processor. This approach removes many of the possibilities for subtle, difficult to debug errors common in shared memory programs. The penalty is in a slightly higher software overhead and a more active roll of the programmer in keeping track of a distributed data structure.

We choose a hypercube or binary n-cube as our model because it has both good local and reasonable (log in the number of processors) global communication. Further, commercial hypercubes are now available. However, we will see that simpler architectures are also adequate (and may even be superior).

2. Background. In order to discuss the reasons for our choice of data structure and algorithm, we need to model our parallel processor. There are two parts to this model. The first is the performance of a single processor. This can be expressed by three parameter: f, the time to do a single floating point operation, β, the time to transfer a single word from this processor to a neighboring processor, and α, the time to start up a transfer to or from a neighboring processor. In this paper we are concerned only with the management of the adaptive method, and so the floating point time f will not enter our calculations. However, β is roughly the same size as f. For many systems, $\alpha \gg \beta$ because of significant software overhead. Typical numbers are $\beta = 10\mu$ seconds and $\alpha = 6500\mu$ seconds.

The second is the properties of the interconnections between the processors. The hypercube is rich in structure; only a few of its properties interest us here. One property is that a k dimensional grid may be imbedded in a hypercube of dimension $\geq k$ as long as the lengths of the sides of the grid are powers of 2. The other property we will need is global communication, which is possible in $\log p$ time for a hypercube with p processors.

3. Adaptive methods as graph manipulation. Consider the data as a graph. A vertex of graph represents "point" of computation. The edges of the graph represent the sharing of information between vertices. These edges are determined by the difference stencil for finite difference methods and by the finite element footprint for those methods. For example, the "usual" 5-point difference stencil for an elliptic PDE is a piece out of this graph, and a step of the solution at each vertex consists of using information from the adjacent vertices.

Because a non-adaptive method is often highly ordered, the graph is represented implicitly, for example, through the way in which data is stored. In an adaptive method, the generality of the graph often requires that the graph be represented explicitly. The operations on the graph are refinement and derefinement. Refinement replaces one vertex with 2 or more vertices, with those vertices connected by edges (not necessarily a complete graph). De-refinement replaces 2 of more vertices with a single vertex. Of course, edges must be properly merged if the computational domain which the graph represents is to remain correct.

Thus managing an adaptive grid is the same as managing a dynamic grid.

In practice, it is more efficient to allow each vertex to be a "cubical" subgrid, as this reduces the size of the graph and the amount of "pointer-chasing", as well as providing opportunities for vector processing within a vertex.

Once we view an adaptive method as a graph manipulation, we need to consider how to map it onto a parallel processor. And more than that, we must try to pick a graph which *can* be mapped efficiently onto the parallel processor we are considering. For example, Berger and Bokhari [1] consider one particular method of refinement using "binary decomposition". Other partitionings are possible, and may be more suitable for different adaptive algorithms. The point is that, as with many parallel algorithms, the best choice for a parallel processor is not necessarily the best serial algorithm.

In order to help decide what sort of graph and graph manipulation to use on our parallel processor, we need a criteria to use in selecting among the possibilities. There are several criteria to consider:

- cost of graph, including changes to the graph
- suitability for solving PDEs with the graph—matrix solvers, explicit finite difference schemes
- simplicity of code for simplicity of user interface

The last two items here are very important but hard to quantify. Perhaps most important is that the the graph must be compatible with the solution algorithms. Given the complexity of parallel computing, the structure of the graph must be simple enough to allow easy integration with a wide variety of solution algorithms and with developing linear equation software. In addition, a problem with MIMD parallel computers is that each processor has a copy of the program. This can rapidly chew up a lot of memory if a 1024 processor system is running a program which takes half a megabyte, for a total of half a *gigabyte* for the parallel program. This emphasizes the need for a simple program.

The first point is the easiest to get a handle on. To determine the cost of manipulating the graph, we note that there are 3 sources of cost:

- Cost of communicating information along edges
- Cost of re-arranging the graph. This may include moving vertices to another processor.
- Cost of computing the configuration of the graph

The goal is to minimize the cost

$$\text{cost} = \sum_{\text{steps}} \max_{\text{processor}} (\text{cost of adjacent edges})$$

$$+ \max_{\text{processor}} (\text{cost of computing graph for each processor})$$

$$+ \max_{\text{processor}} (\text{cost of re-arranging graph for each processor})$$

Here, "steps" refers to the time or iteration steps taken by the PDE solution algorithm. Since any processor will likely have more than one vertex, we take the maximum over each processor rather than over each vertex.

Fortunately, choosing the graph that minimizes this cost is impossible. If nothing else, the changes in the graph depend on the solution, and can not be predicted. So, we must use heuristics. We will try to make the cost of re-arranging the graph low or zero; to control the cost of edges we will enforce data locality. The cost of computing on the graph will be large, consisting as it does of many floating point operations. However, this term can be made as small as possible by *load balancing*; distributing the vertices among the processors so that each has almost the same amount of floating point work to do.

Also, we want to keep in mind that what we want is the best way to solve PDEs, not a way to sell a particular style of parallel computer. Thus, we would also like to consider the question of what kind of parallel computer is best (shared memory or message passing), and what kind of interconnection (ring, hypercube, etc.). How do the parameters of the machine affect the choice of algorithm? We won't answer these questions here (several years of experience at least will be required), but the work we are doing is aimed at finding answers to these problems.

4. 1-irregular grids. A 1-irregular grid is a special kind of graph which we will use as the basis of our mesh refinement algorithm. We can define it in several ways. One is by the operations which create it:

- Start with a uniform cartesian mesh (of dimension d).
- Replace a node with 2^d nodes. This replacement is itself a uniform cartesian mesh, and the edges are the "natural" edges.
- Allow only 2^{d-1} edges on each *face*. In 3-d, this is in the directions East, North, South, West, Up, and Down.

Such a 2-d graph is shown in Figure 1). Another definition is presented in [2]: In 2 dimensions, given a graph, force additional refinement by applying, as many times as possible, the rule "refine any unrefined element with more than one irregular vertex on one of its sides".

Note that this precludes too rapid refinement refinement

Why do we chose this particular type of grid? One reason is because of the simplicity of the data structure. In particular, the structure can be stored without lists of neighbors because the number of neighbors is limited, and the wasted space is roughly the same as the space used to store the list pointers. For example, in 3-d, the average number of edges is > 6; for a list that would be $6 \times 2 = 12$ words per vertex.

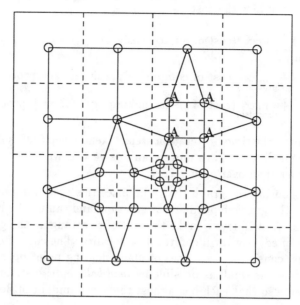

Figure 1: A 1-irregular grid and the associated mesh. The circles represent vertices in the graph; solid lines are edges in the graph. The dashed lines show the associated mesh. The vertices labeled "A" were added to make this graph 1-irregular.

If stored as $6 \times 4 = 24$, or 4 words per face, there is only a factor of two space penalty, and no list is necessary. In 2-d, there are other simplifications [2].

Another reason is that this method automatically excludes overly rapid refinement.In addition, for PDEs requiring the solution of linear or nonlinear equations, the assembly of the matrix of a 1-irregular grid is easier than for a general grid [2].

The disadvantages of this structure are that additional refinement, not necessary for the solution but necessary for the graph, may be required. Also, and this will turn out to be a major problem on parallel computers, a refinement at one point may require massive refinement over a large part of the graph. An example is shown in Figure 2.

5. Mapping graph onto processors. There are many ways to map a graph onto a set of processors. We will be interested only in the two most obvious ways, a random mapping and a local mapping. A random mapping assigns vertices in the graph randomly to processors. The idea is to insure that each processor has the same amount of work to do. The disadvantage is that communication between vertices which are neighbors in the graph is now expensive, since those vertices may now be at opposite ends of the parallel processor.

A local mapping reduces the problem of communication by dividing the graph into "clumps", each of which contains most of the neighbors of the vertices in the clump. This approach however suffers from problems in load balancing. However, it can make better use of the local memory, and in particular can make good use of vector or pipelined processors which may be present. These two approaches are shown in Figure 3.

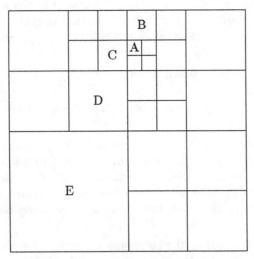

Figure 2: To refine mesh cell "A", cells "B" and "C" must first be refined. To refine cell "C", cell "D" must be refined. Similarly for "E".

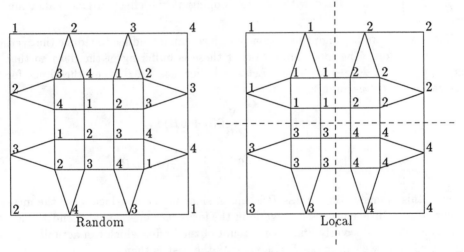

Figure 3: Random and local mapping of vertices onto processors. Mappings for a 4 processor system are shown; dashes in the local mapping show the "clumps".

To understand the magnitude of the tradeoffs involved here, we need to more closely analyze the sources of communication cost in a loosely coupled parallel processor.

5.1. Model of communication cost

We assume that each vertex must trade one item of information with each of its neighbors. For simplicity, we will assume that each vertex has six neighbors, and that there are N vertices in the graph. Recall that α represents the IO startup time and β the time to transfer a single word (not byte).

For the non-local or random mapping, each vertex must send data to its neighbors, over an average distance of $d/2$, where d is the diameter of the *parallel processor*.[1] For example, if there are p processors, then a 2-d grid has diameter $d = \sqrt{p}$ and a hypercube diameter $d = \log p$. The total cost per vertex is then

$$6 \text{ neighbors } \times (\alpha + \beta)\frac{d}{2}$$

Since there are N/p vertices per processor, each processor spends time $3(N/p)(\alpha + \beta)d$ just doing communication.

In the case of a local mapping, only the vertices on the surface of the clump actually communicate to neighbors on other processors. If the clump is roughly cubical, there will be only $6(N/p)^{2/3}$ such vertices. Further, we assume that the clumps are arranged so that the communication distance is one; that is, the clumps fit the architecture of the parallel processor. In this case, the total time per processor is $6(N/p)^{2/3}(\alpha + \beta)$ since the distance is one.

From this, we can see that the communication time for the random mapping is $\frac{1}{2}d(N/p)^{1/3}$ times the time for the local mapping. Since $N/p > 1$ and $d > 2$ for any interesting parallel processor, the random mapping always spends more time communicating than the local mapping. For example, in a 128 node hypercube, with 24 vertices per processor, the random time is ten times the local time. However, in practice, this cost must not be considered without also looking at the effect of load balancing and synchronization.

There are a number of optimizations which we can introduce to reduce the overhead in communication. The most important of these is buffering of the data so that the largest possible messages are sent. Let the buffer size be B, then the times for the non-local and local become

$$\text{non-local} \qquad \frac{N}{pB}6(\alpha + \beta B)d$$

$$\text{local} \qquad 6\left(\frac{N}{p}\right)^{2/3}\frac{1}{B}(\alpha + \beta B)$$

However, this is misleading unless B is small, since in the non-local case the messages are sent to $p - 1$ other processors, while in the local case message are send to only ≈ 6 processors. This can severly limit the amount of the buffer which can actually be used. In the local case, we can make $B = (N/p)^{2/3}$; the cost is then

$$\text{local} \qquad 6(\alpha + \beta(N/p)^{2/3}).$$

In the non-local case, the amount of data for each processor is $6N/p$ which is evenly distributed among $p - 1$ processors, or $B < 6N/p^2$ so

$$\text{non-local} \qquad p(\alpha + \beta 6N/p^2)d$$

The non-local has $dp/6$ more IO starts (α term) and $(N/p)^{1/3}d$ times as much data to send.

---

[1] The average distance is $d/2$ for any parallel processor which has the same number of nodes at a distance i and $d - i$.

- determine where to refine
- while cells remain to be refined *on any processor*
  - for each cell to be refined, either refine it or add the neighbors which must be refined first to the list. If one of the neighbors is a remote cell, send that neighbor a message.
  - send EOD (end-of-data) to all neighbors
  - read data from all neighbors. This includes requests to refine, refinement along borders

- determine where to derefine
- while cells remain and the graph changed last time in this loop
  - for each cell to be derefined, try to derefine it.
  - send EOD to all neighbors
  - read data from all neighbors. This consists of updating vertices along borders

Algorithm 1: Algorithm for managing a distributed, 1-irregular graph

6. Parallel Algorithm. In this section we discuss a parallel algorithm for a local division of the graph among the processors. This algorithm is data driven in that the actions and timing of each processor are determined by the arrival of information for neighboring processors. This ensures that the algorithm is always properly synchronized, and is a major advantage of the message passing paradigm.

There are a number of optimizations involved here. The first is the use of local, read-only copies of vertices on neighboring processors. If a vertex A in processor 3 has a neighboring vertex (determined by the graph) B in processor 7, a read-only copy of vertex B may be kept in processor 3. This copy can be used for references to pointers and data instead of forcing the processor A to send an expensive message to the neighbor processor B. Second, the messages are buffered in the method described above. Third, communication is *predictive*. That is, instead of a processor having to request data, each processor sends the data that will be needed. This can be done because the structure of the algorithm is so simple, and because the local nature of the mapping of the graph across processors makes it easy to determine who needs what information. This optimization reduces the communication by a factor of two by eliminating the request part of a request-reply communication protocol.

There is another consideration in designing the program which has not received enough attention. That is the limited amount of memory available for the program. Despite the fact that a parallel computer may have vast amounts of memory (e.g., 64 MBytes), this is spread over many processors. In addition, this memory must be shared with p copies of the operating system, further reducing the available memory. In the case of the Intel Hypercube, only about 0.25 Mbytes are available for user program and data on each node.

Another concern is for technology transfer. If the program is too complicated, it will not be possible to adapt it easily to "real-world" problems, and hence will have little impact on problem solving.

To keep the program simple, all operations are designed to be as self-contained as possible, and to always leave the data structures in a consistent state. The operations are: `refine-cell`, `deRefine-cell`, `Update-value`, `request-refinement`, `get-value`, and `set/read-global-flag`. All of these operations can be implemented in a simple and functional style, making the code robust and small.

Note that the algorithm terminates because at least one cell in some processor is refined each iteration, and in the worst case we will stop when we have a uniform grid.

7. Experiments. The purpose of the experiments described in this section is to show that the algorithm works and to gain an understanding of the performance in the absence of any load balancing. We also investigated the effect of buffering of data on the communication times.

The two test problems used consisted of (1) refineing everywhere, then de-refining everywhere and (2) refineing in a moving sphere. In case (2), the sphere moves in a circle whose origin is at one corner of the domain and whose radius is half of the size of the domain. The radius of the sphere is half the radius of the circle the sphere moves in. Case (1) is a very basic test and, in the absence of load balancing, is the case to which the theory developed in Section 5.1 is applicable. Case (2) is more realistic and give an idea of how important load balancing is.

These tests are quite limited and leave many questions unanswered. Among the items not tested are multiple levels of refinement. In addition, the code has not been optimized and no floating point operations are included. Only the effort needed to manipulate the graph has been included. The effect of this is to accentuate the communication cost of the graph manipulation.

In addition, we tested various decompositions of the domain. We can divide the domain into slabs (a 1 dimensional partition), into bars (a 2 dimensional partition), or cubes (a 3 dimensional partition). The major effect of these different partitions is to reduce the coefficient of α at the expense of increasing the coefficient of β. Since software overheads make $\alpha \gg \beta$, this can be a useful tradeoff. In particular, the basic estimates for the time spent communicating in these three cases are (in the local, buffered case)

$$1\text{-d:} \qquad 2(\alpha + \beta N^{2/3})$$

$$2\text{-d:} \qquad 4(\alpha + \beta N^{2/3}/p^{1/2})$$

$$3\text{-d:} \qquad 6(\alpha + \beta(N/p)^{2/3})$$

From these formulas we can construct a graph which predicts where each kind of decomposition will be better. Let $\alpha' = \alpha/(\beta N^{2/3})$. We solve the equation

$$6(\alpha' + p^{-2/3}) = 4(\alpha' + p^{-1/2})$$

for α' as a function of p. This curve separates the region where the cube decomposition is more expensive than the bar decomposition. The solution of the equation

$$4(\alpha' + p^{-1/2}) = 2(\alpha' + 1)$$

gives the curve separating the region where the bar decomposition is more expensive than the slab decomposition. The solutions of these equations are shown graphically in

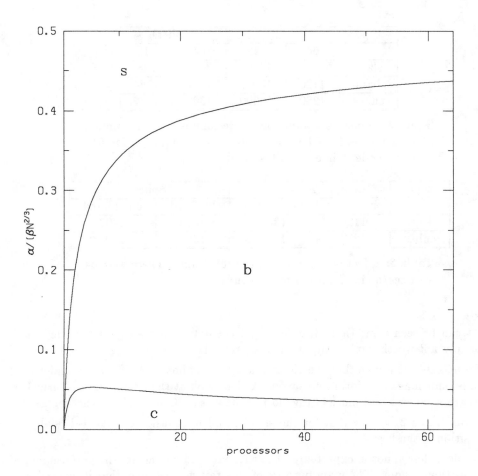

Figure 4: Graph showing where each kind of decomposition of the domain is superior. The region labeled **s** is best for slabs, the region labeled **b** is best for bars and the region labeled **c** is best for cubes.

Nodes	Total Time (ms)	
	All	Sphere
1	12300	1904
64	670	1392

Table 1: Speedup for refinement everywhere (All) and for refinement in sphere (Sphere) for 64 initial vertices.

Figure 4. Note that only for very large problems or very small ratios α/β is the cube decomposition superior.

Each experiment was run on each of these divisions of the domain. The results confirm the predictions in the graph.

In tables 1–3 we present the main results or our experiments. This is additional data which does not change this picture. Also, the problems considered are quite small, with the largest containing only 32768 vertices over the entire parallel processor (64

type	All		Sphere	
	64	512	64	512
slabs	—	12800	—	928
bars	1120	16000	1392	1744
cubes	1280	15300	1392	1872

Table 2: Time as a function of decomposition of domain. 2nd column is for 64 vertices/node, 3rd column is for 512 vertices/node. Times in milliseconds.

type	All		Sphere	
	buffered	unbuffered	buffered	unbuffered
bars	1120	1360	1392	1408
cubes	1280	1470	1392	1392

Table 3: Effect of buffering on the total time. There were 64 vertices/node. Times in milliseconds.

nodes).

As can be seen from Table 3, buffering of the data is not a significant effect, and is probably not worth implementing on this particular hypercube.

From Table 1, we see that the algorithm achieves about 30% efficiency under near optimal conditions of uniform refinement. A close look at the timing data returned by the program showed that much of the "lost" time was in IO waits, i.e., synchronization.

From Table 2, we see that for the small problems considered, the 1-d (slab) decomposition is the best.

Table 1 shows, not unexpectedly, that without load balancing, the performance of the algorithm is poor. The main purpose of this test was to show that it worked, and some speedup was achieved.

The missing values in Table 2 could not be run on the Intel Hypercube because of problems with the system communication software.

8. Some comments on load balancing. In order to load balance, we must move vertices between processors, since in an actual computation, the floating point work in solving a PDE on the mesh will dominate the cost of the calculation. However, using an arbitrary scheme for distributing vertices to other processors has all of the problems of the non-local mesh point distribution. Thus we would like to maintain a local distribution of vertices even in the presence of load balancing. There are several possible solutions to load balancing which maintain the local nature of the mapping of vertices onto processors. One method is to nest grids. View each processor as holding a clump of vertices, arranged as an onion. If a processor has too many vertices, take a small clump from the center of the vertices in that processor, and move those vertices to an adjacent processor. This method can be continued by taking an inner clump from the moved clump and giving that to an adjacent processor. Eventually, the original clump will have shells (onion layers) distributed throughout the processor. This method requires very little interconnectivity; even a ring (linear array) will do. A disadvantage is that though load balancing may be achieved by this method, it makes it very difficult to continue to do load balancing as the computation proceeds, as each processor ends up with a number of shells rather than clumps. Further, these shells have a poor surface area to volume ratio, so that communication costs increase as load balancing progresses.

Another approach is to find a restricted set of vertex movements which maintain the local character of the graph to processor mapping (no links longer than 1). The problem here is that there are some configurations which can't be load balanced, or which can be load balanced quickly.

9. Conclusions. Global communication is a serious problem. Most of the synchronization delay and a large fraction of the communication time in the experiments was due to the global flag check step. There are a number of ways to deal with this problem. One method is to observe that the volume of global data is very low. A hardware solution might use a global bus of bandwidth adequate for the amount of data, and perhaps a 2 or 3-d mesh instead of a full hypercube (since we don't need the $\log p$ diameter of the hypercube if we have the global bus). This could be a big advantage for PDE solution techniques which also require a small amount of global communication, such as Conjugate Gradient methods for solving linear equations.

Alternately, we could eliminate or reduce global communication be either allowing a more general graph since it is the 1-irregular property which introduces the global changes, or by finding conditions is which no global communication will be needed. This later should be the most common case, as in practice the graph will be changing slowly.

Another conclusion has to do with the organization of the software on a parallel computer. The basic communication operation in the algorithm consists of sending or receiving the next message along a particular interprocessor connection. There is *no* communication with non-neighbors in the algorithm. Even the global communication is handled most efficiently by nearest neighbor exchanges. However, the software on the machine we used provides a more general abstract model which presents the user with a completely connected model. This model not only slows down the communication, it actually gets in the way of the algorithm. A more effective approach would be to provide the user with a layered set of software. The lowest level could provide the simple point-to-point communication needed by this algorithm. On top of these routines could be built routines providing a variety of communication models, including the complete connection one Intel provides as the sole model. This is not a new idea; most networking software is designed on these principles. It is time for this same approach to be used in message passing parallel computers.

References

[1] Marsha J. Berger and Shahid Bokhari, *A partitioning strategy for non-uniform problems on multiprocessors*, Technical Report 85–55, ICASE, November 1985.

[2] Alan Weiser, *Local-mesh, local-order, adaptive finite element methods with a posteriori error estimators for elliptic partial differential equations*, Technical Report 213, YALECS, December 1981.

CHAPTER 12

Solving Compressible Euler Equations on a Hypercube Simulator

Jung Pyo Hong*
Bob Tomlinson*
Nisheeth Patel†

ABSTRACT. A two dimensional, time dependent, compressible Euler code using an explicit finite-difference method was executed on a hypercube simulator. The purpose of this work was to understand the code changes required to implement it on a particular hypercube architecture. A shock wave propogating inside a shock tube was used as a test problem. The problem was simulated for a sixteen-node machine.

INTRODUCTION. The simulator was developed for a particular hypercube architecture. Some of the features that will be included in the real hypercube are: large local memory (16MB/node); local disk storage; NSC 32032 processor; AMD 29325 co-processor; and absence of a host machine.

The test code solves the two-dimensional, inviscid, compressible equations of motion using MacCormack's [1] explicit method. This test code was also multi-tasked on a global shared memory multi-processor (HEP). On the HEP, speed-up to about 25 was achieved in going from 1 to 43 processes. This paper describes how a sequential version of the code was modified to execute it on a local memory multiprocessor (hypercube) simulator.

GOVERNING EQUATIONS. The governing equations are two-dimensional and in a strong-conservation form. The compressible Euler equations in general curvilinear coordinates are as follows.

$$\overline{Q}_\zeta + \overline{E}_\xi + \overline{F}_\eta = 0 \qquad (1)$$

*Los Alamos National Laboratory, Los Alamos, New Mexico, 87545.

† United States Army Ballistic Research Laboratory, Aberdeen Proving Ground, Maryland, 21005.

where

$$\bar{Q} = \frac{1}{J} \begin{bmatrix} \rho \\ \rho u \\ \rho v \\ \rho e \end{bmatrix} \qquad \bar{E} = \frac{1}{J} \begin{bmatrix} \rho U \\ \rho u U + \xi_x p \\ \rho v U + \xi_y p \\ (\rho e + p)U \end{bmatrix} \qquad \bar{F} = \frac{1}{J} \begin{bmatrix} \rho V \\ \rho u V + n_x p \\ \rho v V + n_y p \\ (\rho e + p)V \end{bmatrix}$$

$$U = \xi_x u + \xi_y v$$

$$V = n_x u + n_y v$$

$$J = \xi_x n_y - \xi_y n_x$$

The quantities u and v denote Cartesian x and y velocity components, respectively. The density ρ, pressure p and temperature T are related through the equation of state $p = \rho RT$, where R is the gas constant. The total energy per unit mass, e, is given by $e = c_v T + \frac{1}{2}(u^2 + v^2)$. The quantities U and V are the contravariant velocity components.

The explicit finite-difference method of MacCormack [1] is employed to integrate the governing equations in time from an assumed initial condition until a steady-state flow field is obtained.

The test case run on the hypercube simulator used 202 grid points in the ξ direction and 22 grid points in the n direction.

IMPLEMENTATION. A simple rectangular computational domain was divided into sixteen computational subdomains (Figure 1). Each subdomain was assigned to a node of the sixteen-node hypercube. For continuity in solution, each subdomain had one grid-cell overlap with its neighbors. As shown in Figure 2, for an overlapped region, information is passed from the field of subregion A to the boundary of subregion B and visa-versa. This was accomplished in the simulator using SEND and RECEIVE subroutines [2]. SEND is asynchronous and sends information to its neighbors. RECEIVE is synchronous and receives information from its neighbors. The FORTRAN program always waits until a message has been received. The solution algorithm for the test problem is predictor-corrector type. Before entering an iteration loop, the code does initialization and computes metric coefficients. The algorithm for the iteration loop on each node is as follows.

> Start iteration loop.
> Solve for predictor step.
> Exchange information for overlapped regions.
> Compute flux vectors.
> Apply boundary conditions.

Exchange information for overlapped regions.
Solve for corrector step.
Exchange information for overlapped regions.
Compute flux vectors.
Apply boundary conditions.
Exchange information for overlapped regions.
Go back to 'Start iteration'.

The above cycle was repeated for a desired number of iterations.

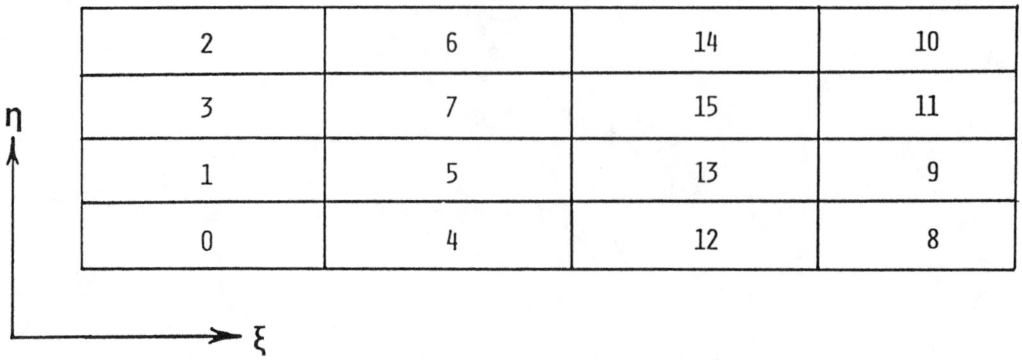

2	6	14	10
3	7	15	11
1	5	13	9
0	4	12	8

η

ξ

Figure 1.   Sixteen Computational Subdomains

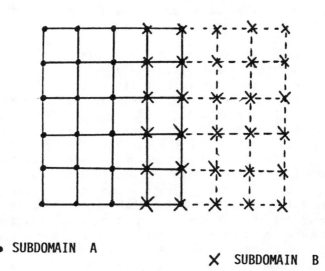

• SUBDOMAIN A

✗ SUBDOMAIN B

Figure 2.   One Grid-Cell Overlap

CONCLUSIONS.   The output from a simulation of a shock wave propagating inside a shock tube on the sixteen-node hypercube simulator was exactly the same as the output from the sequential code.   This validates the algorithm on the hypercube simulator.   However, the hypercube simulator does not provide information about the communication overhead.   Because of lack of timing results information about the speed-up that could be achieved on a real hypercube was not obtained.

REFERENCES

1. MacCormack, R. W., "The Effects of Viscosity in Hypervelocity Impact Cratering," AIAA Paper No. 69-354, 1969.

2. Hong, J. P., Patel, N. R., and Tomlinson, R. D., "An Example of How to Use the Hypercube Simulator with a FORTRAN Program," LA-UR-85-1405, Los Alamos National Laboratory, May 1985.